Seen and Heard
Six New Plays by Irish Women

Women In Arms | MARY ELIZABETH BURKE-KENNEDY

Couch | SÍOFRA CAMPBELL

I Know My Own Heart | EMMA DONOGHUE

La Corbière | ANNE LE MARQUAND HARTIGAN

The Lost Letters of a Victorian Lady | MICHELLE READ

In the Talking Dark | DOLORES WALSHE

Edited, with an Introduction by CATHY LEENEY

Carysfort Press
Dublin
An Chomhairle Ealaíon

A Carysfort Press Book
SEEN AND HEARD : Six New Plays by Irish Women

First published in Ireland in 2001 as a paperback original by Carysfort Press, 58 Woodfield, Scholarstown Road, Dublin 16, Ireland.
ISBN 0-9534-2573-8

This book is published with the financial assistance of The Arts Council (An Chomhaire Ealaíon), Dublin, Ireland.

Cover Design : Alan Bennis
Typesetting : Carysfort Press
Printed and Bound by Colour Books, Ltd.

the arts
council
an chomhairle
ealaíon
50⊦

Contents

Introduction

The energy in Irish theatre is prodigious. The plays in this collection embody and exemplify it. They have all been written and performed over the past fifteen years or so, and they show the richness of work going on in Irish theatre both over the last years of the twentieth century, and also at the beginning of this new one.

In Darwin's book, diversity is not merely the spice of life, it *is* life. It signals success, survival, continuity of change in evolution. The diversity of theatre styles and forms, of stories and moods in the plays published here is exciting. It seems to me a source of great optimism and stimulation that it is difficult to speak generally about this collection of plays. Strangely enough it is their differences that connect them, as well as the confidence and theatrical assurance of the writing. Emphasis on difference resists the sometimes homogenizing impulse of academic critics and commentators, who may be keen to point out the 'sameness' of pieces of writing or performance within an historical period. We all rely on this impulse to make broad sense of the past, to define the 'isms' that categorize theatrical and other histories into manageable units. But the impulse may mask true complexity, editing out all that does not fit some limiting paradigm. Canons are formed, and we are the poorer for them. We have to move on from an idea of Ireland that is requiredly nationalist and masculine. This range of work invites us to make a wider definition of Irishness.

The production histories of these plays show us the crucial role of initiatives such as the Cork Theatre Company's in commissioning Mary Elizabeth Burke-Kennedy's *Women In Arms*. The support that venues like Project Arts Centre, Andrew's Lane Theatre, and Bewley's Café Theatre have offered these playwrights, and the creative initiatives of companies like Glasshouse Productions and Moveable Feast Theatre Company are proof, if proof is needed, of the importance of the work happening outside the larger, more glamourous theatres. Awards and prizes for new writing have a strong part to play too, most especially when, as with Dolores Walshe's *In the Talking Dark*, the prize includes a production. Sadly, the Mobil prize is no longer offered at the Royal Exchange Theatre in Manchester. However, initiatives like Siobhán Bourke's women's playwriting competition in the 1990s led to Rough Magic productions of plays by Gina Moxley and Paula Meehan, and the Stewart Parker Trust continues to support and encourage new playwrights. More recently, the Seeds initiative, organized jointly by Rough Magic and the Dublin Fringe Festival, offers a batch of emergent playwrights valuable access to skilled directors and dramaturgs, and the chance to develop their work for production.

But to the plays themselves. Whether I saw them in performance, or read them, they seemed to me to demand publication.

Women In Arms by Mary Elizabeth Burke-Kennedy re-invents the great heroines and heroes of Irish myth. Its vigour and wit and physicality mark it out as a celebration of performance. It invites us to re-imagine the founding myths and landscapes of Irish identity. Burke-Kennedy effortlessly finds a vivid contemporary idiom that is both moving and funny, and that exploits the Irish story-telling tradition to the full.

Anne Le Marquand Hartigan's *La Corbière* challenges the audience to enter a world of sounds and words that create a fractured series of beautiful and disturbing images. The play's poetry comes from the heart of the nightmare of war-torn Europe. Hartigan confronts us with the language of savage insult and obliteration, and uses the healing sea as a metaphor for the redemption of the lost women. Paradoxically, her abstract theatrical vision reaches deep into the tragedy and damage of war, and the will to negate it in the honour of remembrance.

The twisted destructiveness of racism, which now urgently threatens contemporary Ireland, is the time-bomb in Dolores Walshe's *In the Talking Dark*. It is a compellingly realist piece of theatre, and for a very good reason - it creates an utterly convincing picture of the political reality that was Apartheid, a world so vicious and mad that it is deeply shocking as we confront it in the play. Walshe's characters are complex individuals, subtly and sympathetically drawn, facing the audience with the blinding demands of power and injustice over humanity.

The social and cultural codes, that bound the lived life, form the backdrop to three of the plays: *I Know My Own Heart, The Lost Letters of a Victorian Lady,* and *Couch*. Emma Donoghue's epistolary drama of Anne Lister's sexual adventures, *I Know My Own Heart*, reveals the pleasures and the pain of lesbian passion that were rendered invisible in Regency society. The play lays bare the sexual politics of the period, and draws us seductively into the emotional comedy and drama of Anne and her several loves. The sexual mores of our own period are never far away, nor are the eternal vulnerabilities of the human heart.

Michelle Read's hilarious deconstruction of Victorian ideals of femininity calls on all the resources of comic theatre, as our deliciously gullible heroine rollicks and frolics her way through the perils of life *en famille*, of drug-smuggling, the Irish rebel cause, and the facts of life (gently broken to her by Countess Markievicz). Read's play works brilliantly to entertain and divert, as well as to reflect the absurdities of 'ladyhood'.

The comedy of consumerism, the strangeness and isolation of life in boomtown Dublin is the genius of Síofra Campbell's *Couch*. Campbell manipulates theatrical form and notions of characterization to create an uncanny world of domestic longing and territoriality. It is instantly and unsettlingly recognizable - it is how we live now.

longing and territoriality. It is instantly and unsettlingly recognisable - it is how we live now.

These plays offer wonderful opportunities to actors and directors. Collectively, they develop our idea of what Irish theatre is, re-inventing Ireland as beyond the narrowly national to include our connectedness with other times and other places. Individually, each play makes a valuable and unique contribution to performance possibilities, and fosters that sense of possibility that gives theatre its life.

I would like to thank the playwrights for this collection, which it has been a privilege to put together. Special thanks to Sinead MacAodha, Siobhán Bourke, and Dan Farrelly for their support and encouragement.

Women in Arms

MARY ELIZABETH BURKE-KENNEDY

Women in Arms was first produced by Storytellers Theatre Company at the John Player Theatre, Dublin in September 1988 as part of the Dublin Millennium Theatre Festival with the following cast:

Nessa	Kate Hogan
Macha	Melody McNamara
Deirdre	Bairbre Ni Chaoimh
Maeve	Kay Ray Malone
Fergus	Pat Nolan
Naoise	Robert Byrne
Conchobar	Gerry McGrath
Director	Mary Elizabeth Burke-Kennedy
Design	Robert Armstrong
Lighting	Gerry Maher
Sound	Paddy Gilsenan
Stage Manager	Jim Newman
Costume Construction	Marie Tierney
Administration	Bernadette Cunnane
Producer	Gerry Barnes

Women in Arms was commissioned by Cork Theatre Company in 1984. An early version of the play was produced by the Company at the Ivernia Theatre, Cork and toured to Limerick and West Cork.

Characters

Fergus, King of Ulster until his marriage to Nessa

Nessa, power behind the throne of Ulster and mother of Conchobar, its most distinguished king

Conchobar, King of Ulster and leader of the Red Branch Knights

Cathbad, druid, warrior, prophet

Macha, goddess who curses Ulster

Deirdre, beloved protegée of Conchobar, lover of Naoise

Naoise, most glamorous of the Red Branch Knights, who elopes with Deirdre

Maeve, Queen of Connaught, responsible for the Táin Bó Cúailinge

Ailill, husband of Maeve, bon viveur

Cruinniuc, farmer selected by Macha to be her mortal husband

Fedelm, the Morrigu who haunts the battlefield

Eochaid of the Yellow Heel, Nessa's doting father

Note to Performers

The play is written to be performed by seven actors with the following doubling: Nessa; Macha/Fedelm; Deirdre; Maeve; Fergus; Conchobar/Ailill/Eochaid; Naoise/Cathbad/Cruinniuc

As well as their named roles, the actors are the chorus in the stories in which they are not central. In this capacity, they play not only human characters (courtiers, warriors, farmers) but animals, atmospheres, and landscapes.

The concept of this performance is that it evokes landscapes. The actors are part of the landscape and the elements. The stories arise out of the harshness, the bleakness, the wildness, and the majesty of this terrain. They are connected not just by chronology of plot, but by the texture of the landscape. This texture will be created by the playing, the set, lighting, costumes and sound.

The stage should be raked. The settings are five or six large, unevenly-shaped boulders which allow the actors to stand or sit on them. At the back of the stage is a large canopy, which is erected on two occasions to establish the splendour of Conchobar's court. Otherwise, the set does not change. Specific or individual props and costumes are set simply on the perimeter of the rake.

Prologue

There is the sound of wind blowing over a vast empty space. The actors take their places around the boulders, leaning, curled around them, becoming extensions of the landscape. Each actor speaks as if beginning a particular story. Each story should be allowed to hang in silence for a beat, before the next cue comes in.

Macha: One time ...

Deirdre: Once, there was ...

Conchobar: Now in those days ...

Maeve: Upon a time ...

Fergus: Now there was once ...

Nessa: Then there was the ...

*They keep repeating their lines, letting their voices mingle. As the voices build to a gentle climax, **Naoise** cuts through them.*

Naoise: Now once.

*The actors cease. Sound of church bells clanging. The actors stand to take up positions in a semi-arch with **Nessa** in the centre. The church bells cease. **Nessa** steps out front as she begins to speak.*

Part One: Nessa's Story

Nessa: There was once a girl who lived in Ulster and her name was Essa, meaning gentle or docile.

Conchobar: She was an only child and her father employed twelve tutors for her education.

Nessa sits. The others reach up their arms, forming a cloister behind her. A sustained deep cello chord.

Deirdre: She was engrossed with her teachers. She pulled out of them everything they knew about the five provinces and about Ulster in particular.

Nessa: Who was the most powerful? Who was the most violent? Who owned the most land?

Fergus: Fergus.

Nessa: Who knew the most secrets? Who knew the most music?

Naoise: Cathbad.

Nessa: Who had travelled farthest? What had they seen?

Naoise: Cathbad had seen.

Nessa: What was the best story?

Macha: That remained to be seen.

Maeve: She learned the seed, breed and generation of every important family in Ulster.

Conchobar: Not that wealth interested her much.

Fergus: She knew what people did with it and, for the most part, despised them.

Macha: Surrounded by her dusty old teachers whom she loved, she lived a sequestered life of contemplation and peace.

Fergus: Totally unnatural for a girl of her age or for anyone for that matter. That was the opinion of Fergus.

The cloister breaks up to become Fergus's court. The dominant back-stage centre boulder is established as his throne.

Naoise: The King of Ulster set the standards at the time.

Nessa: Essa went with her father to attend a festival at the Court of King Fergus.

Conchobar: It was the joke of the country that Eochaid of the Yellow Heel had a daughter who was an intellectual. Twelve tutors for the daughter - and no sons.

Fergus: There were no intellectuals at this court. Just men who could fight and drink - and women who could fight and drink - and tell a fuckin' good story.

Naoise: And now in the middle of them was this prissy girl, looking at them with big eyes.

Fergus: Do you know any stories? Or do they tell stories where you come from?

Nessa: Yes, it's what I enjoy most. I compose stories myself and satires.

Fergus: Indeed. And what do you know about satire? You have to know something about life before you can start on the satire. What do you know about life?

Nessa: That I love it. I wish I had a hundred years to live. I'm very happy.

Fergus: *(Derisory, crude)* Happy! Happy! Happy! Happy people don't make good satirists. 'Happy' isn't a word we use around here.

Conchobar: What would you expect with Eochaid for a father?

Naoise: Little happy Eochaid - with no sons.

Macha: It's a long time since we were happy.

Fergus: *(To Nessa)* Tell us one of your stories.

Nessa: Once upon a time - there were -

Naoise: Two Pig-keepers! Once upon a time there were two Pig-keepers! Continue!

Nessa: I can't. I don't know it.

Conchobar: One of them was called Friuch, for he was a bristly boy.

Fergus: And one of them was called Rucht, for he was a grunter.

Naoise: And do you know where he did his grunting? You've never heard the Story of the Two Pig-keepers?

Nessa: I'm not sure ...

Deirdre: She's not sure - that's the best yet.

Fergus: Every night was a big night at Fergus's court. People were expected to enjoy themselves.

Conchobar: And they did too. And their womenfolk with them. Some of those girls would drink you under the table.

Fergus: But what were they to do with this oddity? She wouldn't take a drink.

Maeve: She was aloof with the women. She never gossiped.

Deirdre: She went out by herself for walks.

Macha: She sighed. She blushed if she saw people pissing.

Fergus: She couldn't take a joke.

Naoise: She was *full* of herself.

Nessa *tries to leave.* **Naoise** *bars her way, flings her over his shoulder and parades her around.*

Nessa: Barbarians! Barbarians!

Fergus: That's right. Barbarians. Tell us. Did you ever see anyone swallow a sword?

Nessa: No. And I don't want to.

Macha: Swallow a sword and draw it out again?

Nessa: No. No.

Deirdre: Wouldn't you like to learn to do it yourself?

Nessa: No.

Naoise: *(Grabbing her. Forcing her to her knees)* Teach her Fergus. Teach her a proper lesson.

Fergus jumps up on his throne. He draws a huge long imaginary sword from his hip. Holding is straight up above his head, he feeds it gradually, lovingly down his throat. He clamps the hilt into his mouth. Then he gyrates ecstatically. Then, legs straddled, he begins to draw the sword out from his crotch. The courtiers moan with delight. He pulls the sword steadily and rhythmically. Finally, it is all out and he waves it triumphantly over his head. Pause. He looks at **Nessa***. Using both his hands, he points the sword at her.*

Fergus: Now it's your turn.

Nessa screams and faints. The others break into howls of laughter. They gradually collapse into drunken stupor. Nessa picks her way through the prone bodies. She turns out towards the audience facing home.

Nessa: Her stay at the court was an interminable ordeal. At last the festival was declared over. Business was finished somehow or other, arguments over, territories agreed. She couldn't conceal her joy at her departure. She turned her back on the bleary-eyed, loose-lipped men and their great girls. She vowed she would never set foot among them again.

The others jump up to become her entourage. They form the cloister around her again, urgently trying to protect her.

Conchobar: After three day's ride it was Eochaid and his scouts who first observed from a distance that their home had been attacked.

Fergus: Animals were straying loose, miles from their pens and from time to time wind brought the smell of burning.

Deirdre: They tried to hold her back but she was the first to return home.

Nessa is again in her cloister. This time standing up. The other players crumble individually - burning down. There is a piercing sound of a butcher's saw cutting through bone.

Nessa: She found her hall of study burned to the ground, and her twelve tutors in it, blackened, shrivelled up with open mouths in their necks.

Nessa sits centre stage, the others in a circle around her - dead - the burial mound.

Nessa: She carried their corpses to the grave herself, one after the other till she was as black as they were. She sat there day and night waiting to hear one of them speak from the mound and tell her what to do. She lay in bed for seven days and seven nights. She rose and tried to hear the bird-song in the morning. In the evening by the river the grasses whispered to her. Her father said time would heal all wounds. She must not brood forever about the past. There was nothing she - a woman - could do in the circumstances. Especially if the King had been at the back of it. *(Screams)* Revenge! Revenge!

Everyone springs up to form the hunting party. They beat their hands on their thighs. Pounding horsebeats.

Conchobar: Horrified, her father pleaded with her not to go in pursuit. She set off on her own, so he sent his guard after her to protect her.

Naoise: *(Roaring over the horsebeats)* The murderers seem to have vanished into the hills. After a month riding, turning farms outside in, searching, torturing people for information they hadn't got, all the men were for returning.

Nessa breaks out of the hunting image, tears up, and harangues the others.

Macha: But Essa still had the smell of burning in her nostrils and couldn't rest.

Nessa: She realized that *they* needed to get back to bloat up their bellies again at her father's house and to tell stories of the adventures they had had and feats they had accomplished.

Deirdre: She knew the secret fears of every one of her soldiers.

Naoise: Every man who showed mercy was told he was a coward.

Fergus: Every man who was courageous was told he was a fool.

Macha: So they stayed with her - scared of her bad tongue. And they changed her name to Nessa - the Tough One.

Nessa: Her pursuit dragged on. It was a year now since the murder. But she wouldn't give up.

Delicate wind chimes on tape. **Naoise** *plays* **Cathbad** *the Druid. The others lie down on their backs, arms fully outstretched behind their heads. They lie parallel to the audience in a staggered oval shape - the lake. They make slight ripples with their fingers and knees and a sighing wind sound. Let this image settle.*

Maeve: A soldier's life became second nature to her. She stopped listening for the voices of her tutors in the breeze and in the rivers.

Naoise: She was bathing one day, naked in a lake. Her troop were asleep under some alder trees. Her clothes were on a stone warming in the sun.

Nessa: *(Sitting up at the back of the lake)* A man appeared down among the rocks and stood watching her. It wasn't one of her own men, but she thought she had seen him somewhere before.

Naoise: She watched him in turn, till the lake at his beckoning lifted her and carried her over to him. It was Cathbad the Druid.

The 'lake' roll over on their faces, away from **Cathbad** *and* **Nessa** *- the water receding.*

Nessa: You've a handy way with transport. I've heard you're the most powerful Druid in the country.

Naoise: I want you to come home with me and stay with me. You can bring your troop as well. I'll house them all. If you don't agree, I'll kill you.

Nessa: That's a romantic proposal.

Naoise: I'm glad you see the humour in it.

Nessa: She shook out her hair and invited him to tell her something she didn't already know.

Naoise: Like the Story of the Two Pig-keepers, for instance.

Nessa: I'm not sure I ever want to hear that story. I suspect it's extremely crude.

Naoise: It's much worse than that - which is why you should hear it.

Nessa: Proceed.

Naoise: There were once two Pig-keepers and they were renowned for their excellence, and one lived in Munster and one in Connaught. And they loved each other dearly and delighted in each other and co-operated with each other.

Nessa: So far so good.

Naoise: But they were set against each other and they became enemies. And after that everything changed. The men were no longer men; they appeared in many violent manifestations and the country was devastated.

Nessa: So what was the end of it?

Naoise: That's the worst part of it all. The end has not yet been seen.

Nessa: You mean the story isn't over yet? We're all part of it?

Naoise: Figure it out for yourself.

Nessa *begins to wonder if she is a Pig-keeper*

Nessa: Cathbad then added another challenge. He said Nessa would bear his child and that that child would be a king. A king. Where?

Naoise: You disappoint me. Looking for directions. 'Where' is up to you. Build your own road.

Nessa: Cathbad told Nessa a secret a day while she stayed with him.

Naoise: What he did not say and what she never was to know, was that he was the man who had slaughtered her tutors. A short time later Cathbad died - or disappeared. He would turn up from time to time. But he never bothered Nessa again. Short and sweet.

Nessa: When her child was born she took herself off to live at the court of Fergus. She had a score to settle there and now with Cathbad's prophecy she was armed to avenge herself.

The lake waters curl up into the prone drunken positions we last saw at Fergus's court. **Nessa** *exits.* **Fergus** *staggers to his feet and stumbles to his throne.*

Fergus: Fergus was still the king. A decent big man who cried when he was drunk. He ate meat from morning till night. A couple of pounds of rashers and black puddings in the morning. A calf in the evening. A salmon when his stomach played him up. The cooking stones never cooled at his house.

Naoise: But to give him his due, he provided all the meat he consumed. He was a fierce warrior, led many a successful raid and had a roomful of heads to prove it.

Macha: He was generous to his household. They understood his rough and ready ways.

Nessa *enters to the sound of wind chimes. She is slow, confident, majestic. She holds her arms out, palms upturned, presenting her magnificence to them. The courtiers move backstage and erect the canopy. They take up positions on either side of* **Nessa**, *worshipping the madonna like a Bellini or Ucello triptych.*

Deirdre: They didn't recognize her as the plain girl of three years ago.

Nessa: She recognized them alright. She recognized their smell. She shook out her hair and invited Fergus to play a game with her in the bed.

Nessa *takes over Fergus's throne. Stretches out seductively.*

Fergus: She suggested chess. He suggested a drink. Then fifteen more. He was carried out of the bed every night for a fortnight and eventually he begged her to marry him.

Nessa: She would be his if he would grant her one thing.

Conchobar: Let her little boy rule for a year, so his children could call themselves the sons of a king.

Fergus: Big Fergus laughed. Where do women get their notions! All right. Surely. More drink. Into the bed.

Fergus surrenders, caressing her, kissing her all along her body. He curls up beside her, goes to sleep. The others gradually magnetized by Nessa drift over to her.

Conchobar: So the boy Conchobar became King of Ulster and, a model son, did everything his mother told him.

Naoise: In the course of that year Nessa distributed her private fortune to Fergus's friends and advisors.

Nessa: She admired their women folk.

Maeve: She doted on their beauootiful babees.

Conchobar: At the end of the year Fergus wanted his crown back. Ulster said: You let it go as your dowry. Conchobar bought it. It's his.

Fergus: *(Disconsolate)* They didn't want him back.

Naoise: Too easy-going. Better off with an energetic younger man.

Nessa stands on the throne with Conchobar. He sits in front of her. She controls him from above as if he were a puppet. She jerks up his hands, palms out, fingers tight together, the red hand of Ulster. This becomes the symbol of Conchobar's court.

Nessa: So Nessa took over. She made Conchobar into a king and Eamhain Macha, as his court came to be called, into a palace worthy of the name.

Gradually the others go to join her. She lowers her puppeteering arms and reaches out to them. Conchobar still sits, palms up. The others join up, arms out, fingers touching, forming an echo of Nessa's own cloister. Fergus sits disconsolately.

Nessa: She supervised the building of the three houses of Eamhain Macha. The red branch house became famous for civilized entertainment.

Maeve: No more orgies.

Naoise: Weapons were kept in the second branch. Drink in the third.

Deirdre: Bronze mirrors in Conchobar's apartment; spies in every other.

Macha: She encouraged the visitations of poets and musicians.

Deirdre: She 'invited' the women to take instruction.

Nessa: She had restored her cloister for herself and no-one would threaten it again. She thought of her tutors and their outstretched arms, but she could not bring their faces clearly to mind. Nor could she recall anything about herself at the time when she had been their Essa.

Conchobar: Her son grew to be adored by the whole province. Every bride slept first with him and then with her husband.

Fergus: Fergus decided to leave Ulster. He staggered from this house to that. Till they all got tired of his homesick crying. He went back to Nessa and pledged himself to serve his stepson.

Part Two: Macha's Story

There is a brisk jaunty bodhrán beat. The canopy is lowered and put away. The actors take up positions staggered across the playing area. They sit and lean back sunbathing, listening to the larks and the streams. They are Cruinniuc's sons enjoying their land. **Macha** *stands and surveys them. She decides she wants them.*

Macha: There was once a farmer in the Mourne Mountains. He had seven sons and his wife was dead.

Naoise: He was considered wealthy for he owned a great deal of land. It was mostly mountain, purple and boggy, so he set sheep on it.

Conchobar: In the summer he and the sons followed the sheep up the gradual slopes. They'd lie on their backs and watch the clouds idling above them.

Deirdre: When they tired of that, they'd roll over on their stomachs and look down at the misty blue surface of Carlingford Lough which from that distance seemed quite still.

Nessa: They were content, well-fed, filthy and united.

With the exception of **Macha** *the players move to form a line along the front of the stage, sitting each with his/her legs around the person in front. The family that sticks together.*

Naoise *is at the end of the line. He plays Cruinniuc.*

Naoise/Cruinniuc: One summer day at noon, Cruinniuc, the father, was sitting at his hearth recounting the Story of the Two Pig-keepers.

Naoise: Ah those pig-keepers. They'll be the death of me. Trying to figure them out. The real puzzle is why they fell out in the first place, for they had always been the best of friends.

Deirdre: They were jealous of each other's pigs.

Naoise: Not at first. At one time they did everything for each other.

Maeve: But fell out they did and change they did.

Nessa: They changed into the fiercest fighting eagles ever seen. And if one of their feathers fell on you it burned you.

Fergus: They changed. Into whales. And when they fought off Connaught, the land was flooded. And it hasn't dried out yet.

Conchobar: They changed into stags and they fought and for two years no one slept with the crashing of their antlers.

Naoise: And no one knew what the next of it would be. And while Cruinniuc and his family speculated on this sad fact - a shadow fell across them from his open doorway.

Macha: Macha the woman said nothing, but came in and sat down beside him. She poked up the fire, swept the hearth and laid her hand, companionably, on his thigh.

Conchobar: That evening she baked bread and boiled meat for them.

Maeve: Then she washed their clothes and hung them on the bushes to get a fresh smell.

Fergus: She washed the men themselves and pulled the ticks out of them.

Nessa: When night time came she got into bed beside her gleaming host and put her arms around him.

Macha: Cruinniuc and his sons submitted bashfully to her management. She smiled encouragement at them. They gazed at her, grinning and blushing. They followed her around.

The family all jump up and surround **Macha.** *Their curiosity is wild, voracious. She tries to escape but they run with her, suffocating her.*

Naoise: One day, Cruinniuc cleared his throat to speak.

Nessa: They all looked at him.

Conchobar: Everyone knew he was going to ask her who she was.

Maeve: Where she had come from, how long she was going to stay.

Deirdre: Why had she chosen them?

Fergus: A million questions that were dammed up inside them all.

Naoise: And the end of the Story of the Pig-keepers.

She sinks down, withdrawing into herself, and rejecting them. They go and hide, utterly desolate.

Macha: Macha stopped him on the intake of his breath. She shook her head and laid her finger on his lips. She seemed troubled, nervous.

Naoise: The youngest boy burst into floods of tears. The others all went off and hid in different barns.

Fergus: They had offended her. She might leave them.

Macha lilts Liam Weldon's song, 'Via Extasia'. During the first verse of the song the family stir. They peep out at her. During the second verse, they creep back to her. She accepts them, mothers them. They snuggle up as before.

Conchobar: But that evening, she was at the hearth with baths and towels and she washed them and combed them and she padded them dry.

Deirdre: It was the first time they had heard her voice. Their hearts rose again.

Maeve: There was to be a festival down in the valley, to celebrate the progress of the new king Conchobar.

Fanfare of trumpets. Macha goes and sits. The others form Conchobar's triumphal procession marching behind Conchobar and Nessa, palms up, in the red hand image. They march slowly - step, close, step, close. Conchobar stands on the throne, the others form a semi-circle in front of him - palms out. The royal box at the sports.

Nessa: This was part of Nessa's policy, to introduce her son to each area of his kingdom, with celebration and ceremony.

Macha: Cruinniuc and his sons wanted to go to see the new king, and show themselves off in their new good looks. Macha didn't go. She was expecting a baby and knew that the birth would be any day now. She spoke to them the night before. She said emphatically and crisply that they were not to talk about her at all, to anyone, for any reason. That was it. They promised.

Conchobar *remains standing. The courtiers become Macha's men goggling at the events. The competitors are placed in the auditorium. Actors play the responses straight out.*

Naoise: This was the most astounding spectacle any of them had ever seen.

Fergus: Hundreds of pigeons had been netted and the Druids released them just as Conchobar arrived with his mother - in a cloud of applauding wings.

Deirdre: The whole festival consisted of competitions.

Naoise: Who could balance longest on the tip of his lance.

All: *Gasp.*

Maeve: Who could throw his spear and catch it in mid-flight.

All: *Gasp.*

Fergus: Who could leap from where he was standing, over the tallest beech tree. Backwards.

All: Ooh!

Deirdre: It seemed to Macha's men that everybody could accomplish these dazzling feats except them. Everyone was competing except them. They had no claim to fame.

Conchobar: The highlight of the sports was the horse-racing. The king's gigantic horses won every race. Nessa had seen to that.

In their awe-struck state Macha's men are standing in the middle of the race-track. They scatter in terror as thunderous hoofbeats race over their heads.

Conchobar: They were declared by the presiding Druids to be the most magnificent animals in the country and the fastest ever seen. No creature on earth, declared a red-faced priest, could compare with these horses and they symbolized the might and mastery of their owner, the glorious new King of Ulster.

Naoise: Up jumped the farmer Cruinniuc. My wife can run faster.

Maeve: The Druids were in consternation.

Nessa: Who dared insult the king's horses?

Deirdre: Some queer old mountainy man who picked his teeth with a toe nail.

Naoise: My wife can run faster.

*Nessa distributes lengths of material. **Conchobar** remains on high. The others using cloths as tails, become the horses in the race.*

Fergus: So Macha was fetched and set among the horses.

Macha: She begged them not to make her do it. Everyone could see she was pregnant.

Conchobar: She didn't have to race if she didn't want to. She could take her husband home with her right now, in quarters.

Macha: A mother bore each one of you. Don't ask me to do this. Can't see for their tails. Can't breathe for their tails in my mouth. Scalding my arms with their sweat.

Conchobar: *(Roaring)* Ar agaidh libh!

Macha runs without moving her feet, her head flung back, straining with her chest and arms. The others pound with their feet and crack the tails - at once horses and jockeys. She falls. They roar at her to get up and go on. As she struggles up again, they fall behind her and she wins.

Macha: Let me through. Let me through.

*Collapses at the end of the race. The horses become horrified and mesmerized spectators as **Macha** gives birth. First to one child, then to a second. As they describe her scream they cover their ears. **Macha** should not scream.*

Maeve: Right there in the field in front of them, she gave birth.

Naoise: They watched her in her ordeal. No one dared approach her.

Nessa: Two children came out of her. She screamed, as they came.

Silence.

Deirdre: *(Whispering)* The scream was heard all over Ulster

Conchobar: Every man who heard that scream and his sons for generations after were cursed by Macha.

Fergus: In any time of crisis or threat to their homeland the men of Ulster were made to feel the agony that she had suffered.

Naoise: They would be convulsed with pain, bewildered, bursting. At the very moment you most need your strength, you will go into your pains, and will not be able to move from your beds.

Conchobar: Conchobar called the place after her, Eamhain Macha, the Twins of Macha.

Macha resumes mother position at Cruinniuc's hearth. The others creep up to her again - soberly.

Naoise: She went back up the mountain with her husband, eight sons now and one daughter.

Macha: *(Stridently)* But she left her curse behind her.

Drum beat. Exeunt.

Interval.

Part Three: Deirdre's Story

The actors enter to delicate, sinister music. **Deirdre** *stands on the throne back stage centre the focus of attention.* **Conchobar** *sits on another boulder down right, surrounded by his courtiers, palms up.*

To the set have been added several tall spindly tree shapes. These serve to create the wood, Deirdre's prison, spears of the warriors. There are three attached to the edge of the ramp with clips, back right, and one back left.

Deirdre: The story of Deirdre is soon told. Brought up all alone in the back of beyond beside a waterfall. That was her company. Endless crashing and smashing of water sheeting down and down, over and over. She watched it till the land crawled up beside it and the trees revolved in the hillsides.

Macha: And always Conchobar watching her. Measuring her growth, the size of her teats, licking his lips.

Fergus: At her birth, Cathbad the Druid had foretold that this girl's beauty would be brighter than the sun and deathlier than the moon.

Nessa: He had warned that she would be the destruction of Ulster.

Macha: There would be blood, panic, running, children crying all on the head of her.

Maeve: People were frightened to think of such a creature amongst them. Cathbad was never wrong.

Nessa: At the outset, Nessa said, move quickly. Into a bog. Into a ditch, a big stone on top her. Be done with it quick.

Conchobar: But Conchobar went to see this child and handed his heart into her little fist.

Maeve: He was getting on in years. What could he hope for from this?

Conchobar: He would wait.

Macha: It was completely inappropriate. He had responsibilities.

Nessa: Had he no sense of decorum?

Conchobar: He would wait. And he did. He waited and watched her and loved her.

Conchobar moves upstage to join **Deirdre.**

Deirdre: And she loved her guardian Con who was so good to her. She played with his jewellery, plaited his hair, pushed him under the waterfall where they went to bathe.

He brings her a gift - a cloak. He teases her with it before giving it to her. Horseplay charged with sexuality on his part. The courtiers move to take up position in a line from down right to back right. They are the surrounding wall of the mountain lake and they create the echo.

Conchobar: She loved the countryside with a passion he hoped would soon be fixed on him.

Deirdre: She would drag him off to wonder at black lakes she had found out among the steep stony hills.

Conchobar: Deirdre. Deirdre.

Echo: Deirdre. Deirdre.

Deirdre: Conchobar.

Echo: Conchobar.

Conchobar: Deirdre. Deirdre. Deirdre. Deirdre. Deirdre.

Echo: Deirdre.

Conchobar: And he vowed he would give it all to her one day. Every drop of water, every stone to the lightest scree would be hers.

Deirdre: That meant nothing to her. Owning it. Older people were always on about ownership. Just be.

Conchobar: Then one day she was waiting for him with her hair combed. She didn't want to go climbing or listening to echoes. She wanted to go to Eamhain Macha to see the Red Branch Knights.

Drumbeat. Martial. The courtiers move to take up their 'spears' and strike military positions with them.

Fergus: The finest warriors of Ulster were at the court of Conchobar.

Nessa: On his mother's advice he surrounded himself only with the best.

Maeve: Among them the most magnificent were the sons of Usnach.

Naoise: And of those the most outstanding was Naoise. Fact!

Deirdre: They said his hair glinted in the sun. His eyes glinted in the dark; his body was white as snow with no seams or scars.

Naoise: For no-one could get to him.

Deirdre: His lips were red and his hands ... They said his hands ...

Naoise: Were terrific too. And his hair was black and he had a dimple in his chin. Fact!

Conchobar: And when he sang at night on the ramparts of Eamhain Macha the birds would get up to listen to him.

Deirdre: Really? I want to hear him sing.

Conchobar: You want to hear him sing! What kind of silly talk is this? Do you know you sound like a tawdry serving girl, fit for nothing but gossip and fornication. Why do you think I've had you educated out here by yourself? So as to keep your head clear of such stupid vulgarity.

Deirdre: Don't talk to me like that.

Conchobar: I won't talk to you at all if you choose to go on like a camp follower.

Deirdre: But they're your soldiers I want to see. You're proud of them yourself.

Conchobar: Yes they're mine. What is best in them is what I have given them. So you need look no farther than me. Look at me. Come on. We'll go to the lake and put all this out of our minds.

Conchobar moves to sit dejectedly among his courtiers, down right.

Deirdre: Deirdre had had enough of greybeards and their looks and their silences. Something had happened to the king. He was shrivelling up. His fingers were like iron when he took her by the arm. She had begun - not to - want - to be - with him. His tempers. His outbursts. It was as though ... She didn't want to think about it. One night she jumped down from the old fortress where she lived and set off.

Maeve: Where?

Deirdre: I don't know. I do know.

Macha: She could see well enough by the light of the moon and soon the ramparts of Eamhain Macha rose up on the horizon.

Nessa: This was it at last ... At last.

Maeve: She had to get there and she never felt the stones of the road hitting her feet.

Fergus: Then came the sound of a horse coming behind her at a great gallop.

Deirdre: She looked behind but could see nothing - only the white road.

Conchobar: But the sound got louder.

Macha: They had missed her at home.

Maeve: They were after her.

Still holding their 'trees' the courtiers scatter across the stage. They crouch at the base of the tree holding it erect. They are the wood and the mischievous prophetic spirits of the wood.

Deirdre: She ran off the road into a wood and hid.

Fergus: The hoof-beats grew nearer and nearer.

Deirdre: She held her breath.

Conchobar: They passed by.

Fergus: After a minute she started to return to the road.

Crack - with the trees

Conchobar: *(Crack)*

Deirdre: It was her own footfall.

Fergus: *(Crack)*

Conchobar: *(Crack)*

Deirdre: No, something was coming. Something through the wood. Not behind her now. Towards her.

Naoise leaps out at her.

Nessa: *(Whispering)* A stranger appeared. His hair glinted in the moon.

Fergus: *(Whispering)* In the moon.

Nessa: *(Whispering)* His eyes glinted in the dark.

Macha: *(Whispering)* In the dark. In the dark.

Deirdre: Who are you and what are you doing here in my wood?

Naoise: *(Gazing at her)* A gazelle.

Maeve: *(Whispering)* She'll be the death of you.

Nessa: *(Whispering)* The death of you.

Deirdre: You'd better introduce yourself. You're trespassing and my guardian is with me - you must have heard his horse - he's on the road - he's near at hand.

Macha: His body is as white as snow.

Naoise: The only hoof-beats I heard were my own horse. I saw your shape on the road. Then I saw it slink into the wood. So I passed you out and doubled back.

Deirdre: I didn't slink.

Naoise: Looked pretty slinky to me. You didn't want to be seen, for you know you have no right to be here.

Deirdre: I have every right to be here. This is my place all around here.

Naoise: I am on my way to Eamhain where there is a king who might be interested to hear your claim. I think he is under the illusion that this territory is his. And I am in the business of minding it for him.

Deirdre: He gave it to me.

Naoise: Oh yes. To a little elf with bare feet and untidy hair. You can come with me now and we will see him together - for he is having a celebration. He will be delighted to meet you – if, as you say, you are such good friends.

Deirdre: No. No. Don't bring me to Conchobar. It's him I'm trying to get away from.

Naoise: Then you're running in the wrong direction. What have you done?

Deirdre: Nothing. Deirdre told him who she was and how her guardian had begun to change. Had begun to stifle her. And she told him how she had to see Naoise and how she knew she would meet him just as surely as she knew her nails and her hair would grow.

Naoise: The more he gazed at her face, the more enchanted he became, till he could hardly catch his breath. Do you know you'll be the death of me.

Deirdre: You mean you'll help me, help me to see Naoise.

Naoise: Help yourself.

Deirdre: I guessed it. You see. I was right. I said it would happen.

Naoise: And it has. He called his horse to him and set her up on it and walked slowly back with her, to her own fortress. She fell silent. He said she must be sensible and that it was time for her to grow up. Conchobar was a great king, a great man and a generous master. The Red Branch was the greatest body of men in Ireland. Did she not think that to be their queen was the finest destiny a woman could wish for?

Deirdre: And she told him he had fifteen big freckles on the nape of his neck.

Naoise: The next night he broke into the fortress where she was kept, found her and ran off with her.

Deirdre: For a while they were alone, able to dream together in places only Naoise knew of, where the loudest sound was the rising of a trout.

Naoise: But before long the howls and curses of Eamhain Macha reached them and Deirdre's nightmares took shape.

Fergus: His brothers found him first. They told of Conchobar's fury.

Macha: He had gone for Deirdre in his wedding clothes and when he found she was gone, he had had fits.

Maeve: They had thought he was going to die. He ran screaming through the waterfall as if he might find her there.

Macha: He had threatened to kill Nessa. Everyone was terrified.

Fergus: There were armies of mercenaries looking for the couple. Someone was bound to betray them. They didn't stand a chance.

Maeve: Only for Fergus, Conchobar would have killed everyone in sight. Naoise was in terrible danger. Did he realize he had not just forfeited his position, his honour, but his life?

Naoise: But Naoise knew that he had discovered life with this girl and when they had spent some time with her, his brothers could believe it too.

Fergus: They loved her without reservation, for that was how she gave her own love.

Deirdre: And when Deirdre urged that they should seek refuge away, the brothers came with them.

Conchobar: They took off across the sea to Scotland with nothing other than what they stood up in.

Fergus: They hired themselves out as mercenaries. Degrading. And all over the head of a girl.

The company sits as though in a curragh. They row. **Conchobar** *sits on his throne.*

Fergus: The prophecy about her had come true but she was innocent. And she was theirs. So they went on.

Nessa: They were driven to an island off the coast of Scotland, more seaweed than land. They camped on rocks and the wind blew till they had to cover their mouths to breathe.

Exhaustion.

Naoise: So this was to be their lives. This was what he had heard whispered about her on the soft beds at home, before he had ever met her.

Fergus: But there were times in every single day when she delighted them, then they'd go through ten times the hardship to have her amongst them.

Deirdre: She made a joke or a song about every circumstance. It was her job to conceal the foreboding in her heart from everyone.

Fergus: The news of their situation got home to Eamhain Macha. A major debate ensued.

Break out of the curragh image. The others whisper among themselves, gradually getting louder, ending with violent shouting, until **Conchobar** *calls* **Fergus** *to order.*

Conchobar: That's enough!

Naoise *and* **Deirdre** *remain seated together.*

Fergus: *(Weeping)* Fergus maintained it was a disgrace that any of their own kin should be pushed from pillar to post by a crowd of Scottish red-necks.

Macha: They were only impulsive youngsters and they had suffered enough.

Nessa: There was a chance that further misery could be averted if they were allowed home and if everyone controlled themselves.

Macha: It was possible to put a stop to anything. Just stop it.

Maeve: Conchobar should demonstrate his wisdom and let bygones be bygones.

Macha: They were young enough to forget. Let them come home.

Conchobar: Conchobar invited the assembly to request any other thing they might desire, but not that. Anything else, anything.

Fergus: Their exile is a disgrace on Ulster. Let them back.

All: Yes.

Conchobar: All right. Have it your own way. But secretly he was frightened.

Fergus: Fergus went for them. He found them on a blustery cliff, gazing out towards Rathlin, forever out of reach.

Naoise: They were ecstatic when they saw him. He was father and friend and mother and home.

Deirdre: But behind him Deirdre saw the horns of Eamhain, curled like a wintry moon. And under them the white face of Conchobar.

Fergus: He assured them that all was forgiven and forgotten. They were to come home.

Deirdre: Forgotten! Forgiven!

Naoise: He had arrived at their breaking point. They had borne their homesickness long enough.

Fergus: She must remember how they felt about the place. No water was as blue as Carlingford. No waves so high as Moyle.

Naoise: No cliffs so black. No land so green.

Deirdre: No king so bitter. No, don't go. We mustn't go back there.

Naoise: The brothers were used to Conchobar's passions. So a while ago he could have killed them. Now he was calm and he loved them again.

Deirdre: She knew him too. Knew that mask of a face. Knew what it hid. Didn't they remember being chased; hiding from men who'd been promised farms for her head, or Naoise's?

Naoise: But Fergus already had the brothers laughing at gossip from home. And Naoise felt something stirring too. The need to compete; the need to fight.

Deirdre: No!

Naoise: You'll be with me. You'll be quite safe.

Deirdre: It's not myself I fear for. I dream at night. I dreamed about this. Don't go.

Naoise: We have to settle with Conchobar. We were not born to spend our lives running. He will be magnanimous. Believe Fergus.

Naoise and Deirdre stand together. The others go back upstage to raise the canopy and fetch their spears. They spread themselves out on either side of Conchobar - the watchers on the battlements.

Maeve: Everyone gathered on the battlements outside Eamhain when they heard the exiles were back.

Fergus: The leaders of Ulster stood there in the evening light, shivering in their purple cloaks, watching the four horses and their riders move slowly up over the open landscape.

Naoise: This very landscape had been made by Naoise when he cleared acres of forests to make the approach to Eamhain and Conchobar had said there was no one like him.

Macha: The riders looked tired, their hair frizzy, thick with brine, their tunics bleached and hard.

Nessa: Conchobar and Nessa joined the watchers on the battlements.

Conchobar: Another man came and stood close behind him. He was called Eoin and Naoise had killed his father.

Fergus: Eoin looked at his feet the whole time and whispered to the king.

Naoise goes before Conchobar. Raises his arms in an embrace.

Macha: Eoin ran nimbly down to greet them. He drove his sword through Naoise's back bone. He was about to strike again. This time his brothers flung themselves in front of Naoise to protect him and all three were hacked down together.

Naoise falls.

Fergus: Fergus could not believe what had happened. The king had given his word. To him - to all of them. There was no honour left. He had been a cat's paw. Conchobar had used him for his sentiment and his affection. By the time he caught up with events, the sons of Usnach were dead and Deirdre was a prisoner.

Deirdre is surrounded by others holding spears.

Deirdre: For a year she grieved silently. She never went out of the room she was put in. She never washed her hair. Conchobar shouted at her but she answered him quietly and her voice was steady. She ate little and only to please her jailers who were decent enough men.

Conchobar: Conchobar said, I've had enough of this. You're not going to turn into an old woman on me. You will sleep six months of the year with me, and six with Eoin MacDurtaigh, the man who slew Naoise. That will bring the colour back to your cheeks.

Macha: There was to be a fair at Eamhain Macha. Three years to the day that she had met Naoise. People said that she had grown to look like him.

*Players form a chariot around **Deirdre** and **Conchobar**. Two on each side with spears held out at right angles - the scythes on the wheels of celtic chariots. **Fergus** in front, on one knee with a spear in each hand - the shafts.*

Conchobar: Conchobar drove out in his chariot. He brought Deirdre and stood her between himself and Eoin. There you are now, my darling, a ewe between two rams. Get used to the smell of us both.

*Simultaneously she speaks and moves. She rolls away and lies beside **Fergus**. He stands and gazes at her as the others break out of chariot and re-hang spears - all disturbed, fraught.*

Deirdre: She flung herself out of the chariot and dashed her brains out on a rock.

Fergus: That night Fergus burned Eamhain. The only way to deal with rats is to burn them out. There was nothing worth keeping in a kingdom based on betrayal. Better by far that it be razed to the ground. He left for Connaught with three thousand of the Red Branch warriors, where they offered their allegiance to Maeve of Cruachan.

Part Four: Maeve's Story

*There is a melancholy drum beat and the sound of many voices - arguing, chanting, indistinct, fading away in the distance. The players replace their weapons, fold away the canopy and wait upstage for **Maeve** and **Ailill** (played by **Conchobar**) to collect costume and props (a cushion for **Ailill**). They turn and move downstage together. **Ailill** and **Maeve** detached from the others. The others in a line do a sexy shimmy to a bright bodhrán beat and turn around to form bed-head of Maeve and Ailill's bed, where the pillow talk takes place.*

Maeve: Maeve was the Queen of Connaught; a warm-hearted hospitable woman, as every man who ever stayed at her house could testify, for she went out of her way to fill his plate, his goblet and his bed. And the one man was never enough for her.

Conchobar/Ailill: Her husband Ailill was a powerful man, highly respected - and very understanding.

Maeve: They were delighted with each other and with themselves. The palace of Cruachan was famous for its beds. There were several in every room, for Maeve didn't believe in chairs. She always maintained you could have a much more fertile conversation lying down.

Conchobar: Ailill shared his wife's attitude to chairs, food, wine, nice clothes, horse racing and beds. Two more compatible people never shared the same bolster. He took stock of his Maeve with great satisfaction. Do you know something - it's better you're getting. You've improved since you married me.

Maeve: Maeve was who she was and always had been. What improvement was possible? He'd always said she was perfect. Had he lied? Right so. Back to the beginning. Maeve descended from a line of kings as long as your arm.

Conchobar: *(Reasoning, surprised)* That was why Ailill had decided she was worthy enough to marry him. He was, after all, the most spirited, robust and generous man of his generation.

Maeve: Which meant he was her equal and that was why she married him. She had brought to him the most magnificent dowry ever heard of. The entire province of Cruachan and nine thousand nine hundred soldiers.

Conchobar: Were they back to the dowry again? Had she taken leave of her senses to think her fortune was greater than his? If he'd left her to her own devices, she wouldn't have a halfpenny to her name.

Maeve: Jealousy talking. There wasn't a tree or a bit of scenery in Connaught, until they had included Cruachan within its boundaries. And she had given it to them. A decent place to be. And beds. Who had brought the beds?

Conchobar: Before I met you, I didn't sleep so much.

Maeve: What's that supposed to mean?

Conchobar: It *means* you're a very tiresome woman.

Maeve: And a very rich one. That's what galls you. Admit it.

Conchobar: These protestations of wealth are not impressive. You're trying to convince yourself.

Maeve: I know what I know.

Conchobar: And I know what I know.

Naoise: They sent to Leinster for auctioneers to evaluate their two estates.

Deirdre: Every item each of them owned was counted, weighed, measured and compared.

Maeve and Ailill sit. The others - the auctioneers - stand around them announcing their tallys.

Macha: As far as land was concerned, they were neck and neck.

Nessa: Neck and neck in herds of swine.

Fergus: Neck and neck in flocks of sheep.

Naoise: Neck and neck in cattle.

Deirdre: Neck and neck in flocks of geese.

Macha: Neck and neck in swans.

Maeve: Neck and neck in fish.

Naoise: How do we count the fish?

Maeve: Get into the rivers and the lakes and count them. That's what you're being paid for.

Nessa: Neck and neck in rings and bracelets.

Fergus: Neck and neck in necklaces.

Maeve: Say that again.

Fergus: Neck and neck in necklaces.

Deirdre: Neck and neck in furniture.

Macha: Neck and neck in bolts of cloth.

Naoise: Neck and neck in dishes.

Nessa: Neck and neck in soldiers and servants.

Conchobar: Shear the sheep and weigh the wool.

The auctioneers: Neck and neck, neck and neck, neck and neck.

The bull is presented. The largest actor stands upstage, facing upstage, slightly bent over with arms up and wide as horns - quivering. Three actors stand behind, bent over from the waist, bums out to audience, the body; the smallest actor leans over the middle one of them and swishes one leg behind as the tail, trailing on the ground.

Conchobar: And then they discovered Finnbennach, a white-horned bull which had been born to one of Maeve's cows but had gone over to Ailill's herd and had refused to leave it, because it wouldn't follow a woman.

Maeve: There was nothing to equal him in the Queen's herd. She was beaten.

The bull goes back to being the bedhead. **Maeve** *flings herself into bed for her tantrum.*

Maeve: She might as well have been a pauper. She couldn't lift up her head. She felt like a child who'd been humoured into thinking she was important. She felt that everyone had been laughing up their sleeves at her for the last twenty years.

With all her airs and graces, she was no more than a kept woman.

The bedhead group around her now as her cronies, patting her, soothing her, encouraging her.

Naoise: Then she was told of the existence of another bull in Ulster. A big brown one, the Dun Bó Cúailinge, bigger, fiercer, more stupendous than Ailill's white one. If she got the seed of that for her herd, she'd be equal to anyone.

Maeve: She would send off for the loan of it for a year. In return she would offer fifty yearling heifers.

Nessa: A farm of land the size of the Ulster farmer's own, in Connaught.

Macha: A chariot worth twenty-one sewing girls.

Deirdre: And a sample of her own famous hospitality to round everything off.

Maeve: Maeve waited impatiently for the arrival of the bull. She would have to get it to the heifers at once. It was all taking too much time. She wanted immediate results. She was ready to explode with frustration. Any one who looked sideways at her was dismissed from her service.

Conchobar: Ailill looked on sympathetically. He didn't like to see her suffer. And he missed her. But she would have to accept the facts of life. He was in the lead. He worried, though, about the eruption he could see coming. He hoped she'd get the Dun Bó Cúailinge and then nature could take its course. He waited as anxiously as the next man.

Deirdre: The messengers returned, shifty, and reluctant to speak.

Everybody: Well? Where's the bull?

Maeve: Speak up. Tell the story.

Naoise: Well, first of all the Ulster farmer had been so delighted with her proposition, he'd burst the cushions under him with his bouncing.

Maeve: So far so good. Where's the bull?

Deirdre: There was a lot of drink taken then.

Naoise: To celebrate the bargain.

Deirdre: And to let the Ulstermen show how hospitable they were.

Maeve: That shouldn't have taken too long.

Naoise: Oh no, no, they were very open-handed.

Maeve: So? In that case, where's the bull? Have you lost it?

Deirdre: In a manner of speaking.

Naoise: With our tongues loosened we said ...

Deirdre: He said ...

Naoise: I said ... I said it was just as well the oul' fella agreed to our terms for the bull, for if he hadn't, I would have taken it anyway. That's what I said.

Maeve laughs.

Maeve: So then what?

Deirdre: The Ulsterman said get out to hell – you'll have no bull of mine and tell that woman she's lucky I don't cut your throats.

Maeve: 'That woman' indeed. I'll show him 'that woman' with a vengeance!

Nessa: Maeve wasn't too worried about the diplomacy of the situation.

Macha: The messengers had told no more than the truth.

Maeve: She had to have that bull, even if it meant the inconvenience of going to war.

Ailill joins Maeve. The others go and take up positions around the big centre-back boulder which will become Maeve's chariot. They are her soldiers waiting for the call to arms.

Conchobar/Ailill: Ailill wanted to keep an eye on her so he said he'd been slighted too by this upstart of a farmer. Who did he think he was, refusing a request from the greatest lady in the land? He should have been honoured to send his bull without any compensation at all. Maeve's problem always was that she was too good-natured. It allowed her inferiors to take advantage of her.

Maeve: He was the only man who really understood her. The only man she really loved. And so it was more imperative than ever that she prove herself equal to him. She would fight to the death to get the bull.

Conchobar: And he would fight with her. They'd raise an army. Fergus was obviously the person to lead them. He'd be able to take them to Cúailinge in the cleverest way, for he knew the whole province like the back of his hand.

Maeve: Besides, he owed it to them. They had sheltered him for years and never called on his services before.

Fergus: Fergus had known such an expedition would occur sooner or later. That at some time, as sure as winter ended the year, he would be required to turn on Ulster. But when Maeve came to him he was taken unawares. He took his time to muster his soldiers and to prepare his chariot and his weapons.

Conchobar: Ailill was complacent. His wife knew well how to inspire men. He would leave it to her to select the moment to provide encouragement.

Ailill brings Maeve to her chariot. She mounts ceremoniously and he stands to her right, her principal general. Fergus calls the others down front. They crouch in two groups of two, the team of horses drawing Maeve's chariot. Fergus begins a heaving, stamping rhythm. Conchobar joins in.

Nessa: As they set out, Maeve's army was filled with foreboding.

Deirdre: Fergus still had loyalty to home. There were people still there whom he loved.

Naoise: He was afraid of the morning he would wake up and see the land of Ulster rising to meet him.

Deirdre: He fancied it was a different colour. Had a different smell.

Fergus: It was the light. There was a different light.

Macha: He knew that as soon as news of an approaching army reached them in Ulster, they would all fall under Macha's spell, and would take to their beds, gasping and vomiting with labour pains.

Nessa: And old Nessa would be getting Cuchulainn - the only one free from the curse - down to the border to take on the men of Connaught.

Fergus: So Fergus gave Cuchulainn time to get going. And himself time to think about what he was going to do.

Naoise: He led Maeve's army up and down and round about. They were stuck for months on the shores of midland lakes, where eels choked the watering horses and fish bit the bathing men.

Conchobar: The nearer they got to Ulster, the more he thought of Cuchulainn. He could talk of nothing else.

Fergus: He could think of nothing else.

Nessa: Maeve's army could think of nothing else.

Naoise: At the age of four, with a hurley, Cuchulainn destroyed an entire troop of armed men.

Macha: He has seven pupils, like seven stars in each eye.

Maeve: He squints.

Deirdre: At the age of seven when he was embarrassed at the sight of women's breasts, they put him in a vat of water to calm him down. He boiled the water in the vat with his sheer temper and it burst and scalded fifty people. Seven times over.

Macha: He has seven fingers on each hand and seven toes on each foot.

Fergus: By the age of eleven there wasn't a fortress built that could keep him out. By fifteen he could see the soul of every weapon and no weapon disobeyed him.

Macha: He has four dimples in each cheek.

Deirdre: He goes into battle in a monstrous contortion. He shakes from head to toe, a shaking that would stop the heart of a lion.

Naoise: His body twists inside his skin. He is inside out and back to front.

Conchobar: One eye is sucked to the back of his skull, the other dangles on his chin.

Nessa: A straight column of black blood shoots up from the crown of his head and hangs in a cloud of sparks and smoke.

Maeve: No wonder he squints.

Fergus: And returning from battle a flock of swans fly with him over his chariot.

Macha: And a wild stag trots beside, calmed by one look from Cuchulainn's eye.

Maeve: I never want to hear that name again. You're obsessed with a boy, a brat without hair on his chin. There's to be no more about eyes or fingers or toes or any other part of him. Thinking to clear her soldiers' minds, Maeve sought out the prophetess Fedelm.

Macha plays Fedelm. She takes a red cloth from behind a downstage rock and kneeling, makes movement of washing and wringing it out, twisting it above her head, bathing in what flows from it.

Maeve: When they found her, she was washing clothes and the water that ran from them was red. *(Moving among the army)* There's blood on you. There's blood on you.

The army are horrified, panic-stricken. They examine themselves to see blood seeping through their clothes. They echo **Macha** *. 'Blood on you'. 'Blood'. 'Blood'.*

Macha/Fedelm: *(Shrieking)* I see you crimson! I see you red!

Maeve: *(Jumping up. Shattering the spell)* What's all this? Pull yourselves together. You've let yourselves be shaken by an old black crow. Soon Conchobar and his men will be over their cramps and they'll swarm down on us. We have to move. We can't be held at bay by a whippersnapper who paints stubble on his chin with berries. We've got to get rid of Cuchulainn.

Fergus: She began to bribe men to meet him in single combat.

Maeve: She offered them money.

Naoise: *(Listlessly)* Money!

Maeve: Cattle.

Deirdre: *(Interested)* Cattle?

Maeve: Land.

Nessa: *(Very interested)* Land?

Maeve: And her daughter Finnabair in marriage.

All: *(Incredulously)* Marriage!

Maeve: And she promised to tell them the end of the Story of the Two Pig-keepers.

All: *(Emphatically)* We'll do it.

There is a fast martial beat on the bodhrán, gradually becoming wild and convoluted to suggest the confusion of the battle. **Maeve** *watches while the others line up, three facing three to perform the single combat. It is like a dance in which they gradually collapse and fall, still preserving some contact with one another: the first two in an embrace, the second couple, one holding the other by the legs, the third couple, their legs intertwining.*

Macha: Finnabair was engaged twenty-seven times in one month.

Naoise: All her fiancés were delivered back from Cuchulainn to the camp with their entrails around their feet.

Deirdre: Fergus was leading them astray.

Conchobar: He and the other Ulster exiles were up and down to the border calloguing with the enemy. Running with the hare and hunting with the hounds.

Nessa: Something would have to be done.

Maeve: She took him off to a wood and lay down with him.

Maeve grabs Fergus by the hand and dumps him unceremoniously on his back. All the others come and watch.

Maeve: She went off to find Fergus. She knew right well that he was beginning to dither. She reminded him that this was his chance of getting his revenge on Ulster .

Deirdre: On Conchobar for having stolen his throne.

Macha: For having murdered Deirdre and Naoise.

Fergus: As if he needed reminding. But though she reiterated everything he knew in his heart of hearts to be true - she couldn't get him into the right frame of mind.

Naoise: He had too many friends there.

Deirdre: He couldn't contemplate the slaughter.

Fergus: People he had lived his life with.

Naoise: He hated their king. But they were all right.

Maeve: He was just a big duck-egg sitting on the border and no matter which way he fell - he would break. She had cajoled, bribed and bullied every way she knew how. There was nothing for it but to lead the army herself. She set off with her own troop.

Naoise: They eluded Cuchulainn. They crossed into Ulster.

Macha: There it snowed on them to the height of ten men.

Deirdre: They made a city in the snow and sat in it and argued with one another, for months.

Nessa: Then it rained on them till their city melted and their arguments melted and they almost melted into wrinkles.

Conchobar: They trudged on and, within a short march, they found - a bull.

Fergus: It was sitting in a flooded field with a retinue of wet cows.

Maeve: (*Making up her mind*) It was the Dun Bó Cúailinge.

The company all raise their arms to suggest the horns of a bull. But they are tired. It is an anti-climax.

During the ensuing seven speeches, the company take the positions and grouping of the characters of Picasso's 'Guernica'.

Naoise: *(The bull)* The bull was trundled down from his pasture.

Macha: *(Woman with Child)* The men of Ulster rose from their pains and pursued them.

Conchobar: *(The Man on the Ground with Sword)* They mixed their enemies' brains with lime and used them in their slings.

Fergus: *(The horse)* Fighting, not over a woman, not over a bull. Fighting for the sake of killing.

Nessa: *(The Head with the Lamp)* There was nothing but darkness and floods of blood.

Deirdre: *(Woman with Up-flung Arms)* If only this battle were the end of the world.

Maeve: *(Woman Running and Falling)* But it was only the end of Maeve's campaign. She went back to Connaught with the brown bull, half her army dead and the other half, silent.

*The 'Guernica' image is held. Then **Maeve** sits up - back in her bed in Cruachan. On their lines, the others break out of the 'Guernica' and assume the opening image of this story - Maeve and Ailill's bed and the pillow-talk.*

Maeve: Ailill stayed on to fight. Months later he returned - with no stories.

Conchobar: Conchobar had defeated them. He was king of kings. No more to be said.

Fergus: Fergus trailed back too. His mind was - not made up.

Macha: Finnabair stayed on with Cuchulainn. She liked the taste of berries.

Nessa: Nessa was blind. But her secrets kept her going.

Deirdre: Ten thousand cattle had been rustled, to plump up the Connaught bellies.

Naoise: Twice that many bellies had been slashed in the getting of them.

*The bed head is now in place. **Maeve** and **Ailill** are in the bed as before. She looks at him in silence. He turns his back on her and rests his head on his arm. Eyes open.*

Epilogue

The cloister bell rings as at the beginning of the play. The company take up their positions, as in the prologue.

Macha: One time ...

Conchobar: Now there was once ...

Nessa: Then there was ...

Maeve: Upon a time.

Deirdre: Once. Once.

Naoise: Once ...

As they start into the Story of the Pig-keepers, the company move downstage telling the story directly out to the audience.

Fergus: There were once two Pig-keepers and they were great friends. And one lived in Connaught and one in Munster.

Maeve: They were the best men of their kind. They respected and loved each other.

Macha: They visited each other with their herds. If one had a good mast of acorns he invited the other to share it.

Nessa: But then ... But then they were set against each other. They were told one was taking advantage of the other. They became suspicious. They became enemies.

Conchobar: They transformed themselves into ravens. For two years the skies in Connaught and in Munster thundered with the sound of their combat.

Deirdre: They transformed into sea-beasts. For two years the seas around Connaught and Munster heaved to the pulse of their battle.

Naoise: They transformed into warriors. For two years the air in Connaught and Munster was thick with their screams and their clashes.

Fergus: They transformed themselves into maggots and slipped, each, into a river; one was drunk by the cow who calved Finnbennach.

Maeve: And one was drunk by the cow who calved the Dun Bó Cúailinge. And those two bulls ripped each other to pieces.

All players raise their arms to form horns, heads down. They jump legs apart - facing out front - one heavy solid movement - locking into battle.

Blackout.

Afterword

Women in Arms

Although I come from County Derry, I discovered the Ulster Cycle of Irish mythology in Kerry. The excitement of first seeing Mount Brandon and the Slieve Mish Mountains led me to excavate the legends and histories associated with these breath-taking places. The promontory fort on the top of Caherconree was, in ancient times, the home of Curigh the Shapeshifter. It had been taken by surprise and all its inhabitants massacred by Cuchulainn, who had lurked for months on Brandon, plotting with Curigh's wife, awaiting his chance to avenge a slight to his vanity.

This complex tale led me to Eamhain Macha in Armagh, to Conchobar and the Red Branch Knights and a wealth of fascinating stories drenched in blood and bombast. In spite of all the competitive posturing of the Red Branch warriors, it struck me that it was the women in this cycle of stories who engineered the destinies of their men, and of the country. Once the wily Nessa got on her way, she established a new dynasty at Eamhain Macha and from then the major turning points in the cycle revolve around women.

I wanted to retell these stories from this perspective, and looked for a fresh theatrical idiom in which to present them, free from the shackles of naturalism, poetic drama, or pageant. I chose the vigorous colloquial language of rural Northern Ireland, much of the turn of phrase being direct translation from Irish. The staging of the play does not rely on formal choreography. The images are in turn suggestive and stylized, playful and prophetic. The narrative is an extension of traditional storytelling, and has the the capacity to allow the audience to traverse time and distances as freely as the Red Branch did when all of Ireland was their playground. The play came out of the landscape.

Mary Elizabeth Burke-Kennedy
Dublin
2001

Couch

SÍOFRA CAMPBELL

Characters

Leah

Rachel

Bob, Rachel's boyfriend

Grandmother, Leah's

Andrew, Leah's brother

Anna, Andrew's girlfriend

Simon, Bob's friend

Note

All the characters should be played by two actors, without interchanging the parts of Leah and Rachel.

Couch was presented at the Dublin Fringe Festival 2000 in a version modified from the original.

Leah is at the front door of her flat, talking to Rachel who is standing in the hall.

Rachel: So do you mind if I check yours, then?

Leah: Eh. No, not at all. Come in.

Rachel: Is this a bad time?

Leah: I was just - Not at all. It's through there.

Rachel: Yeah. We've the same layout.

Leah: Of course you do.

Rachel: Great.

Rachel goes through to the other room. Leah remembers she was speaking to someone on the phone.

Leah: Oh.

She picks up the receiver.

Leah: Sorry. My neighbour was just at the door. She's having problems with her -

Leah listens.

Leah: Mam. Stop. You know what the answer is. Well, I can't talk to him either, he doesn't listen to me. I haven't conveniently forgotten. Yeah. OK I will. Bye.

She hangs up the phone.

Leah: D'YA WANT A CUP A TEA?

No response.

Leah: RACHEL.

No response.

Leah: D'YA WANT ONE?

No response.

Leah: HELLO?

No response. Leah gets a bit concerned.

Leah: I'M MAKING A CUP A TEA.

From the other room:

Rachel: LOVE ONE.

Leah *goes and comes back with two mugs of steaming tea. She sits on the couch.* **Rachel** *comes out.*

Rachel: Oh my God.

Leah: What happened?

Rachel: This.

Leah: What?

Rachel: Where did you get it?

Leah: Em. It might have been Arnott's. Or it might have been Habitat.

Rachel *strokes the back of the couch. She sits into it with great tenderness.* **Leah** *hands her her tea.*

Rachel: Thanks.

Leah: Any luck?

Rachel *looks at her blank.*

Leah: The -

Rachel *looks at her tea.*

Rachel: Oh. Yours seems to be fine.

Leah: So what do you think it might be then?

Rachel: I don't know. It's a mystery.

Leah: Maybe it's rot.

Rachel: Could be.

Leah: Maybe.

Rachel: Maybe.

Leah: Maybe you should ring a someone.

Rachel: That's the next step, yeah. Yeah.

Leah: Yeah, I think so.

*Rachel leaps up from the couch without touching it. **Leah** is alarmed.*

Rachel: I don't know whether to sit on it or look at it. Which is better?

Leah: It's only a couch.

Rachel: But which is better?

Leah: I usually sit on it, usually.

Rachel weighs it up.

Rachel: You're right.

She sits back down.

Leah: So you were living in London?

Rachel: Yeah.

Leah: So how was that?

Rachel: Fine. Yeah, London's grand. Some things are better, some things are worse. Better things include British Gas, the mix of people, High Street Kensington, sterling and the way there's no doors on the buses, some of them, and the way people don't talk to each other on the buses. That's great. And when they do talk, I could hardly keep a straight face sometimes. But they do know how to hit them t's. Tite as opposed to tigshhhh. That's good.

Leah: So what made you come back?

Rachel: Couldn't get a boyfriend.

Leah: Really?

Rachel: Yeah. It's desperate over there.

Leah: And it's better here?

Rachel: Ah yeah.

Leah: Really?

Rachel: Ah yeah. Irish fellas are more -

Rachel searches and searches for the right expression.

Rachel: Willing.

Leah: Willing how?

Rachel: Just.

Leah: I never found them that willing.

Rachel: No?

Leah: Easy, maybe. But very unwilling.

Rachel: Unwilling how?

Leah thinks.

Leah: Generally. You never know where you are with them.

Rachel: Ah, they're grand. I came back, scored almost immediately.

Leah: Yeah?

Rachel: Just over a week it took me.

Leah: Is he nice?

Rachel: Ah, alright. It's a start. D'you have a fella?

Leah: Just got dumped.

Rachel: You're better off. Fellas are eejits.

Leah: I know. But getting dumped by an eejit is no laugh.

Rachel: I've a few eejits I could fix you up with.

Leah: Yeah?

Rachel: Ah yeah.

Leah: How come?

Rachel: I just know a lot of them.

Leah: Great.

Rachel: Ah yeah. Not my kind of eejits but decent sorts all the same.

Leah: Great.

Rachel: Ah yeah.

Leah: But not just any eejit.

Rachel: Ah no.

Leah: Because the last eejit -

Rachel: I can imagine.

Leah: As soon as we -

Rachel: You don't have to tell me.

Leah: And then he -

Rachel: It's desperate.

Leah: So I tried to -

Rachel: Go'way.

Leah: And then of course -

Rachel: Sure I know.

Leah: What a disaster.

They sit in silence.

Rachel: I think the room would work better if you moved it over there.

Leah *is puzzled.*

Rachel: The couch.

Leah: I kind of like it where it is.

Rachel: Doesn't work.

Leah: I like it.

Rachel: Doesn't work.

Leah: Well.

Rachel: I'm only saying.

Leah: We'll agree to differ.

Rachel: But it doesn't work.

Leah: Well.

The atmosphere gets frosty.

Rachel: I should go.

Leah: Alright.

Rachel: Thanks for the tea.

Leah: No problem. Come back again.

Rachel: Don't be a stranger you either.

Leah: I won't.

Rachel: When would it be all right to pop round again, d'ya think?

Leah: Well, what were you thinking?

Rachel: I'll play it by ear.

Leah: Well, OK.

Rachel: Bye.

Rachel leaves.

*Rachel and **Bob** in Rachel's flat, **Bob** is sitting on their couch reading the newspaper.*

Bob: I says to myself, Bob, the woman is only relaying the information, don't take it out on her. She doesn't make up the rules. Sure enough, that's the next thing she says to me, I don't make up the rules, all hassled with herself. I almost had to lean over and stroke her hair to let her know it was alright, I wasn't holding rules against her. She had lovely frizzy hair and I was wanting to touch it anyway but either way I didn't. I filled out the thing and gave it back. There's no knowing how these things will go but with any luck we should be approved by the end of the month. Get ourselves out of this kip, somewhere nice. I'm sick of looking out that window. Rachel?

Rachel: Yeah?

Bob: I thought you weren't listening to me there for a second. So anyway, I dropped six or seven hints today about the promotion and I think they got through. I was afraid I'd get slagged but actually no. The three of them nodded like they were taking it serious. If some young whippersnapper arrives in off the *Irish Times*, that's it. I mean - who knows the company better than me? Hah? I was there before all of them, you know? People have came and went and Stalwart Bob. Stalwart. Stalwart Bob. Yeah. So.

Bob *thinks about this.*

Bob: Rache?

Rachel: Yeah?

Bob: What was I saying? Bob. Yeah. Anyway. Nobody's better at minding their own business. And if there's needing to be depended on, Bob's your man. Bob. Yeah. Things keep happening to me, it's funny. Yeah. Like you know the way - it's just funny. Yeah. Funny.

Rachel *kicks the couch.*

Bob: Rache?

Rachel: I mean, there's ugly you can live with but really.

Bob: If there's someone else, just tell me. Bearing in mind that you told me you wanted to spend the rest of your life with me and said I was the only man in the world for you. Women are such liars.

Bob *sticks his fingers in his ears and closes his eyes.*

Bob: I can take it. Speak up.

Rachel *opens her mouth to speak.* **Bob** *buries himself under a cushion. He stays there a minute and then resurfaces.*

Bob: Have you finished?

Rachel *nods.* **Bob** *takes his fingers out of his ears.*

Bob: What?

Rachel *laughs.* **Bob** *drops his head in his hands and thinks what to do. He jumps up accusingly.*

Bob: Where did you go last night really?

Rachel: I went next door.

Bob: You told me you were checking the -

Rachel: I was.

Bob: I'm going to bust down that door and roar in there and -

Bob *heads for the door.* ***Rachel*** *blocks him. They tussle.*

Rachel: Something's burning, Bob.

Bob: No it's not.

They keep tussling.

Rachel: It is, I swear.

Bob: I have it on low, it couldn't be burning.

They tussle some more.

Rachel: Can you not smell it?

Bob: No.

Rachel *gives up and jumps back.*

Rachel: Let it be noted that it was me saved the dinner. Six points.

Rachel *goes to save the dinner.* ***Bob*** *looks triumphant.*

Leah *and her* ***Grandmother*** *in Leah's flat.* ***Leah*** *is dragging a hoover out.*

Granny: Can you not wait till I'm out the door?

Leah: I'm only taking it out to remind myself.

Granny: He's a nice young lad if only he wouldn't keep -

Leah: Nice me arse.

Granny: Ah Leah. There's no harm in him apart from -

Leah: There's no harm in him? A big dose of that fella would - would - and you'd be -

Granny: Sure it's the same as anyone, really.

Leah: Are you alright?

Granny: Of course I'm alright. Why wouldn't I be?

Leah: Well, you know with your -

Granny: I'm grand.

Leah: OK.

Granny: Mrs. Dolan's dog is destroying my flowerbeds, I don't know what to do.

Leah: Poison it.

Granny: Leah.

Leah: Little runt.

Granny: Do you not get lonely?

Leah: No.

Granny: I think it's unnatural, living by yourself.

Leah: I prefer it.

Granny: Yeah, but still.

Leah: It suits me.

Granny: I worry about that.

Leah: I'm not lonely.

Granny: What are we going to do about this young fella at all?

Leah: She should throw him out.

Granny: Ah Leah.

Leah: See how he likes that and not be doing her head in.

Granny: I have a better idea.

Leah: What's that?

Granny: He can come and live with you.

Leah: No way.

Granny: It's a great idea.

Leah: No no no.

Granny: Burglars would be afraid.

Leah: You're out of your mind.

Granny: He's your little brother.

Leah: He's a little rip.

Granny: So were you at that age.

Leah: Not half as bad.

Granny: Twice as bad and twice again.

Leah: I was not.

Granny: Don't talk to me about what you were like at that age.

Leah: Granny.

Granny: I think it's a great idea. Young fellas are happy to doss down anywhere and this is a comfy one.

***Granny** bounces up and down on the couch. **Leah** switches on the hoover to drown her out. **Granny** starts to shout for help. Something horrible is happening to **Granny** on the couch. She sits and suffers it. Eventually, **Leah** turns off the hoover. **Granny** is frozen in terror.*

Leah: What's wrong?

Granny: I -

Leah: No.

Granny: Yes.

Leah: No.

Granny: I -

Leah: You didn't.

Granny: Yes.

Leah: No.

Granny: I did.

Leah: You promised you'd tell me when you needed to -

Granny: Sorry.

Leah: It's alright.

Granny: I got upset.

Leah: It's alright.

Granny: When I get upset -

Leah: Do you need to -

Granny: No.

Leah: Are you sure?

Granny: If you haven't of upset me being so mean about your little brother.

Leah: I'm sorry.

Granny: A glass of water till I take my pill.

Leah: Of course.

Leah gets a glass of water. Granny puts it on the floor.

Granny: And I need my coat.

Leah gets Granny's coat and gives it to her.

Granny: Now, if you wouldn't mind.

Leah: Of course.

Granny: I just need to -

Leah: Of course.

Leah leaves the room. Granny heaves herself out of the couch. She checks to see that Leah is out of sight and pours the glass of water on the couch, making a little neat puddle. She ties her coat around her waist.

Granny: Alright love.

Leah comes back, all sympathetic. Granny gives a suffering smile.

Granny: Sorry about that.

Leah looks at the wet patch, pained. Through gritted teeth:

Leah: It's only a couch.

Granny: If only I hadn't the worry.

Rachel at the door of Leah's flat again. Andrew, Leah's gangly teenage brother, answers it.

Rachel: Oh. Is Leah in?

Andrew: No.

Rachel: D'ya know where she is?

Andrew: No.

Rachel: When will she be back?

Andrew: Don't know.

Rachel: You've no idea.

Andrew: No.

Rachel: You look really like her, actually. You must be her brother.

Andrew: I am.

Rachel: I thought so. Same nose, same eyes.

Andrew: Same only better.

Rachel: Are there any more?

Andrew: Why?

Rachel: I was just wondering.

Andrew: No. Andrew is the last of the line.

Rachel: Listen, would it be alright if I came in a second? I'm her next door neighbour. I need to check something.

Andrew: What do you need to check?

Rachel: Well. We're having problems with something and I just wanted to check and see was Leah having the same problems.

Andrew: What kind of problems?

Rachel: On-going problems.

Andrew: What kind of on-going problems would they be?

Rachel: Well. I'd rather not say.

Andrew: In my book, that's a bit suspicious.

Rachel: It's private.

Andrew: And you think that Leah might have the same kind of private problem?

Rachel: Exactly. And if she is, then we can go to the landlord.

Andrew: I see.

Rachel: Are you a Gard or something?

Andrew: They threw me out of Templemore.

Rachel: I'm sorry to hear that.

Andrew: Said I was trouble.

Rachel: Can I come in please?

Andrew: OK.

Andrew lets Rachel in. The couch has been cordoned off. Rachel is aghast.

Rachel: What happened the couch?

Andrew: Accident.

Rachel: Is it serious?

Andrew: Granny.

Rachel: Oh no.

Andrew: Yes. She has problems with her -

Rachel: The couch.

Andrew: I have to sleep there when it dries out. How disgusting is that?

Rachel: The couch.

Andrew: So what is the nature of this private -

Rachel: Oh that doesn't matter.

Andrew looks at her very suspiciously. Rachel squirms and changes her mind, pointing to the other room.

Rachel: : Actually, I just need to check in the -

Andrew: Go on ahead.

*Rachel goes through to the other room. **Andrew** stands watching her. She comes back.*

Rachel: No. Leah's seems to be fine.

Andrew: That's a relief.

Rachel: So you don't know when she'll be back?

Andrew: No.

Rachel: Do you mind if I sit down a second? I'm knackered.

Andrew: Can you not sit in your own house?

Rachel: Just for a second.

Andrew: Suit yourself.

Rachel sits looking at the couch, swinging her leg.

Rachel: So have you moved in?

Andrew: Against my better judgement.

Rachel: Oh.

Andrew: We're very worried about her.

Rachel: Oh. Why's that?

Andrew: Family matter.

Rachel: Oh, I'm sorry.

Andrew: So here I am.

Rachel: God love you.

Andrew: I know.

Rachel: So how long do you think you'll be staying?

Andrew: It's not easy to predict that right this minute.

Rachel: Oh.

Andrew: Could be a day or two, might be a few years. Depends.

Rachel: I see. So what are you doing with yourself now that you're not a Gard?

Andrew: My Leaving.

Rachel is confused.

Rachel: I thought you said -

Andrew: I only said they threw me out. I went in over the fence one night, locked. Scars to prove it.

Bob is in the shop buying tins of things and a few other bits. He spots Leah looking through the magazines.

Bob: Excuse me?

Leah turns around.

Bob: Hi. You're Leah, right?

Leah: Yes?

Bob: Bob. I live next door with Rachel. We're -

Leah: I thought you were about to tell me I had to buy it to read it.

Bob: Oh no, I don't work here.

Leah: I just wanted my horoscope.

Bob: I work in an office.

Leah: There's no point in buying the magazine just for the horoscope.

Bob: Read all you like.

They both laugh.

Bob: So yeah. I'm your next door neighbour.

Leah: That's great.

Bob: Yeah.

Leah: Great.

Bob: So what do you think of the building?

Leah: The building's fine. Absolutely fine.

Bob: Yeah.

Leah: Nice to live in, right?

Bob: I don't find it that great.

Leah: I'm sorry to hear that.

Bob: People have different standards, what they think is good.

Leah: I suppose so.

Bob: We're moving soon.

Leah: Oh, you are? Where are you moving?

Bob: Not sure yet. We're buying.

Leah: Great.

Bob: Just waiting to get the mortgage approved and then we'll get going with it.

Leah: It's never too late.

Bob: Well, it kind of is, you know, the way things are. I came to saving late. We were never taught about piggy banks in our house growing up.

Leah: That's awful.

Bob: That's life. So I'm trying to catch up on all that kind of thing now.

Leah: Well, the best of luck.

Leah puts the magazine back and makes as if to leave.

Bob: I was wondering could I ask you something?

Leah: Yeah. Of course you can.

Bob: You're going to think I'm really daft.

Leah: No I won't.

Bob grimaces, trying to make up his mind will he ask the question.

Bob: It's Rachel

Leah: I was going to say.

They both nod.

Bob: I don't know what to do.

Leah: I'm sorry to hear that.

Bob: Half of me thinks it's because I said Elaine had nice hair.

Leah: Who's Elaine?

Bob: Elaine at the bank.

Leah: Oh.

Bob: You see, what happened was -

Leah: Bob -

Bob: I only -

Leah: Bob -

Bob: I mean -

Leah: Bob, I don't think you should be telling me this.

Bob: That's as far as it went.

Leah: Bob -

Bob: So I wanted to ask you -

Leah: I don't know.

Bob: What?

Leah: I don't know. Haven't a clue.

Bob: But -

Leah: It's between you and Rachel. I really don't know.

Bob: N -

Leah: I don't

Bob: B -

Leah: Really.

Bob: W -

Leah: I'm sorry Bob, I can't help.

Bob: Women are the pits.

Bob *looks very upset.* ***Leah*** *knows she should escape.*

Leah: I'm sorry Bob.

Bob: The total pits.

Leah: Oh. Bob.

Bob: I don't know what to do.

Leah: Talk to her.

Bob: I've tried.

Leah: Bob.

Leah pats his arm.

Bob: Do you remember the first night she went into yours?

Leah: Yes. When you were having problems with the -

Bob: Right.

Leah: Of course I remember.

Bob: OK. Well -

Leah nodding encouragement. Bob takes a deep breath.

Bob: Who else was there?

Leah doesn't understand.

Leah: There was only the two of us.

Bob: Are you sure?

Leah: Yeah. She came in and stayed twenty minutes but there was only the two of us there.

Bob: Women are so conniving.

Leah: Bob -

Bob: Forget it.

Bob backs away.

Leah: Bob.

Bob: Just wait till someone is doing something behind your back and you want to know what it is and no one'll tell you.

Leah: Bob.

Bob *leaves.*

Leah *is just in from work.*

Leah: ANDREW. COME OUT HERE NOW.

Leah *stands with her arms folded.* **Andrew** *appears doing up the belt of his trousers.*

Andrew: What?

Leah: You know what. I come home from work -

Andrew: Keep your voice down.

Leah: I'LL TALK AS LOUD AS I LIKE IT'S MY HOUSE.

Andrew: Leah. Let's be reasonable here.

Leah: Reasonable? I'll give you reasonable.

Andrew: Point taken.

Leah: I come home from work -

Andrew: Alright.

Leah: And find -

Andrew: Point taken.

Leah: You and -

Andrew: POINT TAKEN.

Leah: You cannot bring cider-drinking trollops the like of that into this house.

Andrew: That's my girlfriend.

Leah: The third one in as many days.

Andrew: You know what your problem is?

Leah: It's not fair and it's not on.

Andrew: I'll tell you.

Leah: We're not talking about me here.

Andrew: Just because -

Leah: THAT'S MY ROOM.

Andrew: I heard you the first time.

Leah: MY ROOM.

Andrew: Well I could hardly entertain her on the couch.

Leah: MY HOUSE.

Andrew: Would you prefer if you walked in and I was -

Leah: I'D PREFER IF I WALKED IN AND IT WAS ONLY ME LIVING HERE.

Andrew: You've always hated me since I was born and then it wasn't just you getting all the attention.

Leah: SHUT UP.

Andrew: It's true.

Leah: Get her out. OUT.

Andrew: You've made my life nothing but misery.

Leah: OUT.

Andrew: From Day One.

Leah: OUT.

Andrew: Misery.

Leah: OUT.

Andrew: And finally I find a way to let some love in.

Leah: OUT.

Andrew: Finally.

Leah: OUT.

Andrew: And you just can't.

Leah: OUT.

Andrew: You just can't.

Leah: OUT.

Andrew: Well fine. Fine. I can't believe how selfish -

Leah: Selfish?

Andrew: Yes.

Leah: You're such a teenage twit.

Andrew: Oh that's low.

Leah: Please don't start going on about your feelings again. I can't stand it. Just get her out of here and that's the end of bringing anybody back ever.

Andrew shrugs.

Andrew: Well, can you go for a walk or something?

Leah: Go for a walk?

Andrew: She's afraid to come out now. I know I would be if there was a pissed-off sister waiting in moral judgement.

Leah glowers. She grabs her coat.

Leah: I'll be back in ten minutes. Ten minutes. And you better have the place cleaned up.

Leah leaves. Andrew sinks on to the couch. He picks up the newspaper. Anna comes out of the bedroom.

Anna: Hiya. Is everything alright?

Andrew: You have to go.

Anna: Yeah. But I can't find my -

Andrew: Where did you put it?

Anna: I don't know. I think you had it last.

Andrew: Oh. Have another look.

Anna goes to have another look. She comes back.

Anna: No. I can't find it.

Andrew goes to have a look. Anna sits on the couch to put her boots on. Andrew comes back.

Andrew: No. It doesn't seem to be anywhere around.

Anna: What'll I do?

Andrew: Well you can't sit here until it decides to show up.

Anna: I think you're a big ride.

Andrew: Really?

Anna: Yeah.

Andrew: Well thanks very much.

Anna: And?

Andrew: What?

Anna: Do you think I'm a big ride?

Andrew: Of course I do.

Anna: You don't really.

Andrew: I do.

Anna: Great. So will you come and meet me Ma?

Andrew: Do you not think it's a bit soon?

Anna: Is it?

Andrew: Well, I only met you -

Anna: I suppose. She'd like to meet you but. Youse'd get on.

Andrew: Maybe on Saturday.

Anna: Seriously?

Andrew: I have to, you know, do things today.

Anna: So what do you do?

Andrew: What do you mean?

Anna: For a job, like?

Andrew: Oh. I'm doing my Leaving.

Anna: Should you not be in school then?

Andrew: Eh.

Anna: How many honours are you doing?

Andrew: Eh. About four. Yourself?

Anna: I'm only in second year.

Andrew: Second year is great.

Anna: It is yeah. I like it.

Andrew: What's your favourite subject?

Anna: Maths.

Andrew: Maths?

Anna: Yeah. Maths is great. And science.

Andrew: Maths is my worst subject.

Anna: You see the way we'd balance each other out. What are you good at?

Andrew: Eh. History.

Anna: And what else?

Andrew: Eh. Geography.

Anna: And what else?

Andrew: Eh.

Anna: We'd get by on that. We'd be very happy.

Andrew: Maybe so.

Anna: I could take care of all the money and you could worry about where we live and who lived there before us.

Andrew: Yeah.

Anna: I'd better leg it.

Andrew: Alright.

Anna: So you'll come round on Saturday?

Andrew: I might have to study. I'm a bit behind.

Anna: OK. Yeah, no more bunking off school now.

Bob and ***Rachel*** *are looking at a new house.*

Bob: So what do you think, Rache?

Rachel: I don't know.

Bob: Why not?

Rachel: I just don't know, Bob.

Bob: What's wrong with it? It's a perfectly good house.

Rachel: Yeah.

Bob: So what's wrong with it?

Rachel: It's just -

Bob: What?

Rachel: There's something -

Bob: What?

Rachel: I don't know. It's awful far away.

Bob: What are you talking about?

Rachel: It just is.

Bob: OK. Use your imagination here a second. Carpet.

Rachel: OK.

Bob: Have you got it?

Rachel: Yeah. A blue carpet.

Bob: No. The carpet's green.

Rachel: It's blue, Bob.

Bob: It's green.

Rachel: It's blue.

Bob: I'm telling you it's green. We have a green carpet.

Rachel: OK for the sake of argument.

Bob: Now. The curtains.

Rachel: No curtains.

Bob: We have to have curtains.

Rachel: Blinds, Bob.

Bob: Blinds are rubbish for keeping out the draft.

Rachel: Blinds are all in.

Bob: Who cares about what's all in?

Rachel: Let's just forget about it, OK?

Bob: Why are you being so difficult?

Rachel: I'm not being difficult.

Bob: You are.

Rachel: I just don't want to live here.

Bob: Why not? What's wrong with it?

Rachel: It doesn't feel right.

Bob: A lick of paint and it'll feel right.

Rachel: Yellow walls.

Bob: No. Green walls.

Rachel: You can't have green walls and a green carpet.

Bob: Yes you can.

Rachel: Are we living in St Patrick's Day?

Bob: It's about bringing the mood of the tree in the garden into the house.

Rachel: That little scut of a yoke?

Bob: We've a mortgage sitting there, Rachel.

Rachel: Yeah but you don't have to buy the first house you walk into, Bob.

Bob: All my saving up. I'm excited.

Rachel: This is not the right house.

Bob: You're being unreasonable.

Rachel: Am I not allowed have any say?

Bob: You are, of course.

Rachel: Well, I don't like this house.

Bob: Why not?

Rachel: Too far away.

Bob: Too far away from what?

Rachel: Things.

Bob: There's loads of amenities.

Rachel: Not amenities that I'd be interested in.

Bob: What's this about, Rache?

Rachel: It's about I don't like this house and I don't want to live here is all.

Rachel *is silent.* ***Bob*** *paces.*

Bob: I'll concede you the paint.

Rachel: How many points?

Bob: Three.

Rachel: How can the paint be three points? Bringing back the videos is four.

Bob: Surely that's in your favour then.

Rachel: Damn.

Bob: So you pick the paint.

Rachel: And the blinds.

Bob: You can't afford blinds.

Rachel: Yes I can.

Bob: You're in minus points.

Rachel: No I'm not.

Bob: Yes you are. And do you know why that is? Because I do everything.

Rachel: Oh get over yourself.

Bob: I have seventy-three points and you're minus seventeen.

Rachel: Oh. Who's keeping count?

Bob: Minus twenty with the paint and that's the cut-off.

Leah *comes back from her holidays. The couch has been moved. She puts down her suitcase.*

Leah: Andrew!

She picks up her post and starts to go through it. **Rachel** *appears.*

Rachel: Hi.

Leah: Hi Rachel.

Rachel: How was Morocco?

Leah: Nice enough. It was alright yeah.

Rachel: Snogs?

Leah: Ah. A couple.

Rachel: Any use?

Leah: Ah. Alright.

Rachel: Where were they from?

Leah: Germany.

Rachel: You didn't get much of a colour.

Leah: The weather wasn't that great. What are you doing here?

Rachel: Well -

She sits down on the couch and starts to weep.

Leah: Rachel. What's wrong?

Rachel: Bob threw me out.

Leah: Oh, love.

Rachel: He told me to get lost.

Leah: Oh. Rachel.

She stops crying.

Rachel: I'm fine. It just takes a bit of getting used to. You know, when you've been with someone seven weeks and come to depend and suddenly -

Leah: Oh.

Rachel: Andrew was - Andrew was kind enough -

Leah: Oh, love.

Rachel: He's lovely, your brother.

Leah snorts.

Leah: Where is the little rip?

Rachel: At school.

Leah: What's he doing at school?

Rachel: He turned over a new leaf.

Leah: What do you mean?

Rachel: He's at his books till all hours.

Leah: Really?

Rachel: Oh yeah. Especially maths. He was telling me he wants to be an engineer.

Leah: An engineer?

Rachel: Yeah. I agreed with him it was a good idea. I'm not sure what engineers do - have you any clue?

Leah: All kinds of different things.

Rachel: I'm taking Bob to court.

Leah: You are.

Rachel: Thinking about it.

Leah: What are you taking him to court for?

Rachel: My name is on the lease as well. He can't just throw me out.

Leah: I suppose.

Rachel: He has his savings, you know? And what do I have?

Rachel hugs the couch.

Rachel: He's such a - He's such a - He's such a -

Leah: Shh, love.

Rachel: He's such a -

Leah: Shh.

Rachel: He's such a -

Leah: Love.

Rachel: He's - He's - He's - He's - He's such a -

Leah: Shh.

Rachel: A - A - A - A -

Leah: Wanker.

Rachel: Exactly. You thought he was a wanker all along, didn't you? You were thinking, why is Rachel going out with a wanker?

Leah: No. Not at all.

Rachel: That's how women are. No loyalty.

Leah: Why did Bob throw you out?

Rachel: He - He - He - He - He - He - He - He - He - He - He - He - He-

Leah: Not to worry.

*Leah shakes her head, giving **Rachel** a hard look.*

Leah: So, I see the -

Rachel: What?

Leah: I see you moved the -

Rachel: Oh. Yeah. Much better, don't you think?

Leah: I don't know.

Rachel: You don't know?

Leah: No. I don't.

Rachel: Feels a lot more joyous.

Leah: Yeah? What joyous?

Rachel: The couch. Do you -

Leah has double had enough. She leaves the room and comes back.

Leah: Rachel -

Rachel: I know what you're going to say.

Leah: Rachel -

Rachel: I know. I know.

Leah: I don't mean to be mean.

Rachel: I know you don't.

Leah: But.

Rachel: But. Hmm. Do you need the bathroom for anything?

Leah: Not this second.

Rachel: I was just about to hop in the bath.

Leah: Hop ahead.

Rachel: I shouldn't be more than an hour.

Bob *is in the pub with **Simon**.*

Simon: That's what happens when you issue ultimatums, Bob.

Bob: I know, Simon, but -

Simon: Cheers anyway.

Bob: Yeah. Cheers. But -

Simon: You'll be back out drinking with the lads in any case. They'll be delighted.

Bob: She left me for a - . Engineered it so -

Simon: What d'ya call a hamster crossed with a pigeon?

Bob: You should have seen this place. It was perfection.

Simon: I don't know either.

Bob: And you should see her skipping up the stairs now, all happy. In to the next door like a -

Simon: You know what you should do.

Bob: What?

Simon: Get a horse.

Bob: What?

Simon: It's only a suggestion.

Bob: Where would I keep a horse?

Simon: Well, you said there was a little garden with the place.

Bob: And what would I do with it?

Simon: Ride it.

Bob tries to digest this.

Bob: Well, thanks for the idea.

Simon: No problemo.

Bob: They take a bit of looking after.

Simon: Yeah but they're lovely but.

Bob: Will you have another?

Simon: I can't, Bob. The missus is expecting me home.

Bob: And will she have the dinner ready?

Simon: For sure.

Bob: It's nice to have someone to look after.

Simon: Yeah, but if you got a horse. Have you ever kissed a fella?

Bob: No I have not.

Simon: It's one of them things, isn't it? I'm not gay, by the way. Not that there's anything wrong with it. They're awful screechy when there's a gang of them and they're all fixing each other's collars. They probably say the same thing about us that we roar our heads off and thump each other until we fall down. Maybe it's better behaviour now that I think of it. I just wonder would I regret it when I'm lying there dying that it was the one thing I should have tried the once. Like test-driving a convertible.

Andrew is studying. **Leah** *is tidying up. The couch is back where it was.*

Leah: It's your responsibility.

Andrew: Why is it my responsibility?

Leah: Because you let her in.

Andrew: So? You let her in the first time.

Leah: You let her in.

Andrew: I will tomorrow.

Leah: You said that yesterday.

Andrew: I promise tomorrow.

Leah: And while we're on the subject, when are you moving out?

Andrew: What do you mean?

Leah: You heard.

Andrew: But my new leaf.

Leah: What about it?

Andrew: Well, does that not entitle me to something?

Leah: What had you in mind?

Andrew thinks.

Andrew: Breakfast in bed.

Leah: Would you get out of it.

Andrew: I'll be a degenerate again in five minutes. Is that what you want?

Leah: I want my flat back.

Andrew: You'd be responsible when I became a repeat offender.

Leah: Rubbish.

Andrew: Think of how lonely you were.

Leah: I wasn't lonely at all.

Andrew: Yes you were. We were worried sick.

Leah: I'm giving you a week. One week.

Rachel knocks at the door of her own flat. **Bob** *answers.*

Rachel: Hi Bob.

Bob: Rachel.

Rachel: Hi.

Bob: You're back.

Rachel: Can I be back?

Bob: Well let's discuss it we'll see.

Rachel: OK.

Bob: Did you miss me?

Rachel lies.

Rachel: Something shocking.

Bob: Come in.

Bob *lets* **Rachel** *in.*

Rachel: The place looks the same.

Bob: Why wouldn't it?

Rachel: You know the way when you go back somewhere you used to live and it looks smaller.

Bob: That's from when you were little and you grew up. You were only gone a week and two days.

Rachel: Did you miss me?

Bob: I'm not saying.

Rachel: Fair enough. Did you buy the house?

Bob: I'm not saying.

Rachel: How's work?

Bob: Same.

Rachel: That's a comfort.

Bob: It's a cold comfort when you've to work through all your lunchbreaks.

Rachel: Have you not complained yet?

Bob: I'm getting round to it.

Rachel can't bear to sit down.

Rachel: You wanted to discuss.

Bob: Yes.

Rachel: Well, go ahead.

Bob: You first.

Rachel: You're the one that wants -

Bob: Oh, and am I supposed to discuss alone, is that it?

Rachel: OK Bob. Do you want to get married?

Bob: That's my question.

Rachel: I only -

Bob: You've ruined everything now.

Rachel: I'm sorry.

Bob: Why are you being so nice?

Rachel: That's how relationships work, Bob. Someone has to be nice some of the time or it's a complete disaster. If both are nice at the same time, that's having a good relationship. If both are horrible all the time, that's called Old Habits Die Hard.

Bob: Alright. Hug.

Bob and Rachel hug. Rachel kicks the couch.

Rachel: There's one condition.

Bob: What?

Rachel: I want that couch Bob.

Bob: What are you talking about?

Rachel: That's the deal.

Leah is huddled on her couch wrapped in a blanket. She is sick.

Andrew: Should I call the -

Leah: No. I'm fine, Andrew. Really I am.

Andrew: Isn't it lucky I'm here to mind you?

Leah snorts. It turns into a sneeze.

Andrew: Em. So Anna's coming round.

Leah: When?

Andrew: About in twenty minutes.

Leah: What?

Andrew: She's dying to meet you.

Leah: Why would she want to meet me?

Andrew: Because, you know - You're my -

Leah: I'm not your Mammy.

Andrew: Yeah, but -

Leah: Take her there instead.

Andrew retreats and pauses.

Andrew: Yeah, but you see -

Leah: No.

Andrew: But -

Leah: No. Absolutely not.

Andrew: Seeing as you're on the couch.

Leah: No way.

Andrew: D'ya not remember what it was like when you were our age?

Leah: No.

Andrew: Bitch.

Leah: No squared.

Rachel and *Bob* in *Arnott's*.

Bob: It's not here, Rachel.

Rachel: She only said she *might* have got it in Arnott's.

Bob: Yes and here we are and can you see it anywhere?

Rachel: Or it might have been Habitat.

Bob: Habitat.

Rachel: One or the other.

Bob: Was it more likely to be Arnotts, or was it more likely to be Habitat?

Rachel: One or the other she said.

Bob: This is rubbish.

Rachel: We made a deal, Bob.

Bob: I know. What was I thinking?

Rachel: I'm going to live in that horrible house. How's that for compromise?

Bob: I don't understand it. What is so great about that horrible couch?

Rachel: You've never even seen it.

Bob: I can imagine.

Rachel: I know what your imagination looks like. IT'S ALL GREEN.

Bob: Please stop embarrassing me.

Rachel: WE MADE A DEAL.

Bob: Rachel.

Rachel: It's not here anyway. Let's go to Habitat.

Bob: Look why don't I meet you in the pub after.

Rachel: No.

Bob: I'll even buy you a pint.

Rachel: That's generous but no.

Bob: Why do you want me to come?

Rachel: We made a deal.

Bob: OK I'll do all the cooking for the next month if -

Rachel: What have you got against Habitat?

Bob: It's miles.

Rachel: Well, we'll get a taxi.

Bob: That's stupid, that is. I can't stand the sight of that Stephen's Green.

Rachel: We made a deal.

Bob: I don't want to go to Habitat.

Rachel: Why not?

Bob: There's a fella works there and I had a run in with him.

Rachel: A fella?

Bob: No, a girl.

Rachel: What kind of a run in?

Bob: I'd rather not say.

Rachel: I'm your girlfriend. You're morally obliged to tell me everything.

Bob: Since when?

Rachel: What else have you not told me?

Andrew is packing up his schoolbooks. Leah is standing up wrapped in her blanket.

Andrew: YOU'D THROW YOUR OWN BROTHER OUT IN THE STREET.

Leah: I'M NOT THROWING YOU OUT IN THE STREET AT ALL. MAM IS LONELY. SHE MISSES YOU. SHE WANTS YOU BACK.

Andrew goes off and comes back with the rest of his belongings in a bin sack.

Andrew: You've no idea how hard it is being the youngest.

Leah: And what about me? What about how hard on my nerves I have it being the eldest?

Andrew: You're going to make me fail my Leaving.

Leah: Oh please.

Andrew: And then when I get arrested for the third time, it'll be your fault.

Leah: I won't be blackmailed.

Andrew: The one chance I had to make a go of my life.

Leah: I don't know what you're talking about.

Andrew: It's misery there. You know what she's like. If only Da had never left.

Leah: You can't blame your laziness on being from a broken home.

Andrew: It's lucky I've any motivation at all.

Leah: Andrew -

Andrew: I'm serious. What's the point of getting up in the morning if when you fall in love and you've all that hope and you're so happy but at the end of the day, you're never going to get on for fifty years and if you've that gene that we have you're going to be an alco anyway. Life has no happy ending. I grew up too fast. Most people don't realize how miserable they're going to be until they look back and it was total misery.

Leah: Andrew.

Andrew: So fine if you want to throw me out.

Leah thinks. Andrew slows down his packing in anticipation of a favourable decision.

Leah: Go home to Mam.

Andrew: Bad things are going to happen to you now.

Leah: Andrew -

Andrew: That's not a threat. But it's a proven fact that that's the laws of the universe. I'm doing physics, I know these things.

Leah: You can come and stay here at the weekends. How about that?

Andrew: Friday, Saturday, Sunday?

Leah: Friday, Saturday.

Andrew: No deal. Friday, Saturday, Sunday or I won't bother me arse.

Leah: Alright.

Andrew: Then there's bank holidays. And mid-term breaks.

Andrew leaves. Leah buries her head under the blanket. Time passes. There's a knock at the door. Leah slowly lowers the blanket.

Leah: Who is it?

Bob: It's Bob.

Leah: Bob, I'm kind of under the weather and not fit to be seen.

Bob: I don't want to see you.

Leah considers this.

Leah: Well Andrew doesn't live here anymore. He left a few days ago.

Bob: I don't want to see Andrew either.

Leah: Oh. Is there another problem?

Bob: I want to see that couch.

Leah: Why ?

Bob: Because.

Leah: Bob, can you come back tomorrow? I'm seriously under the weather.

Bob: I'll bust the door down.

Leah: I'll dial 999.

Standoff.

Bob: Please.

Leah does a big cough.

Bob: Please.

Leah drags herself to the door.

Leah: Between your girlfriend and my brother and this lump of stupid furniture.

Bob: You see, the thing is -

Leah: I don't want to know.

Bob: But -

Leah: I don't want to know.

Leah lets Bob in.

Bob: Hello there again.

Bob sizes up the couch and leaves.

Rachel is sitting on the couch, happy as a bunny. Leah is at the other end looking into a large envelope.

Leah: There must be five grand in here.

Rachel: Six.

Leah: I can't take this off you.

Rachel: It's Bob's, it's fine. You're not taking it off me at all.

Leah hands her back the envelope. Rachel won't take it. Leah puts it in her lap. Rachel stands up so it falls on the floor.

Leah: I don't understand.

Rachel: Did you never want something?

Leah: Of course I did. I robbed my mother to buy a dress once. And then another time, I robbed Andrew's lunch money for two weeks so I could buy a record.

Rachel: Then you know what I'm talking about. You had to have those things, right?

Leah: Well -

Rachel: So take the money, why don't you?

Leah: You could buy ten couches for that.

Rachel: That's not the point. I want this one.

Leah: No.

Rachel is desperate.

Rachel: I'll trade you.

Leah: I don't like your couch.

Rachel: You don't?

Leah: No.

Rachel: What about Bob then?

Leah: Are you serious?

Rachel: Yes.

Leah: No.

Rachel: You said you wanted a boyfriend.

Leah: Yeah but Bob's too old.

Rachel: He's only forty-five. And he still has all his hair. He's a bargain.

Leah: No thanks.

Rachel: Just give him a trial run.

Leah: No.

Rachel: Remember them Germans and multiply the ecstasy by two hundred.

Leah: No.

Rachel: Having a boyfriend is the bees knees.

Leah: You said it wasn't.

Rachel: D'ya not remember how great it was at first?

Leah: Yeah, but only at first.

Rachel: That was then.

Leah: And?

Rachel: Now, it's even better when you get used to them because we're older and being from Dublin we like familiar things.

Leah: Bob is not my type.

Rachel: Another thing about being Irish is that we adapt well.

Leah: No.

Rachel: And women are often surprised when they acquire a taste for things.

Leah: No.

Rachel: People who live in this part of town especially are partial to their neighbours.

Leah: No, cubed.

Rachel: I'm not saying that there aren't more fish in the sea. I'm not saying that.

Leah: I'm not interested.

Rachel: Of course there are loads of fishes. Defective ones.

Leah: Rachel -

Rachel: He really does like and respect you, Leah.

Leah: He does?

Rachel: Yes.

Leah: Oh.

Rachel: Ever since he met you at that party.

Leah: I never met him at any party.

Rachel: I mean, at the thing.

Leah: What thing?

Rachel: The -

Rachel thinks.

Rachel: He's been going on and on about you in any case.

Leah: No he hasn't.

Rachel: He doesn't like many people.

Leah: I don't want to be stuck with some fella that nobody likes.

Andrew on the couch. He puts down his maths book and gets up. He shouts to the other room.

Andrew: I WAS GOING TO MAKE A CUP OF TEA. D'YA WANT ONE?

Rachel comes through.

Rachel: That would be fantastic.

He shouts through to the other room:

Andrew: ANNA. D'YA WANT A CUP A TEA?

Rachel: Anna's great.

Andrew: She is, isn't she?

Andrew goes off and comes back immediately with steaming tea.

Rachel: You're a treasure.

Andrew looks at her suspiciously. Rachel sips her tea.

Rachel: Who says be careful what you wish for? The same pack of liars as the people who say that getting what you want won't make you happy. There's so much to go around so there's no point in being mean about it.

Andrew: Yeah, but -

Rachel: No, but really.

Andrew: Yeah, but -

Rachel: No, but -

Andrew: But, Rachel -

Rachel: Yeah, but -

Andrew: But, Rachel.

Rachel: What?

Andrew: Well - . But what about when we fall out with one another? What then?

Rachel: You're too much of a worrier, Andrew.

*Leah is on a date with **Bob**. He has brought her to see the house he was thinking of buying.*

Bob: So I was thinking, green carpet, green walls.

Leah: That would look nice.

Bob: Do you think it would really?

Leah: You wouldn't have them the same shade of green, now, would ya?

Bob: Two different kinds.

Leah: Yeah. That would work.

Bob: Because you see the tree there -

Leah: Yes. That's a brilliant idea.

Bob: And did you see the supermarket as we went by on the bus?

Leah: I did.

Bob: It'd be handy if you had a car.

Leah: Yeah.

Bob: Save on the lugging, you know the way them handles cut into your hands.

Leah: Yeah.

Bob: And you saw the pub.

Leah: I did.

Bob: So I'll get a car.

Leah: What kind of a car?

Bob: I've never thought about it. D'ya know, I've never thought about it. What kind of a car would you get?

Leah: Some class of a Mercedes convertible.

Bob: I could go a Mercedes I suppose.

Leah: I suppose any kind of a car is better than no car.

Bob: And you can always sell it on if you turn out not to like it.

Leah: Of course you can.

Bob: No harm done. Should we be kissing about now?

Leah: It might be a bit soon.

Bob nods.

Bob: Kissing is alright though, no?

Leah: I have nothing against it.

Bob: And you honestly think green would work?

Afterword

Couch

This play started out as a set of formal challenges: to write a multi-character piece for two women actors, which had no bad language and which required minimal staging. These concerns met a preoccupation with home furnishings. As a rite-of-passage, the couch represents the first truly adult purchase beyond the realm of strict necessity, and signals a willingness to be domestically anchored in some way at last. In the land of rented accommodation occupied by Leah and Rachel, it takes on a disproportionate significance by virtue of being the only thing in sight. For both women, it becomes a source of anxiousness and insecurity. Rachel has one by default (Bob's) but disdains it, and covets another's. Leah's couch is pissed on, hijacked, and ultimately swapped for a man she doesn't really want simply because she should have one of those too.

Everybody worries a terrible lot. Trying to find a home for consolation, they instead flap about undermining each other. Virtually everything is barter; Leah is the only one who (grudgingly) gives, expecting nothing back. While each of them is their own comedy, there's an ultimate ruthlessness to their striving - which is not to say that the characters are manufacturing all the time. There are degrees of feeling: Andrew's teen passion for Anna is genuine, Bob is 'fond' of both women, the complex sibling relationship between Leah and Andrew is underpinned by commonality and not just obligation. But there is a feeling that they are all out to get what they can while they can - relationship as a means to an end laid bare.

As each scene turns on a hair's breath and dives into another, there should be a feeling that anything can happen next, either of the actors could become any character. There should be a charged moment of pause as means of identity is with-held from the audience before being signalled again. The narrative structure should even feel a little bit random, as if the scene taking place is almost arbitrary, but that the actors happened to find themselves doing this particular one. It should be about the actors forging a more intimate pact with the audience, a mutual seduction for the best part of an hour.

Síofra Campbell
New York
2001

I Know My Own Heart

EMMA DONOGHUE

I Know My Own Heart was first produced by Glasshouse Productions at Andrew's Lane Theatre, Dublin. A one-act, lunchtime version had been produced in April 1993 at Project Arts Centre. The full-length (evening) version, which is published here, was produced in November 1993 with the following cast:

Anne Lister	Claire Dowling
Marianne Brown	Eunice McMenamin
Nancy Brown	Aisling Cronin
Tib Norcliffe	Orla McGovern
Director	Katy Hayes
Designer	Peter Courtney
Lighting Designer	Marcus Collier
Costume Designer	Sylvia Callan
Graphic Designer	Margaret Lonergan
Producer	Caroline Williams

Characters

Anne Lister, a Yorkshire heiress-in-waiting

Marianne Brown, a farmer's daughter

Nancy Brown, a farmer's daughter

Isabella (Tib) Norcliffe, a woman of independent means

ACT ONE

Anne: *(At her desk, murmuring at the same pace as she writes)* Anne Lister of Shibden Hall, Halifax, Yorkshire. *(Amends it proudly)* *Miss* Anne Lister. Wednesday the third of April, in the year of our Lord 1811. *(She looks up and addresses the audience)* My friend Tib brings me a present whenever she comes to stay. This time it's a journal. *(Reading from the inscription)* 'In the fond hope that through a thoroughly honest account of your days, you might come to know yourself.' I am acquainted with myself already, of course, but that is merely the skin. I intend to probe down to sinew and bone. And I have devised the most secret of cryptic codes to protect my journal from any prying eyes - even Tib's.

Marianne: *(In the Browns' parlour, writing a letter)* 'Dear Miss Lister.' Do help, Nancy.

Nancy: Go on, thank her for the book.

Marianne: *(Trying out the words)* 'Kindly allow me to take this opportunity to offer you my most humble appreciations ... '

Nancy: No no, keep it graceful and simple, Marianne.

Marianne: 'Dear Miss Lister. Thank you for the book.'

Nancy: Too simple. She'll think you a child.

Marianne: I may not have attended your fancy boarding school, Nantz Brown, but I am still your elder by eighteen months.

Nancy: No need for peevishness; I'm only trying to be of use.

Anne: *(Writing diary again)* The lecture on electromagnetism lasting longer than usual, and I staying on afterwards to look at the apparatus - or rather, at that girl with skin the colour of fresh cream - I did not get home till near midnight. Though I woke at six I lay dozing till eight, remembering her. According to my aunt, the girl's name is Miss Brown. Elder daughter of Mr Copley Brown, of West Farm. Oh dear.

Nancy: Try this: 'My dear Miss Lister, allow me to thank you for your most kind gift of Miss Seward's *Poetical Works*. My sister and I read aloud from the first volume after supper last night, and we particularly enjoyed *(Picking it up and scanning the contents page)* the "Ode to Content".'

Marianne: Did we?

Nancy: They all seemed pretty much alike to me, but the important thing is to make you sound like a woman of discernment.

Marianne: Oh indeed. Carry on.

Anne: *(To her diary)* Considering her low station in life, Miss Brown is quite wonderful. I wonder what she thinks of me? She must be flattered. What girl would not be? My attention to her at church yesterday was certainly marked enough to attract her notice; Tib had to give me a great jab with her elbow when it came to Holy Communion. I fear I never received the sacrament with less reverence, Miss Brown being directly opposite me at the altar rails.

My Euclid class with the vicar made not a whit of sense to me this afternoon. Somehow Miss Brown steals my wits away. Was it going too far, to send her that book of Miss Seward's poetry? Well, let me dream and scheme what I may, I shall never permit myself to do anything beyond exchanging a civil word with her in the street. Now and then. When our paths happen to cross.

Nancy: What else is there to say?

Marianne: What do you think she'd like to hear?

Nancy: You forget that I've never met Miss Lister.

Marianne: But you must have remarked her at church, on your visits home.

Nancy: Is she so remarkable?

Marianne: Oh yes. Tall, strong, distinguished. She wears a great black cloak, and rides a horse called Lord Byron.

Nancy: Pretty?

Marianne: Handsome, more like.

Nancy: And her manners, are they similarly mannish?

Marianne: *(Peeved)* Her manners are ... softly gentlemanlike.

Nancy: Speaking of manners, how shall we end this letter? 'My family would be charmed to welcome you to our ... '

Marianne: 'Humble abode.'

Nancy: You've been reading too many sentimental novels again. The correct phrase is 'modest home'. 'My family would be charmed to welcome you to our modest home, should you happen to be passing through the village. Your kind gift has won you the eternal gratitude and esteem of your servant, M. Brown.'

Marianne: She'll know I didn't write that. I don't speak a bit like that.

Nancy: Nor do any of us; it's merely a polite code.

Marianne: You make a fair copy, Nantz, your hand is so much neater than mine.

Nancy: But what if she sees your scrawl somewhere else and notices the difference?

Marianne: You're right, as usual.

Nancy: Why this timidity, Marianne? She may be Squire Lister's niece but she's unlikely to bite you.

Marianne: You don't know her.

Nancy: Is she so frightening?

Marianne: *(Gladly)* Oh yes.

Tib: *(Entering **Anne's** room)* Your lady aunt says Betty is busy helping her make plum jam, so you must mend your leather stays yourself.

Anne: Oh Tibs, it's all so small. *(Yawns)*

Tib: If you find my company tedious ...

Anne: You're always so touchy before luncheon. The fact is, I didn't sleep at all well last night.

Tib: I knew those walnuts would give you wind.

Anne: Nonsense, I can digest anything. In fact I was fast asleep at half past three when Betty came rapping at my door to say there was a shabby-looking man interfering with the hens.

Tib: Why didn't she wake your uncle?

Anne: My aunt will not have him disturbed; that inflammation of the bowel is troubling him again. Besides, I'm the only one with a pistol.

Tib: A pistol?

Anne: *(False innocence)* Surely I mentioned it before. Perhaps it slipped your memory?

Tib: You are the most outrageous ...

Anne: Calm yourself, Tibs. I bought it in Halifax on Tuesday, because that same man - or some similarly shabby vagrant - had been seen snooping round our stables the night before. I haggled it down to sixteen and six.

Tib: I don't care what it cost, Anne; what matters to me is that my dearest friend is becoming more eccentric by the day.

Anne: My hens needed protection. When the tramp came back last night, I leaned out the parlour window and shouted 'If you do not go about your business immediately, I will blast out what few brains you possess'. But he paid me no attention, so I fired off the pistol.

Tib: *(Dry)* And shot him dead?

Anne: I'm afraid not. The pistol bounded through the window and broke the lead as well as two panes of glass. My hand felt stunned for some time.

Tib: No doubt the shabby-looking man was equally stunned. Tell me, my dear, have you heard that the townsfolk have taken to nicknaming you 'Gentleman Jack'?

Anne: Oh, that's an old one. Have they invented nothing new?

Tib: Does it not discomfit you?

Anne: Why should it?

Tib: Well, the fact that your somewhat ... masculine demeanour has provoked disapproval even in the lowest ranks.

Anne: Disapproval is too strong a word; I'd call it affectionate mockery. They know I'll be their master as soon as my uncle ... *(Lowers her voice)* passes on.

Tib: And is that how you want to spend your prime of life, Squire Lister - overseeing farmhands?

Anne: On the contrary. After the ... unhappy event, I intend to get things into shipshape order here, then convert half my fortune into francs and set off for Paris.

Tib: Will I never cure you of your dreaming habit?

Anne: You went to Paris. And Brussels, and Rome, and Athens ...

Tib: I had independent means.

Anne: It won't be long now.

Tib: Your uncle could live for thirty years more. You feed on hypotheticals.

Anne: Because nothing ever happens in Yorkshire.

Δ

Anne: I offered Miss Brown my arm at the bottom of the High Street. I regretted it the moment I did it. Think what damage this acquaintance might do to my dignity, my social standing. I offered her my arm; a slight readjustment of the muscles, no more. Such a small gesture to bear so much weight.

Marianne: *(Joining her)* Oh, Miss Lister.

Anne: I spotted you by your drooping ribbon, Miss Brown; it is quite the prettiest I have ever seen.

Marianne: I thought you didn't notice such feminine fripperies.

Anne: Not in general; other girls might have sacks around their heads, and I wouldn't notice, but there are some whose ribbons I could recall in detail after seven years. You never do respond to a compliment, Miss Brown. I missed you at church last Sunday; I hope you were not unwell?

Marianne: *(Whispers)* A female complaint.

Anne: Ah. After the service - you must excuse the impertinence, but as I was passing the pew where you sit I peeped into your prayerbook.

Marianne: Whatever for?

Anne: Simply to discover your first name, but it was not on the flyleaf.

Marianne: It's Marianne. You're very kind to take an interest.

Anne: *(Savouring the consonants)* Marianne ... I must fill the name in the blank in my diary.

Marianne: *(Alarmed)* What did you write about me?

Anne: Several things that would make you blush.

Marianne: For shame?

Anne: For pleasure. They are much too flattering to be repeated.

Marianne: That journal of yours frightens people. At the lecture I overheard Miss Caroline Greenwood say she dreaded to open her lips in front of you, for fear of your pen.

Anne: I record only those remarks that are worth remembering; Miss Caroline Greenwood need have no fear.

Marianne: I believe you have an exquisite garden at Shibden Hall, Miss Lister. I love to walk round our little kitchen garden by moonlight, it makes me deliciously melancholy.

Anne: Ah, so I've found you out: you are a romantic. *(Evasive)* I should have had great pleasure in inviting you to see Shibden, were it not that, my uncle being old and sickly, we scarcely ever make new accquaintance.

Marianne: But my mother would be delighted to have *you* call on *us;* that should not trouble your uncle.

Anne: I have not said I will never call.

Marianne: Indeed. Good day, Miss Lister.

Anne: Good day. The impertinent little baggage. How dare she adopt such pettish manners with her betters? Presuming and demanding and sulking and waving her creamy neck about like a constipated swan. Well, the townsfolk will have nothing to gossip about now. I will waste no more nights dreaming of Farmer Brown's daughter. I will keep out of the girl's way as much as possible, and devote myself entirely to the study of great literature.

Δ

Tib: *(Looking up from her book)* Have you seen anything of your little friend from the lecture recently?

Anne: Miss Brown is only an acquaintance, not a friend. I did pass her in the street today, as it happens, but she returned me only a cold little nod.

Tib: Why so?

Anne: Well, perhaps I am being fanciful, but it occurs to me that she is hurt because I haven't called on her.

Tib: Surely a girl of her station would not presume to expect a call from you.

Anne: But I may have - unintentionally - led her to hope for one. Over the past few months, we - Miss Brown and I - we have met once or twice accidentally at the library. And occasionally walked together on the moor.

Tib: How nice for you.

Anne: *(Anger breaking through her caution)* I'll not have you mock me.

Tib: *(Tinged with sarcasm)* But I'm more than glad that you've found a congenial friend in this 'wretched little village'.

Anne: It's not that, Tibs; you are all I require in a friend. But with Marianne ...

Tib: Do you like her as you liked Eliza when you were at boarding school?

Anne: Much more. She fills my head the way the scent of a bowl of roses fills a room. One does other things, one occupies oneself ...

Tib: ... and one's thoughts drift back to one Miss Brown.

Anne: You *are* mocking me.

Tib: God help me, I'm not. I remember just how addlepated I was when I first knew Charlotte.

Anne: The thing is impossible. For weeks now I've been worrying over it, but I still cannot understand why I feel such things for a girl completely outside my social sphere.

Tib: There are more important things than understanding yourself, you know.

Anne: Such as?

Tib: Happiness. *(Long pause)* Why don't you call on the girl?

Anne: *(Sullen)* Because she expects me to. Besides, that family.

Tib: I believe they're worthy folk.

Anne: Oh yes, very worthy and obliging, but low, Tibs, the Browns are undeniably low. From the hue of her nose one might even suspect Mrs Brown of a taste for spirits.

Tib: You're so intolerant of those of us who drink the least drop more than you do!

Anne: Tipsiness is undesirable in any woman, Tib, but quite unacceptable in the mother of the girl I ... have a growing regard for. *(Pause)* Besides, my aunt would never permit me to call.

Tib: Then don't ask her.

Anne: It's out of the question, Tibs. *(As **Tib** exits)* I have far too much respect for the family name.

Δ

Marianne: *(Leading **Anne** into Browns' parlour)* Pray sit down, Miss Lister. Oh, I expect you'll find that one more comfortable.

Anne: I would much rather sit here beside you.

Marianne: You look most distinguished today, Miss -

Anne: *(Interrupting)* You promised to call me Anne.

Marianne: Anne.

Anne: Will I tell you a secret? I have made up my mind always to wear black.

Marianne: Oh do. It brings out ... it suits you.

Anne: What does it bring out?

Marianne: You'll laugh.

Anne: I swear I won't.

Marianne: It brings out the fire in your eyes.

Anne: You think it's the colour of my clothes that does that, Marianne?

Marianne: Nantz would mock me for my flowery language.

Anne: Nancy is your little sister, I take it - the one at school?

Marianne: Yes. When she comes home on visits, she shows me no mercy.

Anne: Tib and I are just the same. Our letters are courteous, but whenever we meet the sparks fly.

Marianne: So Miss Norcliffe - Tib - does not actually live at Shibden Hall?

Anne: Certainly not. We've been exchanging visits for years now, but as to living together ... how could you have thought that?

Marianne: You seem so well-matched. Comfortable.

Anne: Oh, Tib and I jog along well together, all things considered. But only after my uncle's death will I be finally free to choose.

Marianne: Choose what?

Anne: A companion. As long as my uncle lingers I am his dependent. You seem to think me rich, Marianne, but I am obliged to beg and wheedle for every guinea. Sometimes I mend my stockings over and over again because I have too much pride to crawl to him for the money.

Marianne: So if he passes away -

Anne: When he dies a small but comfortable fortune will be mine, and I will choose a companion to share my life at Shibden. Someone who touches my heart far more deeply than Tib ever will.

Marianne: I see. *(Long pause)* I was so surprised when you knocked on the door this afternoon.

Anne: So was I.

Marianne: I'm sorry about my mother. She's always been that way.

Anne: It doesn't matter. Truly. I'm so glad to be here, to see where you eat, where you sew, where you ... wake.

Marianne: If you'd not called today you would have missed me; I go to stay with my cousins in Sheffield tomorrow.

Anne: *(Teasing)* Ah yes, a little bird told me that you are expected to make a good match there.

Marianne: Well ...

Anne: *(Stiffens)* You mean it's true?

Marianne: Oh no. There is a gentleman - a Mr Charles Lawton - but nothing has been said. In all likelihood nothing will come of it. *(Lightly)* Why would he stoop to me when he could have his choice of fine ladies with fat dowries?

Anne: Lawton Hall is a prosperous estate; I seem to recall visiting it as a child. I should rejoice at such a marriage for you.

Marianne: Would you?

Anne: I said should, not would. I ought to rejoice at it, and I would certainly seem to. And you?

Marianne: I am not sure whether I want to be anyone's wife just yet.

Anne: Well then. Bring your heart back safe from Sheffield.

Marianne: What must I do with it?

Anne: Just don't throw it away. I must go, my aunt expects me. Au revoir, Marianne. *(Exits)*

Marianne: *(Can't pronounce it)* Aw ... Awwah.

Anne: *(To her diary, bleakly)* Seven weeks she's been gone now. *(Pause)* Received a letter from Tib, suggesting I go to hers for Easter, but I haven't the heart. Oh, my daily routine keeps me busy enough, from going to check Lord Byron's been well groomed at six in the morning, through Greek, French, overseeing the workmen if my uncle's unwell, paying a tedious call or two, then dinner and smoking a hookah with my aunt before retiring at ten. If I have any difficulty in sleeping, I lie on my back and practise arithmetic.

Δ

Marianne: I love the wind in my hair.

Anne: So do I.

Marianne: But you've got a hat on.

Anne: I meant so do I, love the wind in your hair.

Marianne: *(Giggles)* How long have I been gone? It seems like months.

Anne: Three weeks and four and a half days. I hope you received all my letters.

Marianne: They made me pine for a walk on the moors; the air tastes so sweet after the grime of Sheffield.

Anne: *(Reproachful)* Why did you stay away so long?

Marianne: Mama has scores of friends there. And I suspect she kept delaying our departure in the fond hope that Charles would - as she put it - 'speak'.

Anne: And did he not? I notice you are on first-name terms.

Marianne: I gave him no chance to 'speak'. Whenever it seemed that we were being left tête-à-tête, I fetched my cousin Lucy to play duets.

Anne: That must have pleased your mother.

Marianne: Oh, she's worse than ever. I had to promise to be home by five o'clock today; my time is never my own.

Anne: My aunt never interferes directly in my life, but I can sometimes sense her disapproval.

Marianne: You mean because of me.

Anne: *(Unconvincingly)* No, not in particular. She has always been made uneasy by my 'takings-up' as she calls them; the way I set my heart on a friend at first sight and feel for them ... more than is quite correct.

Marianne: So there have been others.

Anne: Never like this. I had a friend at boarding school, her name was Eliza Raine. We used to dream of running off to Paris together when we were of age. I invited her to Shibden for the holidays twice a year, and my aunt became increasingly irritated; she used to refer to the friendship, even in front of the servants, as 'Anne's little infatuation'.

Marianne: Where is Eliza now?

Anne: In York, being taken care of by relatives. *(Painfully)* She was always a nervous girl, but now she has completely lost her wits.

Marianne: Do you visit her?

Anne: On occasion; sometimes I think she recognizes me. Once we had five minutes of lucid conversation, till she shattered the illusion by addressing me as Mr Smith and bursting into tears.

Marianne: Poor girl.

Anne: Am I boring you?

Marianne: Never. I'm honoured that you confide in me.

Anne: Oh, Marianne - confidences are the least of what I'd like to offer you.

Marianne: *(Awkward pause)* You know, I thought of you so much last night that it prevented me from sleeping. It almost gave me a pain.

Anne: A pain? Where?

Marianne: *(Genuinely naïve)* I don't know exactly. Above the knees.

Anne: *(Delighted)* Oh dear. You must never think of me after going to bed in future.

Marianne: And I have strange thoughts. Sometimes, I cannot help wishing that you were somehow ... a gent.

Anne: A what?

Marianne: A gentleman. Rather than a lady.

Anne: Your strange thoughts are no stranger than mine.

Marianne: But on the other hand, if you were a gentleman we could never have become such friends.

Anne: Can you bear me as I am?

Marianne: Oh Anne, what a thing to say!

Anne: Will you take me as I am?

Slowly pulls her close, kisses her throat. Blackout

Δ

Marianne: *(She is lying in Anne's arms)* I shall have to find a different name for you now, my beloved; you see, my mother calls me Mary-Anne.

Anne: And we can't have two Annes on one sofa.

Marianne: Would you like a long name or a short name?

Anne: Short. Anything but Bartholomew.

Marianne: A feminine name or a masculine name?

Anne: You choose.

Marianne: Hmm. *(Giggles)* Stop that at once, I can't think. I know: Freddy.

Anne: That is the most undignified name I've ever heard.

Marianne: But I've always loved it; I mean to christen my first son Freddy. It sounds so gentle and trustworthy-

Anne: Well then, I must live up to my new name.

Marianne: You will. This should all feel so frightening, but I know I'm safe in your arms. *(Sudden thought)* Are we sinners, Anne?

Anne: We are all sinners.

Marianne: But is this ... an unnatural sin?

Anne: *(Improvising)* Surely our conduct is natural to us, because it is not taught, but instinctive.

Marianne: I suppose so. Certainly, if I didn't believe us bound together in heart and soul, I would never think it right to, to ...

Anne: Kiss me?

Marianne: Is that the word for it?

Anne: One of them. *(Trying to distract her from morality)* Do you know what I want?

Marianne: What?

Anne: I want to bite your left breast exceedingly gently. I want to slip my hand under your petticoat and slide it between your knees.

Marianne: Stop, I can't bear it.

Anne: I want to kiss your soft thighs.

Marianne: My mother might come in. Where did you learn such language? *(**Anne** whispers in her ear)* You didn't!

Anne: I did.

Marianne: At fourteen?

Anne: Only above the waist. *(Sobers up)* But do you know what I want most?

Marianne: What?

Anne: One whole night with you. No petticoats, no listening out for mothers or aunts. I want to peel you like a grape.

Marianne: Oh. Let's.

Anne: It's impossible; we've aroused enough suspicion already.

Marianne: But Freddy, it wouldn't occur to my mother. The generality of people don't suspect that such a thing exists. I'd never heard of it myself till ... till I did it.

Anne: Didn't you always, even in childhood, have a vague imagining of what you longed for?

Marianne: No. I shared beds with my friends as girls do, that's all. This sweet intercourse between us must be the best kept secret in the history of womankind!

Anne: You may be right. If we are moderately discreet, and carry it off with confidence, I see no reason why we should ever be found out. *(Holding her close)*

Marianne: Unless my mother takes it into her head to bring me a cup of broth ...

Anne: *(Leaping away)* Oh, it's intolerable to have no place we can call our own. Now I have found you, all I want to do is fall asleep with my head pillowed on your breast.

Marianne: Think of a plan.

Anne: Lord Byron could carry both of us. *(Goes down on one knee)* Would you elope and marry me in disguise at Gretna Green? I'd look rather dashing in a moustache.

Marianne: Perhaps. If there were no other way.

Anne: I love to watch you struggle with your timidity. Don't fret, I'll think of something else.

Marianne: If only one of us had independent means. All we need is a cottage and a hundred pounds a year.

Anne: You couldn't buy many ribbons on a hundred pounds a year.

Marianne: I don't need ribbons. I need you to take me seriously.

Anne: I do. *(Half jokily)* If you'd married that Lawton fellow in Sheffield all our problems would be solved. A married lady is never suspected of anything. We could pay each other endless visits, and in a couple of years he'd die of gout and we could set up home together.

Marianne: It sounds wonderful. But would you still want me as a widow, perhaps with a child or two? You might be disappointed in my looks, having watched me grow old and fat and wrinkly in the service of another.

Anne: I would drown all your children like puppies, and kiss every inch of your body till it was beautiful again. *(Suddenly thinking of it, she fishes out from her bodice a ring on a chain)* This belonged to my great-grandmother.

Marianne: It's much too fine.

Anne: Nothing's too fine for my wife.

Marianne: *(As **Anne** puts the ring on her)* Should it not go ...

Anne: If I put it on your ring finger, my love, people might talk.

Marianne: Of course, how stupid of me.

Anne: Tell your mother it's tin, with gilt on.

Marianne: *(Joining in the joke)* I'll say I won it at the hoopla at Midsummer fair!

Anne: *(Closing her hand over the ring on Marianne's finger)* And now nothing can part us.

Marianne: When we've taken Holy Communion together; then we'll be truly married.

Anne: If only we could be. I'd drive you to church in our own carriage; I'd take you to Paris for the month of May; I'd ravish you on our own dining-room table and no one could call it a sin!

Marianne: What would we live on?

Anne: Air. And kisses. There do be fine feedin' in kisses, Mistress Lister.

Marianne: Call me that again.

Anne: Mistress Lister, giver of the longest, wildest kisses.

Marianne: Freddy, I'm frightened.

Anne: Of what?

Marianne: The future. I can't see it. My mother is talking of sending me away to Cornwall to help my aunt with her inn.

Anne: Tell her you'd pine for the moors.

Marianne: What I pine for is some security.

Anne: The day I inherit Shibden I'll send a carriage for you.

Marianne: But the world would talk, if you took me in.

Anne: What does the world ever do but talk?

Marianne: Would you not care?

Anne: Not unless you did.

Marianne: All I care about is this. But I dread it might all slip through my fingers ...

Anne: Not if I hold them tight.

Δ

Tib: *(Looks up as **Anne** runs in dishevelled and panting)* What in God's name has happened to you?

Anne: I have been grossly insulted.

Tib: How?

Anne: I was walking quietly along the river bank when a little man in a black coat came up beside me. We exchanged a few remarks on the inclement weather, and then he stepped closer and said 'Aren't you the lass they call Gentleman Jack? I'll warrant you could do with a sweetheart to make a real woman of you.' What stinking breath he had, too. Well, I rounded on him, I said 'I'll have you horsewhipped', but the next thing I knew, the brute was trying to put his hand up my skirt. Thank God for my umbrella; I was aiming a blow at the fellow's privates when he ran off as fast as he could.

Tib: You must have been terrified.

Anne: Not in the least. I knew I could knock him down if it came to a fight. I shouted 'God damn you for a craven cur', but he was already out of sight in the bushes.

Tib: 'A craven cur?'

Anne: It was the only phrase that sprang to mind in the heat of the moment.

Tib: I mustn't laugh, you're a heroine.

Anne: I blame myself for speaking to him in the first place, but being so near home I was off my guard. What if my conversation encouraged him?

Tib: What had you said?

Anne: Only 'I think it may thaw soon'.

Tib: That could hardly be deemed encouragement.

Anne: Well, it'll be a lesson to me to take care whom I speak to in future. One cannot keep people at too great a distance in this wretched town.

Tib: I hear you haven't been keeping a certain young farmer's daughter at too great a distance since my last visit.

Anne: Tib, I have endured more than a year of teasing from you on that subject, not to mention my aunt's pursed lips and snide remarks from the vicar's wife. I think you should refer to her politely as Marianne or leave Shibden by the window.

Tib: Yes Master Lister. There'll be no more teasing; I'm just glad to see you happy.

Anne: Is it obvious?

Tib: *(Laughs)* Let's hope the infatuation lasts till Christmas.

Anne: You've got such a shrivelled old heart; you don't remember what it's like to be in love.

Tib: Too true.

Δ

Nancy: *(Coming into the Browns' parlour)* Miss Lister, I presume? I'm Nancy Brown. Oh, no need to rise.

Anne: I'm delighted to make your acquaintance at last; I seemed to keep missing your visits.

Nancy: Marianne has been delayed at the milliner's; she sent me on to reassure you that she had not forgotten the time.

Anne: Your presence will be quite sufficient compensation for the loss of your sister's company.

Nancy: *(Looks down in embarrassment)* She warned me you were gallant. I feel as if I know you intimately, Miss Lister, since Marianne's letters mention little else.

Anne: There is little else to mention; Halifax does not provide much that is newsworthy. You do well to live elsewhere.

Nancy: Ah, but my time at school must soon draw to a close. *(Peeved)* My mother insists on my coming home to help her and generally replace Marianne.

Anne: Replace Marianne?

Nancy: *(Angling to discover whether **Anne** knows)* On the occasion of her marriage.

Anne: I was not aware ...

Nancy: Of course nothing has been quite decided yet. I only mention the matter because you are a close friend of the family.

Anne: Of course. And when exactly ...

Nancy: I have no idea. My father only received the letter from Mr Lawton a week ago, and as for Marianne, she's too bashful to allow it even to be whispered of in her presence.

Anne: But you think she has given her consent?

Nancy: Let me put it like this: I do not think her refusal has been too strenuous. Will you take a stroll in our little garden, Miss Lister?

Anne: *(Mechanically)* With pleasure.

Δ

Tib: Engaged? Since when?

Anne: She sent off her formal consent yesterday. The wedding will take place on Tuesday fortnight.

Tib: How very odd. Did you know about it?

Anne: *(Bluffing)* Oh yes, in fact the idea came from me. I suggested that the only way to free herself from her impossible family and wretched circumstances was to accept a good offer, such as Mr Lawton's. He's an old man ...

Tib: Barely five and fifty ...

Anne: Old enough not to be a trouble to her for too many years. As the widowed mistress of Lawton Hall, Marianne will be elevated almost to my social level, and then I defy anyone to sneer at our friendship.

Tib: Are he and she ... in love?

Anne: God, no.

Tib: Mutually attached?

Anne: Enough to marry, so she says.

Tib: And what do *you* feel?

Anne: Well I really ... *(Deflating)* ... I don't know.

Tib: Poor girl.

Anne: But she is most fortunate.

Tib: I meant you. *(Reaches out)* Come here to me.

Anne: I'm very well where I am.

Tib: *(Drawing back)* As you please. I just cannot believe what you've done.

Anne: What have I done? I'm only the friend, I'm offstage, I have no role to play in this particular drama.

Tib: You could have. Do you think I'd have let Charlotte slip though my fingers?

Anne: But she never had to marry.

Tib: She came close.

Anne: When?

Tib: It's all so long ago.

Anne: Go on.

Tib: It was in her second-last year, if you must know. Her parents received an offer for Charlotte from a rich man of business. They knew full well that she was ill, so they bullied her to accept him before her 'fading charms' might change his mind.

Anne: And did she?

Tib: Charlotte was not made of such stern stuff as you and I. She could never bear to displease anyone. I pulled her one way, Mr and Mrs Threlfall another, and between us all we reduced her to silence, and her health worsened. Well, finally I went to her suitor myself, though we had not even been introduced. I told him bluntly that bearing a child would kill her. And when he expressed some fond hopes about an improvement in her health, I said 'Sir, you may not realize that Miss Threlfall and I enjoy a sincere and tender friendship - a marriage of souls -

Anne: - delicately put -

Tib: 'and that to force us to live apart would be the greatest sin you could ever commit.'

Anne: *(Clapping gently)* What did he say?

Tib: Not a word, poor fellow. He sent a regretful note to her parents and left for the colonies a week later.

Anne: So you and Charlotte ...

Tib: We had eighteen months together. *(An afterthought)* She left me her entire fortune in her will; her parents were incensed.

Anne: I thought you lived on family money.

Tib: Oh no; if it were not for her legacy I'd be a governess by now.

Anne: And you never regretted what you'd done?

Tib: Regretted? She died in my arms. It was what we wanted. *(Pause, comes back to the present)* So you see, sometimes life has to be seized with both hands.

Anne: But your romance depended on money.

Tib: And nerve.

Anne: What have I got to offer Marianne?

Δ

Marianne: *(As **Anne** is pinning on Marianne's wedding veil)* Why don't you say something?

Anne: What would you like me to say?

Marianne: Tell me you're not angry.

Anne: I'm not angry.

Marianne: Well what *do* you feel?

Anne: Nothing. I feel nothing,

Marianne: You do understand that this will make no real difference to us?

Anne: I understand nothing about this.

Marianne: Freddy, I'm *your wife*. Remember that.

Anne: Yes.

Marianne: I wore your ring first, and I'll never take it off.

Anne: Yes.

Marianne: And I'll see you at Lawton Hall in fourteen days.

Anne: Yes.

Marianne: *(Long pause, then bursts out)* Say it!

Anne: What?

Marianne: Say you don't want me to marry and I shall call it off.

Anne: Five minutes before the ceremony?

Marianne: I'll run away with you, I'll do anything you want. Just tell me what to do.

Nancy: *(Calls from a distance)* Marianne, your groom awaits.

Anne: Go to your wedding.

Marianne: *(Shouts)* Just one moment! *(Whispers)* I won't lose you?

Anne: No.

Marianne: We shall be together.

Anne: We shall. *(Watches **Marianne** out of sight, then crumples)*

Tib: *(Entering)* Girl, girl, control yourself.

Anne: I cannot.

Tib: You have no choice.

Anne: The cold, worldly little bitch. To wait till the very last moment, then offer to run away with me. To make me do the refusing.

Tib: If the wedding guests see you cry, they will think you jealous.

Anne: Am I not?

Tib: Of course, but of him, not of her. As one withered old maid to another, I advise you not to let them think you mind.

Anne: You're right.

Tib: Now let's join the bridal party. *(Taking her arm)* Head high.

Δ

Nancy: Have you heard from my sister since her last visit?

Anne: Oh yes, a letter arrived yesterday. All goes on swimmingly.

Tib: Charles sounds highly devoted.

Anne: Indeed. He gives her strengthening medicines and washes her back with cold water every morning; all this in hopes of a son and heir.

Nancy: I believe he's taking her to the sea for three months this summer.

Anne: *(Off balance)* She didn't mention that.

Tib: Of course he may have reformed, but I did hear that Charles Lawton was rather gay in former years.

Anne: Gay?

Tib: A womanizer. A bit of a rake.

Anne: But Charles is a widower, past five and forty. *(Her anxiety mounts)* Why didn't you mention this before the wedding?

Tib: It was only a rumour.

Nancy: I heard it too.

Anne: But I would never have let her marry except that I trusted the man would treat her with the utmost care and respect.

Tib: As, it seems, he is.

Anne: All is well, then. Marianne is adequately happy. Isn't she?

Nancy: I suppose.

Anne: We are all happy.

Tib: Do you miss her, Nantz?

Nancy: One expects to lose a sister if she receives a good offer.

Tib: I don't suppose you're the kind of lady who'd refuse a good offer.

Nancy: It would have to be as good as Marianne's, or better.

Anne: You mean you intend to refuse any suitor whose income is less than Charlie's?

Nancy: Don't look so shocked; I haven't seen you leaping into marriage.

Anne: My reasons are rather different.

Nancy: Yes, but in both cases it's a kind of pride. I won't stoop to a farmer, and you -

Anne: I won't stoop to any man at all.

Nancy: Perhaps we three should form a sorority of Yorkshire spinsters.

Anne: *(Exchanging a glance with **Tib**)* I'm not sure whether you have the stuff of spinsterhood in you, my dear.

Nancy: What do you mean?

Tib: It takes considerable strength to defy the world, when all the time the world will pity you for having missed your chance in it.

Nancy: And you think me lacking in this unconventional strength?

Anne: You have not proven otherwise.

Nancy: I may surprise you yet.

Anne: Please do.

Δ

Anne: *(Writing a letter)* 'My darling Marianne, I can scarcely believe what you tell me about Charles and the chambermaid. Married less than a year to the loveliest woman in England,

and already he's stooping so low. Forgive my bluntness. I meant to soothe your woes, not aggravate them. If only you were here beside me. Of course you were right to dismiss the girl. I advise you to inform Mr Lawton that if you discover any more such goings-on in your own home you will leave on the instant. Sometimes I fear there will be no peace for you and me, my love, as long as that man lives.'

Marianne: 'My dearest Anne, Charles has been in a foul temper all week; the dreadful thought occurs to me that he may have gone rummaging through my bureau and come across your last letter. He has made some sarcastic references to "you and your mannish friend", and congratulates himself on his health in a rather insinuating manner.

I need hardly remind you that if I fail to produce a male heir, the entire estate will go to Charles's cousins after his death. Unless I stay on the best of terms with him, I cannot expect a penny in his will. Till his jealous fit subsides, I will expect to hear from you only every second Tuesday - and perhaps we could use the cryptic code you devised for your diary. Our future depends upon discretion.'

Anne: 'Beloved, I enclose my secret alphabet as requested, but I'm growing weary of discretion. I want to publish our love, Marianne, to have it celebrated in church, to announce it in ecstatic notes to all our friends and neighbours. Aren't there times when you sicken at the thought of sneaking down another corridor, stealing a few hours together, playing at being romantic friends?'

Δ

Anne: Boo! I know you're awake, stop shamming.

Marianne: I've been waiting for you for an hour and a half

Anne: But darling, you said you were going to bed early to take some laudanum for your toothache. I didn't want to disturb you.

Marianne: Then why come in to me at all? You could have sat up cosily chatting to Nantz all night.

Anne: Oho, is that it? Don't tell me you're jealous of your own little sister.

Marianne: She's an incurable flirt.

Anne: We weren't flirting, only ... agreeablizing. Nancy needed help with her Hebrew exercise.

Marianne: What else did you and she talk about?

Anne: You, of course.

Marianne: *(Sweetened)* Love, I wasn't so much jealous as concerned. I know you never mean to flirt, but your eyes do mislead people. You have all the civility of a wellbred gentleman, which confuses these girls; they cannot understand why you make them feel such excitement.

Anne: Do you speak from experience?

Marianne: You know I do. But seriously, now: Miss Caroline Greenwood told me the other day that you looked 'unutterable things' at her in church.

Anne: Miss Caroline Greenwood has an overheated imagination.

Marianne: But won't you alter your manners a little, Freddikins, to please me?

Anne: Very well then, I'll try to be less gallant. But I can't help pleasing girls.

Marianne: Pleasing is allowed, but nothing more. The rule of your conduct should be: what would a married man do?

Anne: That gives me a long rein; married men are not exactly models of fidelity.

Marianne: Must you remind me?

Anne: I'm sorry. But you musn't upset yourself over nothing; I was only talking to Nancy.

Marianne: Yes, but she lives just down the road, and you can gossip with her any time. Whereas I have only a very few precious days with you.

Anne: I'm hardly to blame for that.

Marianne: Of course not. I only meant, let's make the most of our time.

Anne: I quite agree.

Marianne: And now I want to fall asleep in your arms.

Anne: You might sleep better if you were lulled to rest by ... something tenderer.

Marianne: I'm afraid I'm far too fatigued for any of that. And my toothache is bad again.

Anne: Oh. I'm sorry. You must try to sleep.

Marianne: *(A moment later, still sulking)* In most respects, Charles is an excellent husband. He made no objection to my paying another visit to Shibden so soon after the last.

Anne: Very sweet of him. How is his health?

Marianne: Not good.

Anne: *(Grins)* I wonder if he will drag on into his sixties. Not more than five years, surely.

Marianne: Oh Anne, don't be so indelicate.

Anne: It's what we want. Isn't it?

Marianne: All in good time. When God sees fit.

Anne: So here I am wasting my life in expectation of a time which you are too delicate to calculate.

Marianne: You know I long for the freedom to spend the rest of my life at Shibden Hall. But it would be sinful to wish my own husband dead. He's not a bad man; you always think the worst of him.

Anne: On the contrary, I rarely think of him at all. *(Trying to sound casual)* The other day, though, I was wondering, just as a matter of interest: how often are you two ... connected?

Marianne: I'm not sure.

Anne: Twice a month? Three times?

Marianne: About that.

Anne: About which, twice or three times?

Marianne: Several times a month. It would be indelicate to keep account. What's the matter?

Anne: Nothing.

Marianne: Don't let's quarrel, Freddy; you know how my nerves are at this time of the month.

Anne: Don't tell me, tell your lord and master. Has it occurred to you that this is adultery? You are, after all, another man's wife.

Marianne: What do you mean, another?

Anne: What do you mean, what do I mean?

Marianne: You said another man's wife. But you're not a man.

Anne: Do you offer this as some kind of consolation?

Marianne: All I mean is, I am one man's wife, and one woman's ... beloved.

Anne: I fail to see the distinction. You can't gloss over your oddity as glibly as that.

Marianne: What oddity?

Anne: Your feelings for women; the same oddity as mine.

Marianne: *(Shocked)* Oh but *I'm* not - you are the only woman I could ever love in that way.

Anne: Why, what is unique about me?

Marianne: Well, you're a sort of ... female gentleman. If you had been of a feminine nature, I would have been quite content with platonic relations.

Anne: How you deceive yourself ...

Marianne: I'm not -

Anne: *(Interrupting)* Look, you and I and Tib and Marie Antoinette and God knows how many other wives and spinsters were simply born this way.

Marianne: What makes you say that about Tib?

Anne: I've told you about her and Charlotte Threlfall.

Marianne: Just that she lived with a friend, who died young; not that they were ... as we are.

Anne: I thought that much was obvious.

Marianne: Only to you. Most women never go beyond holding hands, you know.

Anne: How can you be so sure? There might be millions of us.

Marianne: Don't be silly. Well now, Tib and Charlotte, who'd have thought it. Just as long as she never finds out about us. Anne, you didn't.

Anne: She's known since it began.

Marianne: How could you put us in such danger?

Anne: Who am I meant to talk to when you're away at Lawton? Besides, she won't breathe a word of it.

Marianne: Who knows what she'll let slip when she's on her seventh glass of wine.

Anne: Tib is no drunkard. *(Voice rising to a shout as **Marianne** rushes out)* She's the best friend I have.

Δ

Anne: *(To her diary)* It is strange that the kisses are always best after we have quarrelled. Saying goodbye in the downstairs hall yesterday morning, while my aunt was looking out the front door for the carriage, Marianne let me gently pull her to me, with her right thigh a little between mine. I could feel the heat of her through my petticoats. My whole frame shakes as I think of it.

This morning before breakfast I locked the chamber door and tried on my new waistcoat and braces over my drawers. The effect was striking, if I say so myself. Spent half an hour in foolish fancies about dressing entirely in men's clothes, driving my own carriage, being my own master. Then Betty knocked, wanting to empty my chamberpot, and once again I was the shabby spinster of Shibden Hall. I pray it will not be many months before I take Marianne in my arms again. Deprived of this intercourse, I am prey to every passing fear and irrational rage.

Δ

Tib: *(Reading aloud, with a hint of innuendo, while* **Anne** *does her darning)* 'Harriet was a very pretty girl, and her beauty happened to be of a sort which Emma particularly admired. Emma was so busy in admiring those soft blue eyes that the evening flew away ... ' Are you listening?

Anne: Mmm. Something about blue eyes.

Tib: You particularly asked me to bring Miss Austen's new novel.

Anne: I'm sorry; I can't settle to anything this afternoon. Do you realize we haven't put a foot out of doors in six days? If this weather doesn't improve by Saturday I shall gallop out on Lord Byron and let the storm do what it will with me.

Tib: I suppose Marianne is holed up in Lawton Hall serving spiced wine to Charles and his friends. *(Pause)* How long has it been now?

Anne: Two months. Almost three.

Tib: What prevents the girl from visiting?

Anne: She fears to provoke her husband's suspicions again. So she says.

Tib: Any hint that she's in an interesting condition?

Anne: No, thank God. I begin to doubt whether Lawton is capable of siring an heir.

Tib: Her letters must be some comfort.

Anne: They're full of local gossip and they bore me to tears. We lead such separate lives. She does love me, but she also loves her house, her fine dresses, her social standing ...

Tib: What about you? Don't you love anything or ... anyone apart from her?

Anne: I feel barren, these days. No love, just need and bitterness. In her last letter Marianne complains that I am growing more 'mannish' by the year; she used to say I was 'gentlemanly'.

Tib: People call you masculine simply because you are more upright and confident than ladies are supposed to be. We all tease you, but we wouldn't want you to be different.

Anne: I'm not so sure. For the sake of female company, I'd almost consider taking to frills and bonnets.

Tib: How very unnatural that would be.

Anne: Don't joke, Tibs. I long for a companion, and I long for an establishment of my own, but by the time I control my fortune I may be too old and odd to attract anyone.

Tib: You will never be anything but irresistible.

Anne: You're mocking me.

Tib: I'm not.

Anne: I can't bear much more waiting. Marianne is teaching me to live without her.

Tib: *(Surprises her with a long kiss)* Then let her be answerable for the consequences.

Δ

Anne: *(Lights up as she groans in exhausted pleasure)* Where did you learn to do that?

Tib: *(Catching her breath)* Paris, of course. *(They laugh)* You taste better than wine. And coming from a lady who likes a fine vintage, that is no mean compliment.

Anne: You're a wicked seductress.

Tib: You provoked me to it. When you hung your head and said you'd soon be too old to attract anyone ... I couldn't resist.

Anne: I used to suspect perhaps you had a slight partiality for me, but no more than that.

Tib: So there I was hungering after your smooth limbs - and you never noticed.

Anne: Why didn't you tell me?

Tib: *(Exasperated)* I've been hinting at it for ten years. But you had other things on your mind.

Anne: I suppose so.

Tib: No sad faces tonight; I feel like champagne bubbling over. *(Pauses to calculate)* Do you realize that no one has laid hands on me since 1804?

Anne: Poor Tib, you have been sadly neglected.

Tib: You were worth the wait.

Anne: Are we bad?

Tib: Very bad.

Anne: I'm glad.

Tib: Do your aunt and uncle have any idea?

Anne: God forbid.

Tib: Your uncle must have some knowledge of such things, his library is full of Lucian and Juvenal.

Anne: Yes, but he's not a thinking man. My aunt, on the other hand, is a thinking woman, but reads nothing but recipes.

Tib: Tell me seriously, though, as a fellow-sinner; does your conscience never prick you?

Anne: No, I cannot say it does. Don't you think our connection with the ladies must be more excusable than, say, self-pollution, which has no affection to justify it?

Tib: That is an attractive argument.

Anne: In any event, I mean to repent at five-and-thirty and retire with dignity. That gives me *(Counting)* nine more years. I shall have had a good fling by then! *(Laughter, then shushes **Tib**)* Is that a carriage, at this time of night?

Tib: Take a look out the window.

Anne: God help us. Get up, Tibs. It's the Lawton crest on the side of the carriage.

Tib: *(Angry)* What in heaven brings her over the moors this late?

Anne: Quick, the butler must have let her in already.

Tib: I'll be in the little room at the end of the corridor.

Anne: Tib? I'm so sorry. I'll try to come in to you later.

Tib: Don't trouble yourself. *(Exiting)* I'll be asleep.

Anne: *(Neatening her hair as **Marianne** bursts in)* What is it, my love?

Marianne: Charles.

Anne: What has he done?

Marianne: I've left him.

Anne: You can't.

Marianne: Why not?

Anne: I mean ... I can't believe it.

Marianne: I gave him five years of my life. And now he's killing me, he's killing us both.

Anne: Sit down and tell me calmly.

Marianne: It's so shameful. I paid a visit to the doctor this afternoon on account of a hot itching sensation in my ...

down there. And he said it was ... venereal. It must have been Charles and that dirty hussy of a cook.

Anne: Damn him to hell for this.

Marianne: I wouldn't mind so much for myself, but what if I've passed the taint on to you? I'll not forgive him this time. *(Big sigh)* Oh, it's a relief to be safe at Shibden. I'll send the carriage for my things tomorrow.

Anne: What do you mean?

Marianne: Well, I'll need my medicine, and some clean linen.

Anne: But dearest, you're not thinking of staying here? My aunt would never permit it, what with my uncle bedridden and your husband likely to ride up at any moment with a brace of pistols.

Marianne: I shall send Charles a note informing him of my decision.

Anne: He'd toss it in the fire. Think, Marianne. Even if you did manage to run away and hide in London, you'd lose all you call precious - your house, your friends, your reputation even.

Marianne: But not you. You're the most precious thing I have, and I wouldn't lose you. We can leave in the morning.

Anne: With what? Seven pounds and ten shillings, that's the sum total of my worldly wealth. So don't taunt me with impossibilities.

Marianne: I thought you loved me.

Anne: I do. That's why I must save you from your own recklessness. Charles is rich enough to divorce you by act of parliament, and your name would be mud.

Marianne: Oh Freddy, you must trust my courage. I'm not a little girl anymore.

Anne: Come here, you're frozen. We'll make our plans in the morning.

Δ

Anne: *(To her diary)* She's gone. It's as if she never came. Just a ghost in the night. Well, what else could I do? A surprisingly humble note arrived from Charles before breakfast; he must be afraid we'll spread the news of his disease and damage his prospects with the young ladies. There was no need for the note; I had already persuaded Marianne to go home. *(Pause, then bursts out)* I never asked her to leave him. I wanted only a fair share of her; a little more time together, a little more hope. Some reassurance that this is not some elaborate game for her. Less discretion and patience and respectability. A little more courage. What am I talking about? Last night she came to me full of courage - and I sent her back. Tib patted me on the back before she left this afternoon; she says I did the only sensible thing. But then, she wants a fair share of me too. What a mess I'm making of our lives.

ACT TWO

Marianne: *(Writing a letter)* 'My dearest, truest husband, here I am back in Lawton Hall. I shrink from sharing a house with Charles, but your will be done.'

Tib: *(Writing a letter)* 'My very dear Anne, I hope this letter finds you well and recovered from the shock of Marianne's little escapade. Since my last night at Shibden, I have been finding it impossible to banish your image from my mind.'

Nancy: *(Writing a letter)* 'Dear Anne, I am sending this note up to the Hall by Billy the butcher's boy to say a thousand thanks for lending me Miss Edgeworth's novel. This is proving such a bleak midwinter that any company, even that of fictional characters, is sure of a welcome.'

Anne: *(To her diary)* The weather continues cold and muddy. I spent the afternoon translating Rousseau. It occurs to me that I may have thrown away my only chance to escape from all this. *(Browsing through letters before she seals them)* 'darling Marianne, keep your spirits up ... enclosed is a little sketch I did of Lord Byron ... the nights are long without you ... Dear old Tibs ... the weather ... the lecture on fossils ... my aunt's rheumatism ... with undying friendship, as ever ... '

Δ

Nancy: Oh, it's delightful to snatch a mouthful of fresh air.

Anne: I thought it would never stop raining; I can't do without my daily walk.

Nancy: I've often seen you striding towards the village, and longed to put on my cloak and join you.

Anne: And why didn't you?

Nancy: My mother always manages to find something useful for me to do instead.

Anne: So how did you elude her today?

Nancy: Well, we've had no letter from Marianne in several weeks, so when we spotted you through the kitchen window I told Mother that I'd run after you to get some news second-hand.

Anne: And was that not indeed why you ran after me?

Nancy: I usually have more than one reason for whatever I do. *(Pause)* Will your aunt be angry to see you walking with another farmer's daughter?

Anne: I am at perfect liberty to walk with a chimney-sweep if I choose. *(Hastily)* Not that the cases are alike. In that pretty gown you'd be an ornament on any arm. I hope the rain holds off, or you'll be soaked to the skin.

Nancy: Oh, I dare say someone might shelter me under her cloak.

Anne: If you asked *very* nicely. *(Approaching with cloak raised)*

Nancy: *(Ducking away)* But as it is presently not raining, there is no need. Tell me, *do* you have any news of my sister?

Anne: None at all; her last letter was three weeks ago.

Nancy: I used to think you and Marianne very silly about each other, but that seems to have blown over.

Anne: Silly in what way?

Nancy: Passionate about the slightest things. Remember the time you two had a tiff, and you tried to make your peace with a bag of barley sugars? She refused to even taste one, and you burst into tears on the spot.

Anne: I had quite forgotten. So it's your impression that Marianne and I have outgrown all that?

Nancy: There has been some improvement; I suppose it's a side effect of age.

Anne: Age?

Nancy: Well, twenty-eight is hardly young. Marianne is settled in married life, and you are almost the mistress of Shibden Hall.

Anne: Master, please. *(They share a smile)* They stare at us as we pass, you know.

Nancy: Who do?

Anne: The townsfolk.

Nancy: Oh, they're nobody.

Anne: Once in Leeds I was waiting by the mail coach, and two bad women took it into their heads that I was a man. One of them gave me a knock on the breast and tried to follow me; her friend shouted out, can you guess what she said?

Nancy: No.

Anne: She shouted 'does your cock stand?' Have I shocked you?

Nancy: *(Unconvincingly)* Nothing shocks me.

Anne: You see, Nancy, I am used to being stared and jeered at in the street, but you are not, and it could happen to you too if you walk with me.

Nancy: That is a risk I will have to take.

Anne: Will you not be ashamed of me?

Nancy: People like you must make their own rules.

Anne: You're not answering my question.

Nancy: You won't take to wearing trousers, will you? The occasional hat or cane, and your splendid cloak, they can be carried off with style, but trousers would be ...

Anne: No trousers. You have my word on it.

Nancy: Then I will walk with you again, if I may.

Anne: The pleasure is all mine.

Nancy: Not all.

Δ

Anne: *(To her diary)* Slept with Tib again on this visit. I had three very good kisses. She had ... not a very good one. She assured me it was not important. In the middle of the night, Tib leaned over and whispered in my ear, 'Do you love me, Anne? Do you love me, damn you?' I pretended to be asleep. Well, what else could I do? *(Awkwardly, as Tib enters)* I called on Dr Simpson today ...

Tib: The whites?

Anne: How ... don't say I've passed it on to you?

Tib: No, but I have noticed you scratching madly whenever you thought I wasn't looking, and you left your uterine syringe in the bureau.

Anne: I didn't want to worry you until I was sure.

Tib: Its source is that lecher Charlie Lawton, I presume.

Anne: I hope his privates rot away.

Tib: Anne!

Anne: The doctor's examination was so humiliating; he averted his gaze and poked his hand up my skirt as if opening a drain. Then he asked if I was married, and I said 'No, thank God,' without thinking. So I told him that I must have caught the infection from a married friend whose husband was dissipated, because I remembered visiting the water closet just after her.

Tib: Oh dear. I believe it's a tedious business.

Anne: I must take sulphate of zinc twice daily, the doctor said, and rub mercury into my skin. *(Suddenly guilty)* I have tried to take precautions, Tibs, the times I've been with you.

Tib: *(Dry)* I noticed. Don't fret, love, we shall be as careful as we can. And speaking of illness, how was Nantz Brown this afternoon?

Anne: Oh, not half so unwell as I had heard, I think she simply wanted a visitor.

Tib: I spotted the pair of you stealing away after tea the other afternoon.

Anne: We only went to the drawing room for a game of chess.

Tib: Ah, but a lot of coquetting can get done over a chess table.

Anne: So you've noticed? I thought it was just my tainted imagination, but no, the girl is making a dead set at me.

Tib: To which you return no encouragement, of course.

Anne: Well, one must be civil.

Tib: One must.

Anne: And she is rather delicious. And she sometimes makes me think of ... what I should not.

Tib: It's understandable. Is she a forward girl?

Anne: Let's put it this way; she has an instinctive grasp of how to play her part. She draws me out, she leads me on ... she asks me to tie her ribbons, for God's sake. If I chose to persevere, I think I could have her on what terms I pleased.

Tib: And she wouldn't run blubbing to Mama?

Anne: Never. She has too much pride for that.

Tib: Well then, you should take the first opportunity of giving the girl a little kiss to see how she likes it.

Anne: I already have.

Tib: When?

Anne: When we were playing chess; I let her buy her queen back with a kiss. A quick one, but moist.

Tib: Was it like this?

Anne: *(Turning her face away halfway through the kiss)* No, it wasn't a bit like that. It was a little soft one with our teeth closed.

Tib: You'll have to educate her.

Anne: All this is a joke, isn't it? Tib?

Tib: That depends on your sense of adventure.

Anne: But you would mind, wouldn't you, if anything did happen with Nantz? You mind about Marianne, even though you try to hide it.

Tib: Nancy is an amusement, nothing worth being jealous of.

Anne: Well then, if anything were to happen, you would be more to blame than I! But nothing will, because my life has been made complicated enough by just two beautiful women.

Δ

Anne: Nancy. Your mother said I'd find you here.

Nancy: Come in. I've been packing my trunks for Sheffield.

Anne: Bridesmaid again?

Nancy: One more time, and you shall have to acknowledge me as an old maid.

Anne: Will it be long before you return to Halifax?

Nancy: Why, would anyone miss me?

Anne: Very possibly.

Nancy: *(Pause)* What are you staring at?

Anne: Your frill, it's a little crooked. There, that's better.

Nancy: Thank you.

Anne: Do you think me rude, Nantz?

Nancy: A little.

Anne: Odd?

Nancy: I'm used to you by now.

Anne: Would you prefer me to be different?

Nancy: Never. I like you as you are. I don't think you have ever fully remarked how much I like you.

Anne: Well, you have always been assured of my esteem and high opinion ... *(Makes her a bow and turns away)*

Nancy: I don't want your esteem and high opinion. I would rather another word.

Anne: You're swimming out of your depth, Nantz Brown.

Nancy: Then hold out your hand.

Anne: You're too cold for my kind of life.

Nancy: Cold, am I? This is just a mask, I could drop it at any time and show you my true face.

Anne: No doubt you could, did circumstances not forbid it.

Nancy: Which circumstances?

Anne: All of them.

Nancy: There is only one circumstance in our way, and it begins with a M. And she is far away and need never know.

Anne: It is a circumstance I cannot forget.

Nancy: For one night you could.

Anne: *(Sits down beside **Nancy**, starts taking off her boots)* I suppose ... for one night I could forget anything.

Δ

Anne: It was the sheets that upset me. The last time I slept in that bed was with Marianne, over a month ago. She had bad cramps; her sobs woke me in the middle of the night, and I remember rubbing her belly with my palm until the pain went away. Today I woke at five, and found myself on the left side of the bed, where Marianne usually sleeps. I looked down at the sheet just beside my hip, and it bore the faint, brown mark of her blood. I could feel Nancy's warmth behind my back, but I got out of bed without looking at her and dressed in the next room. What a paltry lust-ridden creature I am, that I cannot wait a few more years for the woman I love. God have mercy on me and clean my heart.

I had expected to feel low today, but not this low. Strictly speaking, I know the word 'incest' is not appropriate, there being no link of marriage or blood. Nor does 'infidelity' fit, exactly, since I never made Marianne any vows. And why should I worry about Christian taboos when according to the best authorities I am damned for all eternity anyway?

Δ

Tib: *(Yawning, groaning)* Oh, my head. What time is it?

Anne: *(Pulling on her boots)* Late.

Tib: What's the day like?

Anne: Chilly.

Tib: *(Faking a rural workingclass accent)* Come back to bed, Master Lister; it's warm in here. *(Her own voice)* What are you putting your boots on for?

Anne: I have to interview a new farmhand.

Tib: I've seen practically nothing of you all week; I might as well have stayed at home and written you a witty letter,

Anne: I'm sorry you feel neglected, but I have been busy.

Tib: If you choose to fritter away your time on petty chores and parish duties, what can I say?

Anne: Well, Tib, lying in bed all day reading last year's *Ladies' Almanack* and taking vast quantities of snuff has never appealed to me.

Tib: How is it that you are constantly finding fault with me, and never with darling Marianne?

Anne: It's different when one is in love.

Tib: So did you enjoy her sister?

Anne: *(Staggers, then regains control)* Not particularly. She made me do all the work.

Tib: The girl's a little inexperienced, give her time.

Anne: It won't happen again. Tib, why did you push me into it?

Tib: Don't blame me, you're a grown woman. I did hope it might make you a little more realistic. Sometimes your romantic dedication to the unattainable Mrs Lawton turns my stomach.

Anne: *(Wondering, amused)* You're jealous.

Tib: I'm ten years past being jealous. As your friend, I hate to watch you waste your life on a fantasy. Marianne is a happily married woman, and her husband is not going to drop dead on request.

Anne: However long it takes, I shall wait for her. What else can I do?

Tib: Oh, run away to Paris. Become a lion tamer. Come and live with me,

Anne: I am grateful for the offer, but you and I don't suit.

Tib: How can you be so sure that I wouldn't suit you? You've never really looked at me.

Anne: What do you mean?

Tib: Every time you turn your gaze in my direction, a kind of fog intervenes. All you can see are the many ways in which I am not, and never will be, like Marianne.

Anne: Tibs, that's not true; you've always been very dear to me.

Tib: I could get that kind of affection from a lapdog.

Anne: Not affection, then; love.

Tib: How unwillingly you drag the word to your lips. Let's just call it friendship, shall we?

Anne: You must agree that we're better off living apart and paying frequent visits; this arrangement keeps boredom at bay.

Tib: No doubt you've discussed the matter fully with Marianne. Does she know about us yet?

Anne: I hope not. She thinks of you simply as my oldest friend.

Tib: *(Rueful)* A fairly accurate description.

Anne: No - it's not that I am ashamed of our connection, but I would rather Marianne was kept ignorant of it.

Tib: If we can bear the truth, I fail to see why she needs protection from it.

Anne: She's more fragile than we are.

Tib: Fragile? Marianne?

Anne: You must never take it upon yourself to enlighten her without consulting me.

Tib: Oh, I wouldn't. *(Murmurs)* I know my place, Freddikins.

Anne: I beg your pardon?

Tib: It's your pet name, isn't it? It suits you.

Anne: How did you learn it?

Tib: Could I have seen it on a scrap of paper you left lying around? I think the phrase went *(Putting on a childlike lisp)* 'darling Freddy, I miss you so dreadfully'.

Anne: You opened my bureau and read Marianne's letters.

Tib: Only the top few; they soon palled. Epistolary eloquence is not the girl's forté, is it?

Anne: You interfering old hag.

Tib: Well how else do you suggest I pass my days on this godforsaken farm?

Anne: *(Interrupting)* I'm not listening.

Tib: You're out all morning harassing foxes, and at night, if I'm lucky, I get one halfhearted kiss before you're snoring ... (**Anne** *slams her way out)*

Δ

Anne: *(To her diary)* Passing through Cheshire, I stayed the night at Lawton Hall. We all behaved uncommonly well; Charles has been most civil to me ever since I prevented

Marianne from leaving him. He retired at ten. My room was next to theirs. Marianne came in and we had three kisses each, very quietly. We could hear Charles snoring all the while, through the wall. Then she got dressed again and went in to her husband. He is in the best of health, she says. Unlike my uncle, who is not to have any more solid food. He doesn't know us, these days, after his half pint of laudanum. What an ungrateful cub I am, that I can feel no love for the poor old fellow.

Today I got the gardener and five boys to cut the last of the elms into logs, which kind of work always excites my manly feelings. When I saw a pretty young maid go up the lane, I had a foolish fancy about taking her into a shed on Skircoat Moor and being connected with her. I was supposing myself in breeches and having a penis. Just a small one.

A parcel has just arrived from Tib, bearing a little alabaster Cupid from London. I got her picture out of my bureau and looked at it for ten minutes with considerable emotion. I almost managed to persuade myself that I could settle down and be happy with her. I thought of several reasons: Tib's social connections are good, her fortune considerable, her affection beyond doubt, and in bed she is excellent. But my heart has never listened to reasons.

Marianne: *(Looks up guiltily as **Anne** comes in)* I didn't mean to pry. I was just looking for some writing paper and I stumbled across it.

Anne: *(Looks at it)* It's only an old diary of mine.

Marianne: On my wedding night, you wrote about my selfishness, infidelity, the waste of it all.

Anne: I was distraught, I don't even remember what I wrote. You can't be angry with me now.

Marianne: I'm not angry; I just never knew till now how much my marriage cost you.

Anne: What would have been the use in ranting and raving? Your mother was already sewing your trousseau.

Marianne: If I'd known all you felt, I couldn't have gone through with the wedding.

Anne: What else could we have done?

Marianne: Eloped together, like those Irishwomen in Wales.

Anne: I told you, the Ladies of Llangollen had family money as well as a faithful servant. We couldn't even have rented a cottage.

Marianne: I'd have lived with you in a coal hole.

Anne: Let it go, love. I'm sorry about the diary.

Marianne: I don't think I deserved some of the comments. 'Utterly self-absorbed and worldly', that's a little harsh.

Anne: I'll tear the damned page out. There. After all these years, can you doubt how much I love you?

Marianne: When we go to church, you ogle every girl in sight.

Anne: I do not ogle. I merely observe.

Marianne: How can I be sure you don't pay court to all the local ladies when I'm out of the way at Lawton?

Anne: Because you know me.

Marianne: You never promise, though I have often vowed fidelity to you.

Anne: Promising comes easy to you, Marianne. Remember the day you promised to love, honour and obey Charles Lawton? I'm sorry, the words just slipped out. It's the damned itching, it sets my nerves on edge.

Marianne: I don't mind your hurting me if it does anything to comfort you.

Anne: It doesn't. You have to forgive me.

Marianne: Always.

Anne: Do you remember what today is?

Marianne: No.

Anne: The eighth anniversary of our first night together.

Marianne: Eight years? I'm getting old.

Anne: And more beautiful by the day. Listen, tonight I'm willing to promise anything to make you happy.

Marianne: I don't need promises. Just love me.

Anne: I think perhaps I can manage that. Where would Milady like to be loved?

Marianne: You know.

Anne: I haven't the faintest idea. On your ear perhaps? Your elbow? I know, your knee.

Marianne: The place.

Anne: What place? I know nothing about a place.

Marianne: *(Voice near breaking point)* Don't tease me Freddy, not tonight.

Anne: But I am perfectly willing to touch any lady who specifies where and how she wishes to be touched.

Marianne: You know I hate it when you make me ask.

Anne: Ask for what? What is the word you are looking for?

Marianne: There is no word for it.

Anne: Well say please then.

Marianne: *(Explodes)* Oh take your hands off me.

Δ

Nancy: How can you let the sun full in your face? I should be afraid of getting freckled.

Tib: At your age I was equally vain, but nowadays I have no complexion to protect.

Nancy: I'm all bones, though; I'd swap my complexion for your figure anyday.

Tib: You don't seem to be doing too badly with the one you have.

Nancy: *(A startled pause)* She told you, didn't she?

Tib: She didn't need to tell me.

Nancy: You're one too, I suspect.

Tib: *(Amused)* One what?

Nancy: One of her ladies.

Tib: You make it sound like quite a crowd; there are only three of us so far.

Nancy: Three that we know of.

Tib: I think I know Anne pretty well by now.

Nancy: Were you and she - was it always that way between you, even before my sister?

Tib: No, just the last year or so.

Nancy: I suppose between you two, it is more a matter of friendship than of love.

Tib: I have loved Anne Lister since the day she strode into my parlour bearing a large, muddy clump of white heather. And that was ten years ago. So yes, it could be called a matter of love.

Nancy: I didn't mean to offend you; I didn't know.

Tib: She's snobbish, and deceitful, and sometimes cruel, but I don't expect I'll ever grow out of loving her.

Nancy: I quite agree about the snobbery; I could scarcely believe my ears the other evening when she had the family pedigree brought down and read aloud.

Tib: It was not directed at you; she does that on the first Sunday of every month.

Nancy: *(Pause)* I am not exactly sorry for what I did - with Anne - but I do hope I haven't hurt you.

Tib: Not in the least. Only love arouses my jealousy, and there was none of that between you.

Nancy: *(Flat)* I suppose not.

Tib: You simply wanted to steal a slice of your big sister's cake.

Nancy: Is that all it was?

Tib: *(Sharp)* Don't ask me, I wasn't there. Anne was your first, I presume.

Nancy: Oh yes. And my last, I expect.

Tib: Was it so disappointing?

Nancy: Not at all. But it shook me; I felt as if I were being gently dragged towards the edge of a cliff.

Tib: I know that feeling.

Nancy: I think perhaps I may marry after all; it would be so comfortable. Sam Waterhouse would have me at the bat of an eyelid. What do you advise?

Tib: Oh, I never give advice, having made too many mistakes of my own. But I do wish you luck.

Δ

Anne: *(Having a multiple orgasm as quietly as possible)* Oh. Oh my good God. Oh. Oh. Oh Marianne.

Marianne: *(Teasing)* Shh, you'll wake your aunt.

Anne: I don't care if I wake every horse in the stable. *(Panting, laughing, sitting up, regaining some control)* Do you think she heard?

Marianne: She couldn't have, all the way down the end of the passage.

Anne: *(To herself)* No one else *ever* gave me a kiss like that.

Marianne: What do you mean?

Anne: What?

Marianne: You said else. Who else?

Anne: No love, I said no one else.

Marianne: You said no one else had ever given you a kiss *like that*. Well, what kind of kiss *have* they given you then?

Anne: Love, you know I used to flirt with Eliza and kiss her when we were at school.

Marianne: *(Interrupting)* Not that kind of kiss. You meant body kisses, down there.

Anne: I didn't. You're confusing me, I don't know what I meant.

Marianne: You said I was the first ever.

Anne: *(Convincingly)* You were, I swear it. You were the first woman who ever did that to me.

Marianne: And since?

Anne: Since what?

Marianne: Since me, during me. Have you been with another woman?

Anne: *(Pauses a second too long)* No.

Marianne: I don't believe you. It's Tib, isn't it?

Anne: Of course it is.

Marianne: So you've been betraying me all along.

Anne: Oh wake up Marianne, for the first time in your life be frank with yourself. I've been no more unfaithful than you.

Marianne: I never did.

Anne: What do you call your marriage? Any binding engagement between us was cancelled when you walked up that aisle.

Marianne: It's different with a man.

Anne: It is not.

Marianne: How would you know? You've never been with a man, you don't know how ... how nothing it is. A damp fumble in the dark, an insignificant spasm.

Anne: Insignificant?

Marianne: It never really touched me. You know that, and yet you've let a woman inside you, the place I thought belonged to me.

Anne: It's my body, it belongs to none of you.

Marianne: Then I don't want it.

Anne: *(Losing momentum)* I never deliberately lied to you, except by omission. You never asked. I thought perhaps you knew.

Marianne: Did you really? And what else was I expected to know? How many more women are there?

Anne: No more. *(Looks away)* Not any more.

Marianne: *(Tugs off her ring)* You had better have this back.

Anne: Don't ...

Marianne: Consider yourself quite at liberty. You are not mine and I am not yours.

Anne: *(Snatches the ring, then softens, and reaches for Marianne's hand to put it back on)* Yes you are.

Marianne: *(Looking at it)* Yes. Yes I am. *(After a long pause)* It's myself I should blame. If we had our time over again, I swear I'd never marry, I'd not leave you on your own, to be tempted by other women. I was a mere girl when I walked up that aisle, I knew nothing of my own heart.

Anne: Shhh. You could still have all my love, Marianne. If you asked for it.

Marianne: I've not been a very good wife to you, Freddy, have I?

Anne: Don't say that.

Δ

Tib: *(Writing a letter)* 'My dear Anne, the best thing to combat the smell of sickness in a house is dried lavender, sprinkled in the fire. Yes, I did see Nancy's bulging diamond on my last visit. As you say, that Sam Waterhouse does not deserve her, but she tells me that she's made him promise her an extraordinary sum of pin money.

Can Marianne really not contrive to visit you for another three months? You write that you are "worn out pining for the unattainable", which is quite understandable. The important thing is to know exactly what you want. *(With some irony)* As a woman who has for many years known what she wants, and known too that she will never get it, I am, I think you will agree, in the best position to give advice. Yours, as ever, Tib.'

Δ

Anne: *(Sleeping curled around **Marianne**. She wakes up in sunlight, stretches, and lifts the blankets off **Marianne**. She recoils in shock. Loudly)* So that's why you blew out the candle.

Marianne: Mmm? *(Waking)*

Anne: I should have known you were hiding something; I've never known you to want to do it in the dark.

Marianne: What?

Anne: How many months?

Marianne: *(Pulling the blanket around her as she sits up)* Five gone; four to go.

Anne: I don't believe it.

Marianne: You always knew it could happen.

Anne: It had been so many years, I'd stopping fearing it. Twenty-eight is far too old for a first child, everyone knows that.

Marianne: I'll be alright.

Anne: I'm not going to stand around watching you swell up like a brood mare.

Marianne: What on earth can we do about it?

Anne: I can go.

Marianne: *(In the long pause, panicking)* Don't make any rash decisions, my love. This doesn't have to come between us.

Anne: You don't understand me at all, do you? Sharing you with Charles is bad enough; do you think I'd stoop to compete for your attention with a puking infant?

Marianne: I was going to ask you to sponsor it.

Anne: Oh were you? What kind of fairy godmother would I make, grudging the child every soft glance from its mother?

Marianne: I don't know. I never expected you to take it to heart so. After all these years ...

Anne: That's the whole point; the years have worn me out.

Marianne: Am I altered in your eyes?

Anne: You're all you ever were. But you're not just you now, are you? *(Pause)* You'll be choosing a name soon. Another little Charlie, perhaps? A royal George?

Marianne: *(In distress)* Stop.

Anne: Just promise me it won't be Freddy.

Marianne: I ...

Anne: Promise.

Marianne: I can't promise anything. It's the father's right.

Anne: He's no right to any of this.

Marianne: You and I have come through so many storms ... I don't see why we can't weather this one.

Anne: If you don't see, I can't explain it.

Marianne: *(Losing her temper)* Well, whatever I christen it, it can't be more of a baby than you.

Anne: I ...

Marianne: *(Interrupting)* Whining, griping, that's all it's been these last few years. I am sick of feeling like the rope in a village tug-o'-war. At last I have a chance of giving Charles what he wants; *(Holding her belly)* here it is, it's simple, it's right inside me. But you ... I'll never be able to give you what you want.

Anne: All I want is you.

Marianne: That's a damn lie. You want money and freedom and a wife and a mistress, a string of mistresses. You want me, and Tib, and Nancy, and every pretty servant you lay eyes on ...

Anne: *(Cautious)* Nancy?

Marianne: I wasn't going to say anything. I was going to be a good wife and not stir up trouble. But what am I to think when my sister, my own little sister, has to go to the doctor with a mysterious infection ...

Anne: Oh God forgive us. *(Pause)* Did she tell you?

Marianne: My mother told me. Nancy convinced her it's easily caught by drinking out of someone else's glass.

Anne: *(With difficulty)* I'm sorry. For everything.

Marianne: Do you think we're being punished?

Anne: I don't know.

Marianne: Sweetheart, I don't think I can do this any longer. I'm coming apart.

Anne: *(Holds her)* Perhaps you'll find it easier to love me a few hundred miles away.

Marianne: Do you intend to go right after the funeral?

Anne: *(Nodding)* It can't be more than a few weeks now.

Marianne: Paris?

Anne: Of course. Then who knows?

Marianne: I promise I won't let the baby be called Freddy. Nobody else is Freddy.

Δ

Anne: *(Wearing a black lace veil that shows she is in mourning)* It takes a surprisingly short time to pack away thirty years of living. A bare week since the funeral, and my whole life has changed. Who knows but there may be women in Paris like myself? At any rate, I am determined to have a gay old time, and feel young before I have to be old.

I've left a forwarding address with my aunt, and insured my life in favour of Marianne in case I should die on my travels.

I wonder if I will miss my aunt. I think she would like me to fix on a companion before she dies. I did once try to tell her of my nature, but I don't think she understood. 'Aunt,' I said one evening, 'do you know that I prefer ladies to gentlemen?' 'Quite so, my dear,' she replied, 'ladies make much cleaner guests.'

These idle memories will make me late. All I need now is a book for the journey to Dover. I could take Rousseau's *Confessions; I* never did get past chapter one.

(Declaiming from the first page) 'I know my own heart. I am made like no one I have seen; I dare believe myself to be different from everyone else in the world.' Pompous old lecher - but I know what he means.

I feel like a girl again, waiting for everything to begin. What a naïve young pup I was. Each morning I woke up I felt myself to be poised on the brink of an adventure, a story, almost a romance. And now I'm on my own again, as I have always been.

Afterword

I Know My Own Heart is loosely based on the decoded early diaries of Anne Lister (1791-1849). It was produced by Glasshouse Productions at Dublin's Project Arts Centre and at Andrew's Lane Theatre in two different versions in 1993: a one-act lunchtime production in the Spring, and a full-length evening production in the Autumn. The long version was then performed at a rehearsed reading in New York in 1994, and the short one at the Cheltenham Festival of Literature in 1997.

As the self-educated heiress to her uncle's estate near Halifax in Yorkshire, Anne Lister broke all the rules of Regency ladyhood. She cropped her hair short, travelled unchaperoned, studied Greek and geometry, and refused to even consider marriage. Anne Lister was also known for a flamboyant devotion to women that exceeded the 'romantic friendship' considered normal at the time, but only her coded diaries told the whole truth.

This play explores her exciting, dangerous, and sometimes disappointing relationships with three women over a period of ten years. Despite disapproval from friends and harassment from strangers, Lister remained secretly proud of her 'oddity', the fact that from childhood on she had known herself to be (as she put it) 'too fond of women'. *I Know My Own Heart* probes the choices of a woman trying to understand and express herself, in a society based on codes and conventions.

Emma Donoghue
Ontario
2001

La Corbière

ANNE LE MARQUAND HARTIGAN

La Corbière was first produced by Moveable Feast Theatre Company at the Project Arts Centre in October 1989 as part of the Dublin Theatre Festival with the following cast:

Marie-Claire	Eithne Dempsey
Angélique	Virginia Cole
Désirée	Joy Forsythe
Céleste	Clodagh O'Donoghue
Kurt	Joe Hanley
Klaus	Declan Walsh
Man on the Phone	Joe Hanley
Sailor 1	Joe Hanley
Sailor 2	Declan Walsh
Director	Cathy Leeney
Designer	Pauline Donnelly and Dominic Hartigan
Lighting	Paul O'Neill
Costumes	Máire Hearty, Máire O'Higgins, and Kirstie McGhie
Production Manager	Dominic Hartigan

Characters

Marie-Claire, survivor of the wreck

Angélique, drowned woman

Désirée, drowned woman

Céleste, drowned woman

Kurt, young Nazi soldier

Klaus, young Nazi soldier

Man on the Phone

Sailor 1, on the wrecked boat

Sailor 2, on the wrecked boat

Note

The island of Jersey in the Channel Islands was occupied by
the Nazis during the Second World War. The Nazis imported
a boatload of French whores from Normandy in 1941 for the
entertainment of the troops. They were housed at the Hotel
Victor Hugo; there were about forty of them, none of them
young. The project was not a success and the whores were
shipped off again in a Dutch coaster. Fog came down and the
coaster struck rocks and sank in a matter of minutes with the
loss of nearly all on board. The ship sank on the fiercely rocky
coast near La Corbière light. The women's bodies were seen
floating in the sea, sometimes alone and sometimes in
clusters, their long peroxide hair floating on the waves.

Scene One

The Wreck

Foghorn; sea sounds

Désirée: Where am I? I can't see.

Marie-Claire: Give me your hand.

Désirée: What hand. Is that you?

Marie-Claire: I don't know. I can't see.

Désirée: I'm here. Touch me. Where are you for God's sake?

Marie-Claire: All my life it has been like this.

Désirée: This is stupid. I can't find you.

Marie-Claire: All my life, in fog just like this. Dumb.

Désirée: I keep expecting to see the light. La Corbière light.

Morse code received by the **Man on the Phone.**

Man on the Phone: Visibility now nil at La Corbière.

Désirée: *(Sings)* Me and my dog, were lost in the fog, will some kind gentleman see me home?

Angélique: Here we are leaving this bloody island at last, stuck in pea soup. Mother of God.

Céleste: You can always swim for it.

Désirée: When things got really bad at home, my brother and I would swim to the island. We thought nothing of it. Was it a mile or more? I can't even remember.

Man on the Phone receives Morse code message.

Man on the Phone: Distress. Ship in distress. Ship in distress off La Corbière.

Céleste: I can't see, where are you Marie-Claire?

Marie-Claire: Here. I'm here.

Désirée: Where's here?

Céleste: How the fuck does she know?

Angélique: Under this huge tide, rows of rocks ready to eat you. Teeth.

Morse code

Man on the Phone: Warning to all shipping. Dense fog reported from La Corbière.

Céleste: Friendly!

Angélique: Hope this captain knows what he's at.

Céleste: I doubt it.

Marie-Claire: Where are you?

Céleste: I don't know. I can't see. Touch me.

Marie-Claire: Where are you? I can't hear.

Morse code message

Man on the Phone: Warning. Warning to all shipping. Warning. Dense fog reported from La Corbière.

Désirée: Where are you?

The wreck takes place. Sea sounds. Foghorn. SOS in Morse code. Voices of captain, sailors, shouts.

Désirée: Where are you?

Céleste: I can't swim.

Angélique: I can't swim.

Céleste: Where are you?

Marie-Claire: Where are the boats?

Man on the Phone: A coaster has hit rocks off La Corbière. Believe all hands have been lost.

Céleste: I can't swim.

Désirée: Hold on.

Angélique: Marie-Claire.

Désirée: Hold on.

Man on the Phone: Hold on. I can't hear. Hold on.

Céleste: Don't leave me.

Désirée: Where am I?

Céleste: I can't swim.

Marie-Claire: Hold. Hold. Hold.

Sailors: Hold on. Hold on. Hold on. Jump. Hold that. Jump.

Man on the Phone: The lines are down. The lines are out. The lines are bad.

Sailor: Throw a line. Throw, throw a line, throw ...

Marie-Claire: Hold on.

Céleste: Hold on.

Désirée: Hold on.

Sailor: a line.

Man on thePhone: The lines are bad. Hold. Wait. Hold the line ...

Sailor: Throw a line. Quick, quick.

Sailor: Your hand, give me your hand.

Sailor One: Jump. Jump away from the ship.

Marie-Claire: Jump. Jump.

Angélique: Hold out your hand. Where is your hand?

Désirée: Your hand, your hand, where is your hand?

Céleste: Help me.

Man on the Phone: I can't hear. I can't hear you.

Céleste: Oh help me.

Man on the Phone: Hold.

Marie-Claire: Hold on to me.

Désirée: Hold here.

Man on the Phone: Hold on. I can't hear, the conditions are bad, hold on a minute.

Céleste: Hold on. Here, here, here.

Angélique: Give it to me.

Céleste: For God's sake, I can't swim.

Angélique: For God's sake, for God's sake.

Marie-Claire: Where are you? Where? I can't see you.

Désirée: Where have you gone?

Céleste: I'm gone. I can't see, I can't hold on.

Désirée: Can't, I can't, can't.

Angélique: Can't hold.

Marie-Claire: Jump.

Céleste: I can't.

Marie-Claire: You can.

Angélique: I can't.

Marie-Claire: Jump. You can. You can. Do it. Do it.

They are in the water.

Désirée: Throw a line.

Marie-Claire: Throw a line. Where are you? Hang on.

Désirée: Where are you? Where are you?

Céleste: I can't see you.

Angélique: I can't swim. Oh my God.

Désirée: I can't touch you.

Angélique: I can't keep up. Mother of God. Holy Mother.

Marie-Claire: Angélique, Désirée, Céleste...

Angélique: Where is she? She's gone.

Désirée: She's gone

Céleste: I'm going.

Angélique: I can't feel, I can't keep up, God help me.

Marie-Claire: Where are you Désirée, Désirée, Désirée.

Céleste: I can't, I can't swim, I can't hold on.

Man on the Phone: I can't hear. Nothing. Nothing. I can hear nothing.

Désirée: There is nothing to hold, nothing.

Céleste: Help.

Angélique: Help.

Céleste: Help.

Angélique: Don't leave me, don't leave me, I can't.

Désirée: Nothing, nothing.

All Cast: Whooorrre.

Silence.

Scene Two

Marie-Claire Mourns for Those Drowned.

La Corbière light sweeps its light across the stage and audience: Light/dark. Light/dark. Sea sounds. Gull cry.

Marie-claire: Corbière Corbière Corbière,

Désirée: Air

Marie-Claire: Hair

Désirée: Air

Marie-Claire: Hair Corbière Corbière Corbière

Man on the Phone: Requiem aeternam dona eis Domine.

Marie-Claire: Corbière

Désirée: Corpus.

Marie-Claire: Corbière

Désirée: Christi

Marie-Claire: Corbière   **Klaus:** Whore

Désirée: Corpus   **Kurt:** Whore

Marie-Claire: Corbière   **Klaus:** Whore

Désirée: Christi

Man on the Phone: Requiem aeternam
dona eis Domine.

Marie-Claire: Corbière

Désirée: Air Air Air

Marie-Claire: Hair hair hair

Man on the Phone: Requiem aeternam
dona eis Domine.

Kurt: Lot

Klaus: their lot

Man on the Phone: got their lot

Kurt: Deserved

Klaus: their lot

Kurt: harlot harlot

Klaus: harlot harlot

Kurt: Whore

Klaus: Whore

Kurt: Whore

Klaus: Whore

Kurt: Whore

Klaus: Whore

Marie-Claire: *(As a roar)* Whore. Rise up ye strong Whores.
Rise.

Désirée: Whore

Céleste: Whore

Marie-Claire: Whore

Angélique: Whore

Céleste: Whore

Désirée: Whore

Marie-Claire: Whore

Désirée: Whore

Céleste: Whore

Kurt: Har lot har lot har lot

Klaus: Har lot har lot har lot

Marie-Claire: *(Quietly)* Rise up ye strong whores. Sisters rise
up, strong. Strong Sisters. Wronged Sisters. I will weep for

thee, mourn for thee, cry for thee. In the strong salt sea will long for thee, sea sister, water sister, we will howl for thee, banshee for thee, weep for thee, as the salt sea seep for thee.

Sailor One: slop *(As sea sounds: this can be repeated and interwoven)*

Sailor Two: clop, clop

Sailor One: flop

Sailor One: smack lack back

Sailor Two: the rock teeth the rock teeth, the teeth

Sailor One: the grate grind grit growl, the suck back

Sailor Two: shoal grawl, hiss hawl hisshawl, hisshawl

Sailor One: gravel

Sailor Two: drawl

Sailor One: drawldown suckback back

All: Whhoooorrre.

Klaus: Straight.

Kurt: Flat.

Klaus: Empty.

Kurt: Iron.

Klaus: Terrible as tin.

Kurt: A lining fallen from the grey sky.

Klaus: Nothing.

Kurt: All barbarities buried. The rock teeth and ripped flesh.

Klaus: Nothing.

Kurt: There is nothing.

Klaus: Nothing but sea.

Désirée: Our tears are salt

Céleste: and the sea

Désirée: the sea salt

Céleste: and our tears,

Angélique: weep

Céleste: weeping the sea salt

Angélique: and our tears

Céleste: weeping the salt

Angélique: from the sea

Désirée: salt salt salt *(Building up to)*

All Women: Assault

Marie-Claire: *(Low growl)* Assault

Kurt: rape

Marie-Claire: salt

Kurt: rape

Marie-Claire: sea, seasalt

Kurt: rapesalt,

Marie-Claire: rapesalt weep

Désirée: asleep

Angélique: dead

Céleste: beat beat

Kurt: Beat dead

Marie-Claire: deadbeat

Kurt: beatdead

Marie-Claire: deadbeat

Kurt: beatdead beatdead beatdead

Marie-Claire: salt salt salt salt salt

Désirée: Bereft

Céleste: Bereft

Angélique: Bereft.

Scene Three

The Arrival

All bright, sunny; a gentle zephyr. All sing 'A Boatload of Whores'.

All Cast: A boatload of whores
From over the sea
One fine day, one fine day,

A boatload of whores
From over the sea
One fine day in the morning.

Oh they were happy
As happy could be
One fine day, one fine day,

Oh they were merry
As they could be
One fine day in the morning.

You'll come to Jersey
And you'll have fun
One fine day, one fine day,

Men: Just move along
At the butt of my gun
One fine day in the morning.

All Cast: Leave your home
And leave your child
One fine day, one fine day,

The weather there
Is always mild
One fine day in the morning.

Who cares if your mother
Is bombed while you're gone
One fine day, one fine day,

Whores like you/us
Are not worth a song
One fine day in the morning.

Whores like you/us
Are lucky to live
One fine day, one fine day,

Who cares if this boat
Is only a sieve
One fine day in the morning.

Repeat first verse.

*Sudden blackout. The two Nazis shine torches at the women's faces.
One woman shines a torch at the men's boots, and at her own and the
other women's feet. The torches are marked with a cross. Otherwise dead
black.*

Céleste: We've arrived.

Angélique: I hate journeys.
(Together)
Désirée: I hate arriving.

Marie-Claire: We've got here.

Désirée: At least we didn't hit a mine.

Céleste: *(Sarcastic)* We are so lucky, lucky little us, off on our
hols. Oh goody.

Marie-Claire: Belt up.

Céleste: Vive la France. I'm so happy.

Marie-Claire: I'll shut your mouth if you don't belt up.

Klaus: Silence.

Kurt: Pick up your bags.

Klaus: Have your papers ready.

Kurt: Move along.

Klaus: Move. You may not speak to anyone.

Céleste: I'd kill for a fag.

Désirée: It's the end of the journey.

Marie-Claire: You mean it's the beginning.

Angélique: What did I forget?
(Together)
Marie-Claire: What did I remember?

Céleste: Have you a fag sonny?

Klaus: Silence.

Kurt: You may not speak.

Klaus: You will obey orders. There will be silence.

Kurt: You may not show any light whatsoever.

Céleste: They don't understand French.

Marie-Claire: Little shits.

Angélique: I'm frightened.

Désirée: End of the journey.

Marie-Claire: It's only the beginning.

Angélique: It's better to travel than to arrive.

Désirée: It was better on the journey, just travelling.

Marie-Claire: If we'd struck a mine, that would have been that.

Désirée: I've got stomach cramps.

Céleste: I was seasick.

Marie-Claire: Stop complaining.

Angélique: My feet are killing me.

Marie-Claire: Will I see her again?

Céleste: Did we turn off the gas?

Désirée: My head is throbbing.

Angélique: Will she mind him properly?

Désirée: Will he be there when I get home? Will I get home?

Angélique: Hail Mary full of grace, the Lord is with thee.

Klaus: Name, date of birth, nationality?

Céleste: Céleste Vidal, thirty-five, born Lyons, France.

Klaus: Hey, look at this one, says she's thirty-five, forty if she's a day, French whore! Looks like a Jewish whore to me.

Kurt: Very like a Jewish whore, an old bag of a Jewish whore.

Klaus: Make a note of that one, something will have to be done about that one.

Kurt: She'll be for the chop. *(They laugh)*

Marie-Claire: Don't mind them.. They're only whipper-snappers.

Désirée: They took my sister.

Céleste: They took my brother.

Angélique: This suitcase is deadly. My veins are aching.

Désirée: I've got my period.

Céleste: Will they be bombed? They shot the dog.

Désirée: Have you got an aspirin?

Céleste: I hate the sea.

Angélique: I've broken a nail.

Marie-Claire: Listen you girls; if they haven't got nylons on this island I'm hopping on the next boat home. *(Laughs)*

Kurt: Silence.

Klaus: You will proceed to exit 'Y' immediately. Take with you only what you carry. You must not speak.

Kurt: You will show no light whatsoever. It is forbidden to smoke.

Exeunt; two torchlights shining on women's feet. Men sing or hum 'A Boatload of Whores'.

Scene Four

The Whores on the Island; Their Routine Walk.

Kurt: Each day a crocodile of women.

*Quietly, as
water slopping.*

Angélique:	Angélique Duval	**Kurt:** slop clop slop
Céleste:	Céleste Vidal	**Klaus:** slit slut slit
Marie-claire:	Marie-Claire Depret	**Kurt:** slop clop slop
Désirée:	Désirée Montard	**Klaus:** slit slut slit

Kurt, Klaus: Cochon Merde Putain

Kurt: Each day a crocodile of women

Désirée:	Sabine Fournier	**Klaus:** slit slut slit
Angélique:	Adèle Lacoste	**Kurt:** slop clop slop
Céleste:	Thérèse Dupont	**Klaus:** slit slut slit
Marie-claire:	Marie Leblanc	**Kurt:** clop slop clop

Kurt, Klaus: Slit Fuck Cunt

Kurt: Each day a crocodile of women

Marie-Claire:	Catherine Brunel	**Klaus:** slit slut
Désirée:	Suzanne Ratel	**Kurt:** slop clop slop
Angélique:	Brigitte Tonsard	**Klaus:** slit slut slit
Céleste:	Patrice Gassion	**Kurt:** clop slop clop
Marie-Claire:	Dominique Leclerc	**Klaus:** slut slit slut
Céleste:	Françoise Fallet	**Kurt:** slop clop slop

| **Désirée:** | Bernadette Laurent | **Klaus:** slit slut slit |
| **Angélique:** | Juliette Labrousse | **Kurt:** clop slop clop |

Kurt, Klaus: Cochon Merde Putain

Kurt: Each day a crocodile of women. Under Madam's firm eye.

Marie-Claire:	Isabelle Dupont	**Klaus:** slit slut slit
Céleste:	Julie Leplée	**Kurt:** clop slop clop
Désirée:	Sophie Brûle	**Klaus:** slut slit slut
Angélique:	Elizabeth Monnot	**Kurt:** slop clop slop
Céleste:	Monique Cerdan	**Klaus:** slit slut slit
Marie-Claire:	Zoë Barrier	**Kurt:** clop slop clop
Céleste:	Yvonne Préjean	**Klaus:** slut slit slut
Désirée:	Yves Coutet	**Kurt:** slop clop slop
Angélique:	Irma Dubas	**Klaus:** slit slut slit
Céleste:	Elis Meurisse	**Kurt:** slop clop slop
Marie-claire:	Francine Dumont	**Klaus:** slut slit slut
Céleste:	Valérie Robert	**Kurt:** slop clop slop
Désirée:	Véronique Caron	**Klaus:** slit slut slit
Angélique:	Hélène Leduc	**Kurt:** clop slop clop

Kurt: Slit Cunt Fuck Merde Cochon Putain

Klaus: Fuck Cunt Slit Merde Cochon Putain

Kurt: Each day a crocodile of 'girls'. Two by two. In pairs. Docile. Captured.

Céleste: Marie-Claude

Marie-Claire: Marie-Thérèse

Kurt: White veils? Throwing petals?

Céleste: Marie-Claire

Désirée: Marianne

Kurt: Through the flowering hedge-rows, pale voices singing.

Angélique: Marie-Rose

Céleste: Marie-Jeanne

Kurt: Herded, driven.

Klaus: Schoolgirls?

Kurt: Corpus Christi procession?

Céleste: Notre Dame. Notre Dame.

Klaus: Retreads.

Kurt: Old sows. By the bare trees, in bright sun. Two by two they snake the roads.

Klaus: Raddled. Old.

Kurt: Under high hedges, heavy with summer.

Désirée: Désirée

Céleste: Céleste

Angélique: Angélique

Désirée: Désirée

Céleste: Céleste

Angélique: Angélique.

Scene Five

The Women's Dreams

Song: lullaby.

Céleste: I, Céleste, take thee, Armand, to my wedded husband to have and hold from this day forward, for better, for worse, for richer, for poorer, in sickness and in health, till death do us part, and thereto I plight thee my troth.

With this ring I thee wed, this gold and silver I thee give; with my body I thee worship; and with all my worldly goods I thee endow.

The following words float as if blown on the wind by the sea, as if rising up from the unconscious, in a dream.

Angélique: Come home   Mother

Désirée: my child's face   good

Céleste: Sweet

Désirée: Clean

Angélique: Bread   come home

Céleste: Bed   sheetwhite

Angélique: Come home   Mother

Céleste: now

Angélique: found

Céleste: safe

Désirée, Angélique: clean

Angélique: safe   bread

Céleste: found

Désirée: soft warm

Angélique: come home

Désirée,
Angélique: Mother

Désirée: baby's pink

Céleste: sweet

Angélique: home mother

Céleste: soft

Désirée: good baby   warm

Angélique: when   when   now

Céleste: safe

Céleste,
Désirée: Always together

Angélique: warm bread

Désirée: white   now

Angélique: food

Désirée: warm cosy, Mother

Angélique: sister

Désirée: child

Céleste: gently

Désirée: good

Céleste: Holy

Angélique: now gently

Céleste: Never

Désirée: soft

Angélique: always

Désirée: good

Angélique: always

Céleste,
Angélique: Always   always good

Désirée: always

Céleste,
Angélique,
Désirée: Always

Céleste: all

Désirée: ways

Angélique: all

Céleste: ways

Angélique: all

Céleste: ways

Céleste,
Désirée: ways ways ways ways

Céleste: apart

Angélique: ways   apart

Céleste: us do part

Angélique: apart

Désirée: GAP

Céleste: Broken

Klaus rapes Désirée   *Women quietly under rape scene:*

Désirée: Broken. Open   **Marie-Claire:** Gather

Klaus: Now   **Céleste:** keep

Marie-Claire: alert   **Angélique:** stay

Désirée: Not   **Marie-Claire:** hold

Marie-Claire: alert   **Angélique:** belong

Désirée: Not now please.   **Céleste:** trust
                Stop. No.
                Not that.   **Angélique:** trust

Kurt: Here   **Marie-Claire:** collect
                                                    hoard hold
                                                    Stay be long
                                                    long

Marie-Claire:

Désirée: Don't. Please stop.   stay keep trust

Don't. No, not that   be

Mother, said, please don't.   long trust
No. Not. I don't, like this.

Klaus: Like this   **Angélique:** Always

Désirée: Like this   **Céleste:** All ways

Klaus: Like this   **Marie-Claire:** Always

Désirée: Like this   **Céleste:** trust

Klaus: Like this   **Angélique:** Keep

Désirée: Like this   **Marie-Claire:** touch

Klaus: Like this   **Céleste:** be long
Like this
Likethis
Likethis
Like this

Désirée: Not that   **Angélique:** mine

Klaus: Like this   **Céleste:** mine

Désirée: Not that   **Marie-Claire:** mine

Klaus: Like this   **Céleste:** mine

Désirée: notthat   **Angélique:** mine

Klaus: like this   **Marie-Claire:** mine

Désirée: Notthat Notthat   **Céleste:**   mine

Klaus: that that that that that   **All Women:** mine.

Kurt: this this this this this

Klaus: that that that that

Kurt: Whore

Scene Six

Cabaret in Hotel Victor Hugo

Dance music

	Women make the following sounds:
Klaus: Tickle	*Giggles*
Kurt: Slap	*Laughter/ tears*
Klaus: Punch	*Cries/ tears/ protests*
Klaus: Tickle	*Giggles*
Kurt: Slap	*Laughter/ tears*
Klaus: Punch	*Cries/ tears/ protests*
Klaus: Tickle	*Giggles*
Kurt: Slap	*Laughter/ tears*
Klaus: Punch	*Cries/ tears/ protests*

This is repeated getting faster and faster ending:

Klaus: Punch

Kurt: Punch

Klaus: Punch

Kurt: Punch

Klaus: Punch

Kurt: Punch

Klaus: Punch

Silence.

Marie-Claire: Rise up from the bottom of the sea. Rise up from the bottom of their minds. Rise. Up pushing down the sea. Rise. Shout out so loud that the world will burst. From the bottom of the sea the world will burst.

Sounds of jackboots, bursts of machine-gun-fire.

Kurt and Klaus link arms and dance and sing. **Marie-Claire,**
Désirée, Céleste *link arms and dance and sing. Faces masked in*
stockings, soldiers stick out tongues. Two groups confront each other.

Scene Seven

The Healing Sea

Sea sounds. La Corbière light.

Désirée: Shore

Céleste: Whore

Désirée: Shore

Céleste: Whore

Angélique: Swell

Désirée: Shore

Céleste: Whore

Angélique: Drawl

Désirée: Sea Shore Seashore

Céleste: Whore

Angélique: Child

Céleste: Sand

Céleste: Sea

Désirée: Sea Sea Sea

Céleste: Stone

Désirée: Rock

Céleste: Sea

Angélique: Swellchild   swell with child

Céleste: Swell with sea

Désirée: Swell with stone

Céleste: Swell with sea

Désirée: Swell with stone

Marie-Claire: There is no answer but stone.

Scene Eight

Flashback to the wreck

Fog horn. La Corbière light.

Désirée: Where am I? I can't see.

Marie-Claire: Give me your hand.

Désirée: What hand? Is that you?

Marie-Claire: I don't know. I can't see.

Désirée: I'm here. Touch me.

Marie-Claire: Where are you?

Désirée: Where are you?

Kurt: The sea lies flat as tin.

Klaus: Flat as lies told down the black telephone receiver.

Kurt: The sea lies flatter than the earth, its mouth shut tight on the night sky. The sky cannot penetrate and the clouds blot out the moon. An inkstain on grey.

Man on the Phone: Nothing.

Kurt: No where. This is not.

Man on the Phone: Negative. Finished. Silence.

Kurt: No gull cry. No sea sound.

(Shouts)

Marie-Claire: There is no answer but stone.

Scene Nine

The Aftermath of the Wreck

Marie-Claire: sand sand sand sand sand sand sand sand sand sand sand sand sand sand sand sand sand sand

Céleste: Foot

Marie-Claire: sand sand sand sand sand sand

Céleste: Love

Marie-Claire: sand sand sand

Céleste: Breast

Marie-Claire: sand sand sand sand sand sand sand sand

Céleste: Belly

Marie-Claire: sand sand sand sand sand sand sand sand

Céleste: Cunt

Marie-Claire: sand sand sand sand sand

Céleste: Love

Marie-Claire: sand sand sand sand sand sand sand sand sand sand sand

Céleste: Shit

Marie-Claire: sand

Céleste: Rock

Marie-Claire: sand

Céleste: Rock

Marie-Claire: sand

Céleste: Rock

Marie-Claire: sand

Céleste: Slit Rock Crunch

Marie-Claire: sand

Céleste: Rock

Marie-Claire: sand sand sand sand sand sand sand sand sand

Céleste: Rockaby

Marie-Claire: sand sand

Céleste: Rock

Marie-Claire: sand

Céleste: a-by

Marie-Claire: sand

Céleste: Baby

Marie-Claire: sand sand sand

Céleste: Breast

Marie-Claire: sand sand

Céleste: Baby

Marie-Claire: sand sand sand sand

Céleste: Slit Rock Hand Breast Foot Belly Thigh Flesh Smell Rot Gut Rot

Marie-Claire: sand sand sand sand sand sand sand sand sand sand sand sand sand

Céleste: Bone

Marie-Claire: sand sand

Céleste: Finger

Marie-Claire: sand

Celeste: Mouth

Marie-Claire: sand sand sand

Céleste: Lips

Marie-Claire: sand

Céleste: Smell

Marie-Claire: sand

Céleste: Taste

Marie-Claire: sand sand

Céleste: Dry

Marie-Claire: sand sand sand

Céleste: Wind

Marie-Claire: sand sand

Céleste: Cold Dry Cold Dry

Marie-Claire: sand sand sand sand sand

Céleste: Cold Wet Wild Cold Dry Baby Breast Foot Mouth Lips Breast Belly Cunt Love Cunt Breast Lips Mouth Cold

Silence.

Dry

Marie-Claire: sand

Céleste: Bone Dead Breast

Marie-Claire: sand sand

Céleste: Breast Rot Blue Mold Gut Sand

Marie-Claire: sand sand sand sand sand sand sand sand sand sand sand sand sand sand sand sand sand sand sand sand sand sand sand sand sand san sa s s s s s s s s s

Silence.

Kurt: The iron lid is on. The steel grey lid on the sea. Bolted down with rust.

Klaus: The sea is nailed to the shore; the moon at last is powerless.

Kurt: Nailed down. It cannot scream or flap.

Klaus: The last paper bag, blown.

Kurt: The last plastic bottle sucks in its sides. The last black salted shoe loses a sole.

Klaus: Night.

Kurt: Over.

Klaus: Finished.

Angélique,
Céleste,
Désirée: Taboo. Taboo. Taboo.

Marie-Claire: The sea is bolted down, racked, drawn tight in a rictus smile, under this grey teeth of waves, they are buried.

Kurt: They are finished.

Klaus: They are scrubbed out.

Man on the Phone: Not known at this address.

Marie-Claire: This watery arbour, this stiff sea where the rock teeth lie, in unison, chorus.

Man on the Phone: Dateline

Scene Ten

The Drowned Whores' Picnic

Funny song

Désirée: Ripped.

Céleste: Eaten.

Désirée: Digested.

Céleste: Afloat in a shark's belly.

Désirée: The eyeballs float apart.

Céleste: The peroxide hair slimed.

Angélique: Teeth and nose bridges litter the floorbed.

Céleste: Your seabed.

Désirée: Your last bed.

Céleste: What the fuck.

Désirée: Who the fuck. We were the fucking professionals of fuck.

Céleste, Désirée: Fish fuck!

Angélique: Your lovers.

Désirée: Your time-machines. Your nothings. Your holes.

Angélique: Your forgetting.

Céleste: Your guiltholder.

Désirée: Your silences.

Céleste: Your dirt. Your rubbish

Désirée: Your hate. Your violence. Your punchball.

Angélique: Your face, your Mother.

Désirée: Your enemy.

Céleste: Your lies.

Angélique: Your memory.

Désirée: Your toilet.

Céleste: Your headache.

Angélique: Your madness.

Céleste: Your money. Yours.

Angélique: Your expense account. Your throw-away.

Céleste: Your useless.

Désirée: Your dustbin. Your disposable.

Céleste: Your waste.

Angélique: Possessed.

Céleste: Owned for an hour.

Désirée: Bought.

Céleste: Sold.

Désirée: Less than cattle.

Angélique: Herded.

Marie-Claire: Rise up ye strong whores. Sisters, rise up. Strong. Strong sisters. Wronged sisters.

All Women: Whhooorrre.

Scene Eleven

Marie-Claire Laments for the Drowned Whores

Marie-Claire: Corbière Corbière Corbière

Désirée: hair hair hair   hair hair hair

Marie-Claire: Corbière

Désirée: air

Marie-Claire: Corbière

Kurt: lot

Klaus: their lot

Kurt: got their lot

Klaus: deserved

Kurt: their lot

Klaus: harlot harlot.

All Women: Rock and flow

Marie-Claire: In clusters your bodies dance, together you're flowers; yellow hair spread on the sea's time.

All Women: Rock and flow

Marie-Claire: For a time you rest on the sea; balanced over rock caveties.

All Women: No one is coming.

Marie-Claire: No one is coming with arms to dip. No strong arms to dip down you out from the sea's terror. No one. No white arms over the boat's side, to reach over the edge. No one searching. No eyes eager as searchlights, as La Corbière light sweeps its arc over the storm. No one will lay you out in a quiet room. No one will light a candle at your head and feet. There will be no prayers. No one will push their boat out to take your bodies back to earth. You bob your last dance on the sea's foam. Flotsam. Rock and flow. Spreadeagled on the indifferent sea.

No chrism to anoint your brow. No incense around a coffin of wood. No name in the newspaper, no name. Sorrow is a lost word. There are no tears. Can the salt sea weep? Only a harsh gull's cry.

A single gull's cry.

Silence.

The Lost Letters of a Victorian Lady

A Comedy

MICHELLE READ

The Lost Letters of a Victorian Lady was first produced by
ReadCo at Bewley's Café Theatre in Dublin in October 1996
as part of the Dublin Fringe Festival with the following cast:

Edith/Performer 1	Michelle Read
Kelly/Performer 2	Ned Dennehy
Maverick/Performer 3	Mark O'Halloran
Director	Sue Mythen

Characters

Edith; Performer 1

Dorcas; Kelly; Zop; Kloop/Vicar ; Porter; Performer 2

Loxley; Mother; Pieter; Maverick; Performer 3

Historian (Voice-Over)

Note

The set consists of a desk and a chair and three screens depicting a Victorian sitting room. The centre screen is back-lit to create silhouettes. There are two entrances on opposite sides.

Scene One

Backlight up. **Edith** *in silhouette.*

Historian V/O: In the summer of 1993 an interesting discovery was made during renovation work in a Victorian house in Edinburgh's Morningside district. In some respects not an original find, simply letters from a young lady to her former governess, and yet in their content quite revelatory. Edith Lampton lived in a small Shropshire village at the end of the last century and her amazing adventures shed light on a very different side to that supposedly delicate creature: the Victorian lady. The Lost Letters Of A Victorian Lady.

Edith enters.

Edith: Marmsey-on-the-Wold, September the 6th, 1888. *(She sits at the desk and writes)*
Dear Mrs McBride,
Thank you for your kind enquiry after our health. Myself and Sebastian are both well indeed but mother, sadly, is on her deathbed and clings to life but by a short thread.

Oh dearest Esme, how welcome your stoical cheeriness would be at such a time, but of course I am being selfish for we are full grown and there are others now that better deserve your kindly rearing.

Indeed your new wards sound like little treasures and I am so glad you have found Putney to your liking. How did you descibe it again; 'rather like Edinburgh, gladly without the hills but sadly without the kilts'. You are so travelled Mrs. McB, whereas I have never set foot outside Marmsey.

But I am forgetting the sorrowful nature of this missive, dear friend. The strain of mother's sick room is at times overwhelming but I cannot bring myself to act the disciplinarian and slap Sebastian as you have suggested. He is after all a man now and not the little boy you used to chase round the scullery with the carpet-beater. It has taken all my energies to persuade him to enter the Harvest Festival threshing competition this afternoon. His idleness is rather a sore-point with mother and I thought to lift both their spirits with a spot of threshing. Loxley has taught him how it is done.

Loxley *enters in a hurry.*

Edith: Ah Loxley what news?

Loxley: You best come quick mum, it's Sebastian.

Edith: I see the contest is about to start. I'll be along directly Loxley. *(**Loxley** exits)* Do write soon dear Esme, with some of your wonderful advice. Fondest regards, Edith. *She exits following **Loxley**.*

Loxley *enters.*

Loxley: Marmsey-on-the-Wold, October the 1st, 1888. *Exits.*

Edith: *(Enters reading a letter)* Dear Mrs. McBride,
Thank you for these wonderful words of wisdom that many a mickle macks a muckle. Unfortunately mickles are hard to come by in Marmsey just at the moment, but I have put an order in at the drapers.

Sadly mother's condition has not improved which makes her all the more demanding. The third parlour maid in as many weeks has left without notice and mother has taken to flicking porridge at the vicar. Our new cleric is not the most personable of men it is true, but I fear being pelted with cold porridge will do nothing to improve his mood.

But what of little Edith you kindly ask? Well, apart from the stress of mother's sick room and Sebastian losing his arm in a threshing accident,

Backlight up. ***Performer 2*** *screams off and is seen in silhouette for a split second, holding a severed arm.*

I was feeling somewhat unchallenged so I decided to take a job! There I have shocked you, I know it! The idea first came to me when I heard of several mining positions in North Wales and instantly set about attaching a Davy lantern to my bonnet. Unfortunately it was rather unsightly and somewhat crushed the ostrich feather. Sebastian took one look at my attempts and laughed most cruelly. Oh Esme, he said I was the stupidest woman in Christendom. Well, I'd like to see him fashion something elegant from a straw bonnet and a large metal lantern, and in the end I became so cross I took your advice and slapped him hard across the face. Unfortunately I caught his eye with my confirmation ring,

Performer 2 screams off and is seen in silhouette for a split second, holding up an eyeball.

and he has had to have it out. Eventually I decided against the pit as Sebastian informs me nobody in the history of our family has ever stooped to working. *(Enter **Loxley**)* I pointed out that a man with one arm, one eye and one leg since Loxley left his axe in the parlour,

*Performer 2 screams off and is seen in silhouette for a split second, hopping and holding a severed leg. **Loxley** looks at the audience knowingly.*

Loxley do put that somewhere safe.

Loxley: Yes ma'am. *(He exits)*

Edith: ... could not provide for a sick mother and a sister, but I feel he is very sensitive at present, what with all his unlucky little accidents, and so I have deferred to him as the man of the house.

***Loxley** enters and gives **Edith** a pair of sugar tongs. He looks at her longingly and exits.*

But enough of my troubles Mrs. McBride, it grows dim apace and mother's scabs need draining. A fond adieu, Edith. *(**Edith** exits)*

Scene Two

Dorcas enters manically with a tea tray

Dorcas: Marmsey-on-the-Wold, November the 6th, 1888.

Edith enters with sugar tongs, Dorcas puts down tray.

Edith: Well done Dorcas.

During following Edith sits and pops sugar into her cup with the tongs. There is then a tussle over who gets to pour.

Dear Mrs. McBride,
One blessing I have not hitherto mentioned is our new maid Dorcas. She has been with us two whole weeks now and shows no signs of leaving! She is a lovely girl, a little eccentric in her ways by dint of the fact that she was raised by wolves, *(Performer 2 howls)* but kind and helpful and a wonder at keeping foxes away from the chicken coop. *(Edith sips tea)* Mmm, Dorcas well done! Dorcas - kitchen, kitchen!

Dorcas exits with tray and howls for joy.

In answer to your kind enquiry, mother is a little recovered, but Sebastian, I am sad to say, is quite the reverse. He is odd and irritable, I do try to discipline him, but since the eye incident I am rather loathe to adopt anything more than a stern tone.

One ray of sunshine in this otherwise dark world is that we are to have a visitor, a Master Kelly! Do you remember how father was stationed in Ireland when he spontaneously combusted, well apparently it was Master Kelly he was trying to shoot as he burst into flames. I first made the acquaintance of this pleasant Irishman just after the tragedy. He had kindly let bygones be bygones and in a spirit of supreme forgiveness had come to Marmsey to sing at the funeral. After that mother and he became firm friends and ever since she has been sending him large boxes of rifles. Everybody in the village is at sixes and sevens to have a foreigner in our midst - Loxley is as giddy as a goat!

Loxley enters

But speak of the handyman and he will appear.

Loxley: Ma'am, it's time for your lesson. *(He has rope/lassoo)*

Edith: Ah Loxley, you are too good.

Loxley has come to take me in hand, Mrs. McBride. *(He wraps rope around her)* Each week he patiently teaches me a new country skill. Just now I am learning how to hog-tie a heifer. Today it is my turn to be the heifer.

Loxley: There you are, Miss Edith, now off you go. *(**Loxley** slaps her bottom and she moos and runs to stage right)* With all fondest regards, Edith. *(They exit)*

Scene Three

Dorcas enters.

Dorcas: Marmsey-on-the-Wold, February the 15th,1889. *(Exits with teacup)*

'When I'm calling you, and you answer too' sung a capella. **Edith** *enters.*

Edith: Dear Mrs. McBride,
I am sorry not to have written sooner but I have been frightfully busy, what with the crippled widows' Valentine dance and, of course, the advent of the mole shanking season. Poor Loxley has been trying to teach me how to shank a mole for two weeks now, but I am still all fingers and thumbs! You will be sad to hear mother is much worse. She has not been herself since Master Kelly's visit, and I remember it was just before he arrived that she became particularly agitated.

Flashback

Mother: *(Enters distracted)* Edith. Edith is he come yet?

Edith: Oh Mama, you will catch your death.

Mother: Is he come, is he here?

Edith: He will be here any minute Mama.

Mother: Edith I want to tell you something, You know your father's accident ...

Edith: Oh let us not dwell on that sad event. Let us think of happier times. Do you remember when father discovered the shamrock you had planted in his rose garden.

Mother: Aye, that I do. I was lucky his hunting rifle jammed. I hated him Edith, hated him!

Edith: Oh Mama, try not to excite yourself. He was a difficult man, there's no denying it, but I believe it was the tough life of a soldier that made him that way. I worry that Sebastian will follow in his footsteps and run away to the army. Although that's not very likely, as he only has the one footstep and running, sadly, is not an ability he flourishes in.

Horse whinney.

Mother: It's him!

Edith: Just then the tall Irishman entered ... *(**Master Kelly** enters)*

Irish 'sting' and crockery smash.

and I dashed to the kitchen to supervise Dorcas's tea-making.

Edith *exits.*

Kelly: Oh Caitlin, Caitlin is it really you?

Mother: Aye Sean, and on my deathbed in this alien land. You have found me in a lucid moment. My mind is going Sean. The strain is finally too much! But was it worth it? Did I do my part?

Kelly: Aye that you did my darling girl. Your undercover work has saved many an Irish rebel's life. Your sacrifice is hailed throughout the land.

Mother: And what do they say of me, Sean?

Kelly: They sing Caitlin. They sing The Ballad Of The Sweet Rebel Girl. 'Oh, with charms-a-plenty she did woo a British knave. The captain of the garrison became her willing slave. Oh, she ... '

Mother: Sean! There's little time and much to say!

Kelly: Aye, aye. Sorry my love. But I have suffered too. Knowing every minute of every day that you were here in the grasp of our enemy and that man was raising our child. Our daughter! And now it's too late. *(He sings)* 'Her mission was completed, but she was not going home ... '

Mother: Sean!

Kelly: Sorry.

Mother: Yes, Edith is our child but she has been raised as an English lady. I told her nothing for her own safety and now I am dying I fear for her. Oh Sebastian is his father's son: hard, dangerous, mentally deranged.

Kelly: And Edith is our daughter, delicate, vulnerable ...

Mother: ... gullible. Edith is gullible! She needs minding. It's too dangerous for you to stay here, but will you send someone you trust to watch over her?

Kelly: I will Caitlin. I have the very man and I promise by the green, the white, and the gold that I will keep her safe, only don't go, don't die. Don't die my wild, green-eyed beauty.

Mother: *(Gasps)* I must Sean, I cannot hold on any longer. I will never see thee more my love 'til we meet again in Tir na n'Óg. But Sean, one last thing.

Kelly: Yes Caitlin *(Sings softly)* 'She reached her hand out to him upon her dying bed, and with the last breath that she had this is what she said ... '

Mother: Sean! Beware the Vicar Of Marmsey! Remember that! Now go, my love, before you are discovered.

Kelly: *(Overcome, he salutes)* Farewell Caitlin Ní Houlihan! *(He turns, bumping into **Edith** entering with broken tea things)* Farewell Edith!

He presses her hand to his bosom and exits, overcome.

Edith: Master Kelly, Master Kelly? Mother, why has Master Kelly left? What did you say to him? What did he say to you?

*Mother shouts and rambles as **Edith** helps her off.*

Mother: We will be free! Men and women of Ireland unite against the common enemy that holds our country in bondage. 'Seo chugat! Tiochfhidh ár lá!' Eight hundred years of oppression! *(Etc. etc.)*

Edith: Yes Mother. Yes dear. Now don't forget to take your medicine. *(To audience)* Oh dear.

Scene Four

Fade up funeral march.

Loxley *and* **Dorcas** *enter slowly wearing black armbands.*

Loxley: Marmsey-on-the-Wold, April the 11th, 1889

Edith *follows them on and sits. They put an armband on* **Edith**. *Tableau.*

Edith: Dearest Esme,
Sad news, mother finally passed away last night.

Dorcas *and* **Loxley** *exit. Fade out funeral march.*

I took her her usual cup of milky brandy at nine o'clock and found she had wrapped herself in a large green, white and orange sheet, which came, I know not where from. The exertion had obviously been too much for her and she had expired. But she had a placid smile upon her face and her favourite rifle gripped to her bosom.

Dorcas was quite bereft and howled until dawn, then scampered away and hid herself under the stove. Mother was a strange woman in many ways and I often felt I never truly knew her. Still I shall miss her unique Shropshire accent and beautiful clog dancing and know she will long be remembered in Marmsey.

Mr. Nesbitt, the family lawyer, came to offer his condolences this morning, and then we set about the frightening business of money. It seems mother had not left our affairs in good order and although Sebastian had taken on much of the paperwork in recent times, there are certain 'inconsistencies', as Mr. Nesbitt calls them. He wanted to take the books away to ponder over them some more, much against the wishes of Sebastian. Eventually there was an unfortunate tussle in the hall before Mr. Nesbitt showed himself the more determined, and of course the more endowed with limbs.

Dear friend it is all quite ghastly. I am so glad we only have this cosy little manor to maintain or I'm sure I don't know what we'd do.

Thankfully Dorcas is very good at keeping our costs down and makes the most delicious stews from things she catches in the woods. Now if only I could prevail upon her to comb her hair and cut her finger nails for the funeral.

Sebastian has taken the whole thing very badly and I have come to realize he was much more attached to Mother than I had previously thought. He is quite distracted with grief and has taken to hopping round the village streets, at night, on his one good leg, breaking into the vicar's flower garden and trying to smoke the ornamental poppies.

These are sad and trying times Mrs McBride.

Yours in mourning, Edith.'

Morris dance music

Scene Five

Dorcas *and* **Loxley** *Morris dance on,* **Loxley** *ends up centre stage and* **Dorcas** *exits.*

Loxley: Marmsey-on-the-Wold, May the 1st, 1889.

Loxley exits.

Edith: *(Taking second black armband from her pocket and putting it on)* Dear Mrs McBride,
I'm afraid to report, less than a week after we buried Mother,

another tragedy has struck at the heart of our family. I have
had to shoot Sebastian!

Mother's funeral was a touching affair. Several unknown men
fired a volley of shots over her grave and then disappeared
before I could offer them sherry. But Sebastian refused to
attend the ceremony and his behaviour became more and
more odd thereafter, particularly when Mr. Nesbitt
summoned me to his chambers early last week. Dear old
Nesbitt seemed very agitated when I took my seat opposite
him. He told me, in hushed tones and with many a nervous
glance over his shoulder, that Sebastian had invested all our
money in a Dutch business venture. Well, imagine my relief,
dear friend, I had thought Sebastian had blundered over our
finances, but no. Indeed it explained his almost weekly trips
to Holland with his strange wooden leg and false eye. Mr.
Nesbitt continued to talk to me with increased urgency, but
all I could think of was flying home to congratulate Sebastian.
However when I skipped into the parlour, enfolding him in a
sisterly embrace and praising his wise investment he took
great umbrage and unhooking the whaling harpoon rushed
out into the gathering dusk. I, in great consternation, hastened
after him, running into his back just outside the front door;
his hopping is still not the strongest. With all manner of foul
oaths he told me that Mr. Nesbitt had accused him of terrible
things and therefore he intended Mr. Nesbitt terrible harm. It
was then, dear friend, acting quite without thought, that I
wrestled the whaling harpoon away from him and before he
could dive under the privet, shot him through the heart!

For a split second we see **Performer 2** *in silhouette being shot. He
screams for the last time.* **Edith** *looks bashful.*

It was very quick and the new vicar said it was the only thing
to be done. But if all that is not awful enough, mother had
taken the absolute last space in the churchyard and now there
is nowhere to bury dear Sebastian.

Whatever shall I do dear Esme. Please advise me. Your
troubled friend, Edith.

Scene Six

Edith *removes both armbands.*

Loxley: Marmsey-on-the-Wold, May the 4th, 1889

Edith: Dear Mrs McB,
Thank you for your kind letter of condolence and your wonderful suggestion for the disposal of Sebastian's remains. Unfortunately the vicar has advised me that it would not be quite proper to have him stuffed and mounted. But not to worry my dear, the problem is all but solved. Sebastian's Dutch friends have asked to play host to him one last time and give him burial in Holland. I have decided to accept this kind offer and am busy making preparations. Dorcas! Dorcas! Dorcas is helping me with my packing.

Dorcas *drags in a large trunk of neatly folded clothes. She takes an item out and painfully folds it.*

Can I help? *(Dorcas puts it in her mouth, growling.)* No dear, I'll finish it. *(More growling.)* No, I'll finish it. I'll finish it! *(Rips it away from Dorcas. She whimpers and exits.)* Dorcas I am not cross, I am just in a hurry.

I leave straight away and am to travel by myself to the Dutch port, where I am to be met by a Mr. Kloop, an erstwhile friend of Sebastian's. Do you know, dear friend, if it were not part of such a sad mission I would almost be looking forward to my first journey away from Marmsey and all that is familiar. But then I think of poor Sebastian. We have put him in the scullery on blocks of ice and you will be pleased to know I had kept all of his missing limbs in a large pickle jar at the back of the larder, although I couldn't find the eye and I suspect in one of her deliriums mother had mistook it for a gob-stopper. The vicar suggested we surround the body in the coffin with bags of unripened poppy seeds to allay putrefaction. He has kindly supplied the seeds.

Loxley *comes forward sheepishly with a bloody bag in his hand, which he gives to* *Edith.*

Loxley: *(Distraught)* Don't go Miss Edith. You musn't go.

Edith: But Loxley I must.

Loxley: Oh alright then but take this ma'am, for luck!

Edith: Why thank you Loxley. *(She looks inside bag.)* Oh dear. An animal's foot is indeed for luck, dear Loxley, but I fear I shall not be allowed to bring it with me as it is rather bulky, what with the hoof and all. Perhaps it would be best if you kept it here. Now Dorcas *(**Dorcas** enters)*, Loxley. I shall not be gone for very long, indeed I shall be back before you know it and I am counting on you to look after things until my return. I feel sure I can depend on you both. *(To the servants)* Goodbye now, Loxley, Dorcas. God bless.

Loxley/Dorcas: Goodbye Miss Edith.

Dorcas/Loxley love music. **Dorcas** *and* **Loxley** *move the table and place the trunk on it. They then sit down and notice each other.* **Loxley** *offers* **Dorcas** *the bloody bag, she takes it, thrilled. They look at each other adoringly. They hold hands and scamper off together. Although this is basically a set change it should be played as a short scene.*

Scene Seven

Dutch Anthem and market place sounds

Edith *enters, opening the curtains on one screen to reveal a field of tulips and a windmill.*

Historian V/0: Here the story moves to Holland. It was unusual for a country lady of this period to travel unaccompanied, but of course, research has subsequently shown that the unsuspecting Edith Lampton was being used as a drugs courier by the infamous Vicar of Marmsey, later convicted of trafficking in opium.

Edith: *(Holding tulip)* Amsterdam, May the 8th, 1889

Edith *moves downstage, waving and smiling as if she is in the bustling market place and shouts 'Bonjour' a lot, as sound fades out.*

Edith: Bonjour, bonjour.

Dear friend,

(Highly elated) I did it! I have arrived in Amsterdam and it is all so wondrous; pungent cheeses, tulips, strangers and great, long salamis hanging from every rafter. But dear friend, I am getting ahead of myself. The journey itself was far from pleasant. A cold carriage, a storm-tossed boat and finally a horrible, oily, foreigner, or Dutch customs official, as I later understood!

M. Zop, the customs official, comes round behind her.

Zop: Papers!

Edith flinches at the sight of him. He snatches her papers. He reads them suspiciously and eyes her up and down. He then folds them and she goes to take them back.

Zop: Not so fast Miss. Please to raise your arms like so. Pieter!

Performer 3 rushes in stage right, frisks Edith, and rushes out again. Edith is agog, she goes to take her papers again.

Zop: Not so fast Miss. What 'ave we 'ere? *He bangs his fist loudly on the trunk and makes Edith jump.*

Edith: My ... my ... my brother's coffin.

Zop: What is inside?

Edith: *(Confused)* My brother?

Zop: Aha! You don't sound too sure Miss ... ? *(Looks at papers)* Miss Lampton. Pieter! *(Performer 3 rushes back in stage right with an axe.)* Open it up!

Edith: *(Throwing herself across the coffin)* Stop! *(To audience)* I know you, dear Esme, would have reduced them to abject apology within minutes. I took another, less noble, but equally effective tack: I burst into tears. *(Edith bursts into tears. Performer 3 rushes out, M. Zop becomes ostentatiously embarrassed)* Please do not persecute me sir. I am but a woman!

Zop: I am only doing my duty.

Edith: My journey has been long and tiresome in the extreme.

212 SEEN AND HEARD

Zop: This is not my problem.

Edith: Fourteen hours strapped to the top of a coffin with no ladies' facilities and a buffet trolley that passed but rarely.

Zop: What is this to me?

Edith: My entire family dead! *(She drops to her knees grasping his arm)*

Zop: You are touching my jacket.

Edith: My life turned upside down.

Zop: Let go.

Edith: And my unfortunate and short-lived engagement to Leonard Spool, fishmonger to the Queen.

Zop: Shut up! Zat is quite enough Miss Lampton. Talk to me no more of fishmongers! *(He throws down her papers)* Go away!

He exits.

Edith: Thus was customs manoeuvered. Now to find Monsieur Kloop!

Performer 3 *enters as* ***The Maverick.***

Maverick: Miss Lampton? Edith Lampton?

Edith: Monsieur Kloop?

Maverick: No ma'am, I ain't no Kloop! Sean sent me. I'm here to git your ass outta this corn pone mess.

Edith: I'm sorry I don't speak Dutch.

Maverick: Dutch! Lady I ain't Dutch, I'm American, a Yankee!

Edith: Could you repeat that slowly Monsieur Kloop?

Maverick: My name ain't Kloop neither. I'm Maverick. They call me The Maverick. Me - the Maverick!

Edith: How do you do, Monsieur The Maverick? But where is Monsieur Kloop?

Maverick: You don't get it lady. We gotta get outta here. Kloop may be some spotted-assed baboon but the Vicar of Marmsey sure ain't.

Edith: Ah, you know the vicar.

Maverick: Ma'am, you may be the stupidest broad I ever met but I respect the fact that you have led a sheltered life. Now try and understand me if you can; the Vicar of Marmsey is a no-good, low-down, mean-assed son-of-a-bitch who means to git you killed and I have been entrusted by my good friend Sean Kelly, who brung me outta the wilderness when I was wanted in every state in the union for a crime I swear to you I never committed. I have been entrusted to bring you to Ireland and I intend to honour that promise whether you like it or not and you lady, you gotta help me because we gotta go now before this Kloop guy turns up and fills us both fulla holes!

Edith: Monsieur The Maverick was extremely excitable and seemed terribly cross. I could not understand a word he said. His English was evidently very poor, a seemingly common failing among foreigners. However, eventually I managed to discern he was keen for us to depart. I was concerned that we had not yet met Monsieur Kloop, but as luck would have it he appeared at that very moment.

Kloop: Kloop at your service, madam, and may I offer my most heartfelt condolences on your loss.

Edith: Thank you sir. I had all but forgotten poor Sebastian. Allow me a moment, sir, to compose myself.

Kloop: But of course. *(Turning to **Maverick**)* I don't think I've had the pleasure sir?

Maverick: They call me The Maverick and I'm here to look after Miss Lampton's interests!

Kloop: Her interests?

Maverick: I know your game, Mister Kloop.

Kloop: Oh do you?

Maverick: You and your boss the Vicar of Marmsey.

Kloop: Well you had better play along then if you want Miss Lampton to live! Otherwise things could get messy.

Maverick: Why can't you just let her go? You've obviously got what you wanted.

Kloop: She's our cover, don't you understand?

Maverick: I understand one thing: you filled that coffin full of opium, you damn low-life.

Kloop: You're very astute Mr. Maverick, for an American.

Maverick: Yes, I am sir. I'm also one ornery son of a gun. You harm a hair on her goddamn head, Kloop, and I'll stick your clogs where the sun don't shine.

Kloop: Charming, I'm sure, Mr. Maverick, but time is of the essence. Come Miss Lampton, you're carriage awaits.

Edith: Why thank you, Monsieur Kloop.

They help her up onto the table. **Maverick** *sits beside her on the trunk,* **Kloop** *sits in front of the table on the chair.*

Kloop: Giddyup.

Horse whinney and sound of cart, clip clop; establish, and fade down.

Edith: The journey to my brother's final resting place in Amsterdam was uneventful. Monsieur Kloop was skillfully engrossed in guiding our little cart along the narrow road and Monsieur The Maverick seemed lost in thought. Fearing his lack of linguistic ability was making him shy, I attempted, as you would have done, to offer him the rudiments of our language. *(She taps him and points)* WINDMILL, WINDMILL.*(Maverick looks at her and shakes his head in disbelief)* However, I fear he was slow-witted for he would just stare at me uncomprehendingly.

Maverick: Okay, so she's dumb, she doesn't know what's going on. That's good. I'm gonna keep it that way, that'll be better for her! She'll have to see her brother buried, then we'll make our escape! I just gotta keep her happy. Hey, I got an idea! *(He takes a bottle from his pocket, takes a slug and passes it to* **Edith***)*

Edith: Oh thank you. IS IT MEDICINE?

Maverick: *(He nods humouring her. She takes a slug and coughs)* Yup, that's right, little lady. The kind of medicine that makes you feel just fine. Kloop, where the hell are we going?

Kloop: Mr. Maverick, I don't really think that's any of your business. Miss Lampton, as you have ascertained, is providing my cover. You, as I seem to remember, are an uninvited guest!

Maverick: Well this guest is looking to git mighty upset if he don't git some answers right now!

Edith: Oh, look everybody, tulips!

Maverick: I'm waiting.

Kloop: Very well, if you insist. We are merely stopping for the night before going on to 'Sebastian's final resting place' in the morning. Then you will both be free to go. Satisfied, Mr. Maverick?

Maverick: Hell no, Mr. Kloop! I don't make a habit of dealing with the potboy, I wanna know what the head honcho says. I wanna meet the Vicar!

Kloop: Oh you will Mr. Maverick. Have no fear, you will!

Edith: I was tired, hungry and not a little dirty, but as the two men chatted affably I felt an elation deep in my very soul. Oh Monsieur The Maverick, you're not still cross with me, I hope.

Maverick: *(He puts his arm around her)* You ain't so bad with a naggin of whiskey inside you, woman.

Edith: Monsieur The Maverick's attitude had also softened towards me somewhat and, swept along by the moment as I was, I couldn't bring myself to reprimand him for his forwardness; and as the last rays of the sun disappeared *(Night falls)* we finally turned into a stable yard.

Kloop: Whoa!

Edith: I suddenly felt very tired and not a little dizzy and as I stepped down from the cart, Mrs. McBride, I fainted dead away.

She faints into **Maverick's** *arms.* **Maverick** *pulls away and lays her on the desk.* **Kloop** *goes to touch her.*

Maverick: Take your hands off her, Kloop, and keep outta my way. I don't like your face.

Kloop: Very well, Mr. Maverick, but don't try anything silly. I shall be close by. Should you try to make a run for it, be aware that we are surrounded by a labyrinth of dark alleyways, crawling with gangs of knife-wielding psychopaths, all eager to do my bidding! Sleep well. *(He exits with trunk)*

Maverick: When I git my hands on that Vicar, I swear ... Gee you look kinda angelic when you sleepin'. *(He prises bottle from her hand and she wakes)*

Edith: Oh, Monsieur Maverick I have had the most vivid dreams and I feel so happy. Can't you understand me even a little?

Maverick: I can understand you just fine.

Edith: Oh you strange foreign man you are making me feel most peculiar. *(She puts his hand on her breast)* Can you feel my heart beat? - it's going pitter-pat, pitter-pat ...

Maverick: Miss Lampton! ... Miss Lampton ... Oh Edith! *(They kiss)*

Edith/Maverick love music. They dance round the table in a Busby Berkely-style, romantic way and then fall asleep on it.

Scene Eight

Edith: *(Waking)* Amsterdam. May the 8th 1889.
Dear Mrs McBride,
I have just awoken on this beautiful new Dutch day. You will never guess, but last night we slept al fresco on the cart. Oh, it was very cold, but Monsieur The Maverick kept me warm by making himself my blanket and laying close on top of me

and, as we drifted off to sleep, I felt an exquisite euphoria engulf me in great rhythmic waves.

That dear man is still asleep, his head buried deep in my bosom. Oh do not think badly of me dear friend, he is more child than man, more babe even than child. Indeed as he nestles against my breast I can feel all my maternal instincts welling up again ...

Kloop rushes in.

Kloop: Excuse my intrusion, Miss Lampton. We are, as is the custom in this country, to bury your brother at dawn, and so must make all haste to the cemetery. Perhaps you would be so kind as to help me with the coffin, Mr. Maverick.

They load the coffin back onto the desk and get on.

Edith: Dear Monsieur Kloop, I have not yet had a chance to extend my most heartfelt thanks to you ...

Kloop: Thank you. Do get on.

Edith: Indeed, everyone in Marmsey also extends their thanks ...

Kloop: *(He shoves **Edith** up onto desk)* Yes, yes, get on!

Edith: Monsieur Kloop was extremely anxious to leave and as we sped away over the cobbled streets, we narrowly missed a group of militiamen who seemed keen to converse with us.

Chase music. Silent movie style cart chase. Cart stops. They get down.

After a truly hair-raising journey, we have arrived at a large cemetery just outside Amsterdam. It is a lonely and desolate place with three graves freshly dug, giving Sebastian a choice.

Maverick: I'm watching every move you make, Kloop!

Kloop: Well watch this.

*Kloop knocks out **Maverick**. **Edith** is oblivious.*

Edith I can see no sign of a priest so I shall take a moment to pray. *(She kneels and prays. Behind her **Kloop** takes out a cosh and creeps up on her)* I had misunderstood Sebastian. He had been diligently working to increase the family store and all I could do in return was chafe and scold and shoot him with a whaling harpoon.

She prays again. **Kloop** *tries again, but* **Maverick** *wakes up and they wrestle silently behind* **Edith** *until they break as* **Edith** *turns.*

Maverick: Edith, get back, this man is not who he says he is.

Kloop: Brilliantly surmised, Mr. Maverick. *(He uncovers his dog collar)*

Edith: Vicar!

Kloop: Yes, Edith, it is I ...

Maverick: The Vicar of Marmsey!

Edith: Have you come to officiate?

Vicar: You just don't get it, do you, Edith?

Gunfire and shouting.

Vicar: Blast! *(He runs off with the coffin)*

Edith: Vicar, where are you going. Wait for me. Look Monsieur The Maverick, the militiamen. Do you think they are firing a twenty-one gun salute?

Maverick *throws her over his shoulder and runs round desk.*

Edith: Put me down! Put me down, you scoundrel! How dare you sir! *(She slaps his face)* I am missing my own brother's funeral! Vicar, wait for me.

Maverick: Jesus! I cannot believe you, woman!

Maverick *coshes her on the back of the head.*

Edith: How strange the constitution of woman, that emotional fatigue, combined with the constrictures of corsetry, can cause a severe palpitation of the brain.

Edith *collapses into his arms.*

Maverick: Sorry, baby, but it's for your own good!

He lays her on desk and exits.

Scene Nine

The dockside - seagulls etc.

Performer 2: *(In porter's waistcoat. He removes portrait of Victoria on one screen to reveal a woman with a rebel flag)*

Kingstown, Dublin, Ireland. May the 14th, 1889.
Excuse me, ma'am, *(He rouses **Edith**)* we've arrived.

Edith: Arrived?

Porter: Yes ma'am, in Ireland. If you'd be so kind as to disembark, I'll unload your trunk onto the dockside.

***Edith** looks around bewildered.*

Edith: Thank you. *(She feels the lump on the back of her head)*

Porter: *(Moves desk to back of stage)* No trouble at all. All in a day's work. 'Ah, Dublin in the rare oul' times' ...

Exits singing 'Take me up to Monto'.

Edith: Dear Mrs. McBride,
I am writing to you from the dockside in Kingstown, Ireland. I have no idea how I came to be here, indeed I have little recollection of anything except your name and address - perhaps you could send me a postcard reminding me who I am.

Yours ... ? ... Edith.

*She scans horizon with a telescope. **Maverick** and **Kelly** enter.*

Kelly: Is she safe, Maverick?

Maverick: Yes, she's safe and the Vicar of Marmsey is behind bars where he belongs! The only thing is, Sean, it got kinda rough in the churchyard and I had to knock her out.

Kelly: Jesus, Mary and Joseph, you're not bloody bounty-hunting now. She's my daughter, not some desperado!

Maverick: I know, Sean, I'm sorry. It was the only way. You didn't tell me she was so ... so ...

Kelly: So what? She's a lady, Maverick, and don't you forget it! A lady like her mother ... *(Sings)* 'Oh Caitlin was the sweetest girl, as sweet as any lark ... '

Maverick: Sean!

Kelly: Sorry.

Maverick: There's one other thing.

Kelly: Yes?

Maverick: There's one other thing I have to tell you.

Kelly: Well, out with it.

Maverick: I've fallen in love.

Kelly: With who?

Maverick: With Edith.

Kelly: You've what?!

Maverick: I've fallen in love with Edith!

Kelly: Mr. Maverick, as you know, I've great respect for you and not only because your father was from Sligo. You're a great man for the cause with an opinion I trust, sure I'm as fond of you as I would be of my own son - but if you so much as lay a finger on that woman, I'll pull the very spine of your back through the arse of your trousers. Do you hear me?

Maverick: But Sean I love her.

Kelly: I don't care, you lay a finger, one finger on her and I'll rip the ...

Edith: Excuse me, gentlemen. I'm sorry to disturb you, but I seem to have lost my memory.

Kelly: Jesus, what have you done to her? Edith, it's me, Sean Kelly.

Edith: And suddenly it all came back to me, Mrs McBride. As Master Kelly checked my head for lumps, I remembered everything! I had fainted. I had fainted dead away at my own dear brother's funeral and missed the ceremony.

Maverick: It's not your fault ma'am, you were overcome with grief.

Kelly: Sure Edith, a funeral is a very emotional event.

Edith: Ah Master Kelly, Mr. Maverick you are too kind, but what am I to do now?

Kelly: Come child, I'll bring you home.

Edith exits, Kelly gives Maverick a warning look and they exit.

Scene Ten

Irish sting. Edith enters.

Edith: Wicklow, Ireland. June the 5th, 1889.
Dear Mrs. McBride,
I have finally managed to put pen to paper. And what strange revelations I have to tell you. I am staying with Master Kelly deep in the wilds of Wicklow and the truth of the matter is, I cannot leave! Do not think I am being held hostage Mrs McBride for in truth the situation is quite the reverse. My dear host is sheltering myself and Mr. Maverick from the long arm of the law, along with members of the Irish Publican's Army, a renegade brewers' organization. I will explain all: we had just arrived from the dockside and I was most anxious to telegraph to Marmsey when ...

She exits.

Irish sting. Kelly enters followed by Edith and Maverick.

Kelly: You cannot telegraph anyone Edith!

Edith: But why not Master Kelly? I must explain to my servants that I have found my way to Ireland by mistake. I do not blame Mr. Maverick for putting us on the wrong boat - he is after all somewhat feeble-minded and it was a lucky coincidence indeed that led us to meet you, of all people, on the dockside but Dorcas and Loxley will be frantic and I must put their minds at rest!

Kelly: Edith. Sit down and listen to me. Your coming here wasn't exactly a mistake.

Maverick: And I am not feeble-minded, little lady!

Kelly: No, you're not, so you can explain it all to her.

Maverick: Hey, why have I gotta do all the explainin'.

Kelly: *(Under his breath)* Well you're the one that's in love with her, aren't you!

Maverick: Edith, please listen to me.

Edith: Then to my amazement Esme, Mr. Maverick spoke to me lucidly in fluent English. He explained that we had been in the snare of a criminal mastermind: namely, the Vicar of Marmsey.

Maverick: And that's how you ended up here, Miss Edith.

Edith: I can hardly believe it, Master Kelly!

Kelly: It's all true, Edith. He was using Sebastian's coffin to smuggle ... er ... contraband.

Edith: Contraband! Is contraband illegal? Oh poor Sebastian.

Kelly: It's poor Edith I'm worried about. The police think you were an accomplice. They want to put you in prison, Edith, and, Marmsey is the first place they'll look. I'm afraid you're stuck here.

Edith: *(She thinks)* Then I am an outlaw, Master Kelly?

Kelly: I'm afraid so.

Edith: Why, it is quite cosmopolitan. Is Mr. Maverick an outlaw too?

Maverick: Yes ma'am.

Edith: Then we shall be outlaws together! Perhaps you would be so kind, Mr. Maverick, as to show me to my room.

Maverick: Yes, ma'am. *(He offers her his arm)*

Kelly: Maverick!

Maverick: I'll be back directly, sir. *(They exit)*

Edith: Outlaws, what fun!

Kelly: Ah she is a chip off the old Kelly block! *(Exit singing)* 'Oh Edith is the sweetest girl, as sweet as any lark ... '

Scene Eleven

Longer Irish sting. **Edith** *enters in a full apron with pregnancy bump sewn into it.*

Edith: Wicklow, Ireland October 29th, 1889.

Dear Esme,
You will be amused to hear that your beanpole of a friend has become quite stout! It was a great cause of consternation to me at first, as I seem to get fatter by the week, but Mrs. Markievicz has told me that swelling such as mine is very common in Ireland, and afflicts Irish women over and over again!

She starts to get sick and rushes off. **Kelly** *and* **Maverick** *rush on.*

Kelly: *(Livid)* You'll have to marry her!

Maverick: Sean, let me explain.

Kelly: Are you trying to weasel out of it?

Maverick: No! I want to marry her. But let me explain what happened - it's not how it seems.

Kelly: Oh, so that's just a cushion under her dress is it?!

Maverick: It was when we were in Holland. Times were desperate. It was cold. We'd been drinking. She put my hand on her breast. *(**Kelly** chases him off)* I swear it Sean. Sean!

Edith *enters dabbing her mouth with a hankie.*

Edith: Do you know, Mrs McBride, being an outlaw is altogether quite pleasant. I do a spot of gardening in the morning, a little baking after lunch and in the evenings I have been attempting to teach Mr. Maverick how to shank a mole. This evening, however, will be quite different, as Master Kelly has arranged a name-changing ceremony. I believe this is to throw our pursuers off the scent once again. I am to become Edith O'Shaughnessy and Mr. Maverick will be called Yankee O'Shaughnessy. Our 'safehouse' is to be the little gazebo at the end of the garden, which Mr. Kelly has kindly given us for a peppercorn rent. This is very sweet of him but I think we should insist on paying with money.

But what of Marmsey, you ask - well the one joyous piece of information I have managed to glean is that Dorcas and Loxley are to be married. As a fugitive and desperado I have renounced all rights to my little house and so have given it to them as a wedding present.

But now it is with heavy heart, dear Esme, that I must tell you our correspondence must cease. You have put yourself at great risk on my behalf, and your sterling reputation would be tarnished indeed by association with a wanted criminal. Therefore let us write no more but hold each other fondly in our hearts for all time. Do not worry about me, dear friend, I am quite at peace, and once my swelling goes down, as the Countess is certain it will, I will be happy, healthy, and spiritually whole again for the first time since childhood, in Marmsey, with you. God bless you Mrs. McBride, your friend, Edith O'Shaughnessy.

Wedding march.

Kelly *walks* **Edith** *to* **Maverick**, *centre stage.*

Edith: *(As if to priest)* I beg your pardon? Oh, indeed, I do!

Kelly *throws rice. Lights fade quickly as* **V/O** *comes in.* **Edith** *removes her 'apron', bundling it up in her arms reverse side out. The two men either side of her.*

Historian V/0: And this is where the letters sadly stop. We know Mrs. Esme McBride, even under police interrogation, never revealed Edith's whereabouts and continued for many years as a governess before retiring home to Edinburgh. But of Edith there is no further word, except, that is, for one brief communication dated a few months later.

They stand either side of her.

Edith: Telegram: February the fourteenth 1890.
Dear Mrs. McBride. stop. Miracle has occurred. stop. Delivered of a baby girl last Tuesday. stop. One never thinks Second Coming will happen to one. stop. Have named child Jesus Edith Esme Christ. stop. Send bootees. stop.
Edith.

End music: Delightful waltz. Fade to black.

Afterword

Dear Reader,

Lost Letters started life as a faux correspondence between myself and a delusional friend. Sadly an incorrigible fantasist, she quickly eschewed all interest in writing to me of her real life, choosing instead to 'be' Edith Lampton. Such was her perseverance that in the end I forgot her real name, couldn't remember what she looked like and indeed had no idea how we'd met in the first place.

Many a time I considered breaking off this correspondence, sensing, as I did, that its psychic grip was dragging my friend ever deeper into the dark pit of insanity. However, I thought it best to continue the exchange during the compilation of this manuscript, knowing there would be plenty of time after publication (in my name for the sake of convenience), to cut the painful cord of contact.

The play has been a great success I am delighted to say (sales over the million mark, and translations into sixteen different languages), but in spite of my necessary silence, my poor friend has tried to maintain our friendship, clinging like a moth to the lamp of my international celebrity, and sending me a constant stream of missives made up of letters cut from the newspaper. Strangely, her erstwhile gay banter has taken a darker tone of late, and I have been advised by the local constabulary that a change of address might be expedient at this time.

It is a great pity that such a fruitful alliance has thus been lost forever, although I trust that my name and her spirit shall be kept alive in posterity when you, dear reader, hire and perform this 'delightful work of genius' (*Scouting Today*), as often as possible.

Bonne Chance Mes Amies!

The Author
In Hiding
Dublin 6 West
1ˢᵗ April 2001

In the Talking Dark

DOLORES WALSHE

In The Talking Dark was first produced by the Royal Exchange
Theatre in Manchester on 13 April 1989 with the following
cast:

Piet Schuurman	Terence Wilton	
Mia Schuurman	Frances Tomelty	
Jan Schuurman	(Evenings)	Joseph Murray
	(Matinées)	Stuart Pickering
Thulatu Mdala	Norman Beaton	
Paul Richardson	Philip Anthony	
Claus Schuurman	Wolfe Morris	
Babo Schuurman	Jenny Quayle	
Elijah	Joseph Mydell	
Samuel	Alex Tettah-Lartey	
James	Andrew Francis	
Sipho	Wale Ojo	
Vos/Reunert	Peter Rutherford	

Director	Braham Murray
Designer	Johan Engles
Lighting	Robert Bryan
Dialect Coach	Penny Dyer

In the Talking Dark was winner of the O.Z. Whitehead
/Society of Irish Playwrights/PEN Playwriting Literary Prize
in 1987, and won the staging prize in the Mobil
International/Royal Exchange Playwriting Competition in
1989.

Sets   Drawing-room and bedroom of house in affluent white suburb of Pretoria.

              Patio of farmhouse outside Pretoria.

Time   The play is set in the late 1980s, prior to the fall of Apartheid.

Characters

Piet Schuurman	White man, early forties
Mia Schuurman	Piet's wife, white, mid thirties
Jan Schuurman	Their fourteen-year-old son
Thulatu Mdala:	Cape coloured lawyer, early fifties
Paul Richardson	Mia's father, white doctor, mid fifties
Claus Schuurman	Piet's father, white, early sixties
Babo Schuurman	Piet's sister, early twenties
Elijah	Young black servant, real name Thembalethu Mini
Samuel	Black servant, mid sixties
James	Black parolee, mid forties
Sipho	Black parolee, mid thirties
Vos	White farm manager, early fifties
Reunert	Police commissioner, mid fifties

Where German, Dutch and Afrikaans words are used individually and also when they are combined to make a single phrase, their pronunciation should be accented to stress the individual languages.

ACT ONE

Scene One

Drawing room

The room is expensively, tastefully furnished. To the left towards the back of stage, a door leads to dining room. A door in centre at back leads to hall. Two couches at right angles before a coffee table at left front stage. Various other items of furniture including drinks cabinet, bureau, bookcases and miniature Battle of Blood River (laager of wagons, etc.) displayed on table stage right near window.

Piet *and* ***Jan*** *are studying a miniature battle displayed on table stage right before the window.*

Jan: Ten thousand Zulus against a few Boers! And they only got three of us.

Piet: Only wounded, mind. And for each one of the three, we killed a thousand of them. God was on our side.

Jan: They should've had muskets and cannons like us. Stupid using only spears and sticks.

Piet: Savages. God helped us avenge the murder of Piet Retief and his men.

Jan: The battle of Blood River. My favorite story.

Piet: It's no story! That's why you've no school today. All over South Africa the promise the Boers gave God before the battle is being made again just as we did at the Service this morning. Remember the words of the Covenant?

Jan: Of course! *(Stiffening to attention)* Here we stand before God the most Holy in the highest Heaven to make a vow unto Him that if He shall protect us, deliver our enemy unto us, henceforth this day shall be a day of thanksgiving as the Sabbath brings even unto our children in all future generations so that his name may be honoured and the glory of victory be His now and forever.

Piet: Prima. A true Afrikaner. We must never forget that promise, Jan. If we do, we'll forget who we are, we'll be destroyed. We're a tiny country with very few friends. Most of the world is against us now. We've got to be strong, look after ourselves.

Jan: Papa, can I borrow your scouting knife? Grandpa promised me his but -.

Piet: You're not listening!

Jan: I am! But I'll be the only one without a knife.

Mia enters, removing hat. Speaking as she does so.

Mia: Elijah's bringing the coffee. *(Sits sprawling on couch)* That church ... talk about a sauna! Poor Heidi Moulin, did you see her? A mink stole in this humidity! I thought she'd moult ... like a sodden meerkat draped about her neck by the time the service was over. *(Pause)* I've often wondered ... they say there's a dash of the tarbrush, that her mother was ... *(Glances swiftly at Jan)* Hm, never mind what her mother was. Well, thank goodness we won't have to sit through it again till next year. All that gory stuff about the past. *(Shivers)*

Piet: *(Frowns, nods at Jan who is fiddling with the display)* It's part of his history, it's important for him to learn these things.

During the following exchanges, Piet and Jan are absorbed in the battle display.

Mia: Oh, he gets enough of that in school, don't you, Jan?

Jan: Yeah, it's a bore.

Mia: Crashing.

Piet: Will you stop encouraging him?

Mia: *(Speaking as she rises. Moves to Jan)* Oh, don't be such a wet blanket. He'd far rather spend the time on the phone chatting to all his girlfriends. *(Ruffles his hair)* Wouldn't you, dear?

Jan: *(Moves away. Still absorbed in display)* Stop it, Mia.

Mia: Mia? What's this? Whatever happened to 'Mama'? *(Attempts to touch him again)*

Jan: *(Moves away)* It's drippy stuff. Anyway, it's not as if you were my *real* mother.

Mia: *(Hurt)* Yes, well, thanks for reminding me.

Piet: C'mon, he didn't mean it like that ... did you, Jan? *(Piet leans across table, kisses her swiftly)*

Jan: Anyway, Grandpa says I'm getting too big for that now.

Mia: *(To Piet)* Your father. Doesn't surprise me, really. *(Moves away, begins tidying, fussing)*

Piet: Don't make a mountain. I'm sure Papa didn't mean anything.

Mia: Oh no? *(Takes inordinate amount of time arranging a fragile ornament dead centre on a small polished table. Pauses speculatively.)* You think Claus would have felt any different if I'd been one of you? You really think it's just my being English that bothered him so much?

Piet: Water under the bridge. C'mon, forget it, will you? Everything's been fine for ages. *(Pause)*

Mia: *(Nods vehemently)* Yes, it has, hasn't it, Pietie? Really, it's been fine for ages. I'm stupid to worry about these things. *(Holds out hands, examining her nails. Pause)* Silk finish, they said. Exclusive nail artistes. *(Small disgusted sound, holds hand towards Piet)* Look at that one, chipped already! So much for the new salon in Andries Street. Still, the diamanté studs aren't bad. What d'you think?

Piet: Hey? *(Glances up)* Sexy.

Knock on door. **Elijah** *(Thembalethu) enters, bearing silver tray etc. Places it on coffee table.*

Mia: Elijah, do you remember I told you to wear the gloves when you're dusting?

Elijah: Yes, Madam. *(Backs towards door)*

Mia: Well, you forgot to wear them again, didn't you?

Elijah: *(Still backing out)* Yes, Madam.

Mia: Try to remember them next time, will you?

Elijah: Yes, Madam. *(Exit)*

Mia: *(Sighs, begins pouring coffee)* His fingerprints all over the Lladro again. I don't know what I bought those dusting gloves for. Sometimes I wonder if he understands anything I say, or if he hasn't just learned to say 'yes, Madam.' *(Pause)* He's a strange little golliwog. Still, he's clean, and honest, I'll say that for him. I even feel safe leaving my jewellery sitting on the dressing-table. D'you know the Oberholzers up on the hill have had a steel safe sunk in concrete in the bedroom floor? She says she hasn't had one servant she can trust in ten years. Here's your juice.

Jan: Can't I have coffee?

Piet: *(Strolls to couch, sits)* No, it's not good for you.

Jan: Well, I'm not drinking that stuff, it's disgusting. Anyway, it's not fair. You drink tons of coffee.

Mia: *(To **Piet**)* Oh, let him. Just this once. *(To **Jan**)* Go call Elijah, tell him to bring another cup.

Jan: In a minute.

Mia: Did you pack enough socks? What time are the scouts collecting you?

Jan: I told you, Mama, not for hours.

Mia: *(Pleased)* Oh, it's 'Mama' again, is it? Your aunt Babo's coming for dinner, it's a pity you'll miss her.

Jan: And Grandpa. He promised me his scouting knife. I hope he gets here early enough. Can I go to Helmut's for lunch? He asked me.

Mia: Have you packed?

Jan: It'll only take a second. Can I go to Helmut's?

Mia: I thought it'd be nice if the three of us had lunch together -. Grandpa? *(Pause. To **Jan**)* What'd you mean. 'and Grandpa?'

*She turns to stare at **Piet**.*

Piet: *(Draining his cup)* Don't include me for lunch. I've got to get out to the farm. Papa's expecting me. We start harvesting tomorrow, wheat ... just ... ripples! *(Satisfied sigh)* Irrigation spraying's made all the difference.

Mia: Your father is coming to dinner? *(Pause.)* Today?

Piet: Sorry. I forgot to mention it.

Mia: With Babo here? *(Pause)* Does he know she's joined the Black Sash, is that it? *(Sharply to **Jan**)* If you don't get a cup now the coffee'll be too cold.

Jan: Oh, all right. *(Exit)*

Piet: *(Rises)* You'd better tell Elijah, mind – he understands you better than he does me.

Mia: What's up?

Piet: What's the problem? Papa comes to dinner often enough.

Mia: With Babo here?

Piet: So?

Mia: Don't play games with me, Pietie.

Piet: Maybe it's time we tried to ,.. mend some fences.

Mia: *(Rises)* Those kinds of fences don't mend and you know it. Just what is it the pair of you think you're up to?

Piet: *(Moves about)* I don't know what you mean.

Mia: Does she know Claus is coming?

Piet: How do I know? You invited her.

Mia: You told me to. But you didn't see fit to enlighten me about your father.

Piet: I told you, I forgot.

Mia: How convenient! *(Pause)* How can you do that to your own sister! She'd really thank you, I'm sure. They haven't seen each other since the row. *(Pause. Moves towards phone)* I'd better head her off.

Piet: No, don't do that. *(Goes to stop her, leading her away from phone)* C'mon, give it a chance, will you? Wouldn't you be just as pleased if everything was ... patched up between them ... Hey?

Embraces her.

Mia: What's he up to? Tell me.

Piet: Papa isn't up to anything. It was my own idea.

Mia: Then he doesn't know Babo's coming?

Piet: Well ... I probably did mention it, yes.

Mia: You ... probably mentioned it. *(She pushes him away)* Then she deserves to be told. She's the only friend I've got in this family, the only one I can rely on. I won't have her come here with no warning, nothing.

Piet: I've got to go. Papa'll be waiting. Just trust me, will you? He's mellowed a lot in the last year, you can't deny it. *(Embraces her again)* And it'd be nice for us all to be together, one big happy family, you'd like that, wouldn't you?

Ria: Wishful thinking.

Piet: *(Kisses her)* My wishes have a habit of coming true. I got you, didn't I?

Mia: *(Laughs)* I saw you first.

Piet: *(Kisses her again)* I must go. Just leave it to me and everything'll be okay. Let's just play it by ear. *(Releases her, moves to door, hesitates)* Promise?

Mia: *(Nods)* I'll play it by ear.

Piet *smiles, blows kiss, exits. Pause.* **Mia** *listens then moves towards phone.*

Mia: By ear. *(Picks up receiver. Dials)* C'mon, Babo, be there. *(Pause as she listens. Eventually she hangs up. Begins scribbling note on pad, goes to bureau, finds envelope, addresses it. Moves to door. Opening it as she calls out)* Elijah? I want you to go around to Miss Babo's right away.

Exit.

Scene Two

Drawing room.

Babo sitting tensely on couch. Thulatu, equally tense, prowling the room. Pause. Mia enters carrying haversack, clothing, speaking as she does so.

Mia: Babo! ... Thank goodness you've come! You got my note? *(Stops abruptly as she sees Thulatu. Babo rises)*

Thulatu stares intensely at Mia.

Thulatu: *(Low, moved)* A dream ... for bitter eyes.

Babo goes to her, hesitates, kisses her cheek, moves away.

Babo: Isn't your father here yet?

Mia: *(Eyes fixed on Babo)* Paul? Why should he be here? Far as I know he's on duty at the hospital all day.

Babo: He was to meet us here.

Mia: Meet you? *(Glances swiftly at Thulatu, then back to Babo)* Why would Paul want to meet you here? What's going on? Who is this - ? *(She gestures vaguely in Thulatu's direction)* Why've you brought - ? No, don't tell me. You'd better take him -. *(Gestures dismissively towards Thulatu)* Piet and Claus'll be back from the farm soon. *(Indicates Thulatu)*

Babo: Claus? Papa's coming here today?

Thulatu: How can I couch the words?

Babo: You've got to be kidding!

Thulatu: What can I say? I thought this would be easy, my rage would ... burst its banks ... But I'm *(Stares at Mia)* storm-stayed. *(Striking his heart forcibly)* This beat, this ... clamour, *(Intensely)* let it be crushed if I cause you harm.

Mia: What's he rabbiting about? *(Pause)* Where'd he learn to speak like that? Not at a mission school, surely? Is he looking for work, is that it? You should've taken him to the kitchen.

Babo: *(As **Babo** speaks, **Thulatu** raises hand to shake Mia's, breaks off in mid-motion as she ignores his gesture. His humiliation is obvious)* This is Thulatu. He's - with me. About Papa -.

Mia: With you?

Thulatu: Is that so incomprehensible?

Mia: Y'mean one of your political ducks?

Thulatu: *(Low, drawn out)* Quack. *(Pause)* It seems whichever way I play it, I'm sure to disappoint you. *(Bows stiffly)* My apologies. Unfortunately I haven't yet mastered the magic art of changing into a great white swan. *(Pause)* Why won't you look at me? Are you afraid your eyes will shatter? Perhaps you're right. You'd be looking in a glass. *(Pause)* Sooner or later, you'll have to look me in the face.

Mia: Really Babo, I don't want to know anything about the things you get up to. And neither does my father.

Thulatu: *(To **Babo**)* I told you Paul wouldn't show. What'd you expect? He's a coward.

Mia: How dare you speak of my father -!

Thulatu: She sees me -.

Mia: Did anyone see you come in? Any of the neighbours, I mean?

Thulatu: *(Sardonically)* Don't worry. I was wrapped in a white sheet. Babo sneaked me in with the linen.

Babo: We picked a bad day. Let's leave it. Please?

Thulatu: *(To **Mia**)* It's not laundered, I'm afraid.

Mia: If your Papa finds you here with a ... a ... *(Indicates **Thulatu**)*

Thulatu: Yes? Do go on. If you're having difficulty finding a pristine word, I can always supply you with a ... rather varied selection. They're a little tainted, need I say it? But I can promise they'll trip off your tongue ... kaffir, munt, hotnot, koelie, take your pick.

Babo: Thulatu, please, let's leave it till tomorrow?

Thulatu: *(Moving about)* Leave it? Leave it? *(Roars, making **Mia** jump)* Never! All my life I've been waiting. Well, it's time I took the reins. You can leave if you wish. I'll ride it alone.

Babo: Trample, you mean!

Thulatu: I'm not leaving.

Mia: Babo, please! I'll get the blame too. If you have to mix with these people ... that's your business. But me, I'm not even interested in politics, you know that, so please, take ... take him away before Claus gets here.

Babo: *(Stares at **Thulatu**, then goes to **Mia**. Intensely)* I want you to remember something, promise me, later, when it's ... out ... in the open. *(Leads her to sit)* I didn't want this, you must believe that.

Mia: *(Frightened)* What are you talking about? No, don't tell me! Whatever nonsense it is, I don't want to hear! *(Pause. To **Thulatu**)* Will you please leave my house? *(Long pause)* You shouldn't be here. This is a white area. A black spot for -.

Thulatu: Blacks? Coloureds? Ironic, isn't it? *(Pause)*

Mia: If you don't go I'll be forced to ... call the police.

Thulatu: And then what? *(Paces)* Perhaps you could try explaining to them that your sister-in-law brought me here? Right into the marrow of your nice white nest? *(Pause)* They'll ask questions. Awkward questions. *(Pause)* Haven't you even begun to wonder yet? *(Pause)*

Mia: *(Nervously, sitting close to **Babo**)* Piet and Claus will be here soon.

Thulatu: Oh, then perhaps I should wait and tell them instead?

Babo: Take it easy, will you?

Mia: Tell them what ... what does he mean?

Babo shakes her head

Thulatu: Oh, I'll tell you what I mean. I've lost my son.

Babo: Thulatu, please -.

Thulatu: His name was Vusi. Vusi. Memorize!

Mia: *(To **Babo**, relieved)* Are you in some kind of trouble, is that it? To do with this man?

Thulatu *snorts in disgust.*

Babo: Thulatu ... knew your mother.

Mia: You mean he worked for her? *(Relieved)* Oh, I see!

Babo: No, I meant he -. *(Pause)* A long time ago -.

Thulatu: I was a *(Pause)* friend of your mother's.

Mia: *(Sharply, to **Thulatu**)* My mother's dead! *(Pause)*

Thulatu: A very close friend.

Mia: Babo.

Thulatu: *(Pause)* Around the time you were born.

Mia: *(Pause. To **Thulatu**)* She's dead, d'you hear me?

Thulatu: My son is dead. Vusi.

Mia: Yes, well, I'm ... sorry. But it's really none of my -.

Thulatu: Your black brother.

Mia: *(Rises swiftly)* I really think you should go now. *(During following exchanges, she moves about distractedly)*

Thulatu: He was reared in the townships. But you'd hardly know what that is, you'd hardly know the tin and rubble truth that is!

Mia: This has nothing to do with me!

Thulatu: He died ten hours after the police slung him in a fetid donga on the side of the road.

Mia: I don't want to hear! It's none of my business. Babo?

Thulatu: Twelve miles from the nearest hospital. At night, in the heart's ... coldest hour. Twelve miles. Routine procedure in such circumstances, you understand? A case of dumping your black trash in somebody else's precinct. *(Pause)* He lived long enough for the words to stutter past his lips, every tiny detail of what they'd done to him.

Mia: *(Sits, clutching **Babo**)* Babo! Make him stop!

Babo: *(To **Thulatu**)* Please, there's no need for -.

Thulatu: There's every need! *(Points to **Mia**)* Look at her! The bloody demon-child of racism glittering in her eyes. *(Paces)* I've kept silent for thirty odd years. Where's it got me, may I ask?

Mia: *(Rises, moves about)* Get him out! I don't want to hear! *(Low)* Words, just words, that's all they are!

Thulatu: I've lost my children. What've I got left now? My son, cold and flat-eyed as a dead fish. A mulch for worms. And this, *(Indicates **Mia**. She returns to sit close to **Babo**)* this silk madonna in her cocoon!

Mia: *(Hands over ears)* Just words, just words!

Thulatu: A gewgaw living in another world, worse, a shifty little chameleon. Look how well she's adapted, how well suited she is to this, look at the stink in her eyes! *(Pause. Mia's hands fall from her ears. As **Thulatu** continues, she listens, terrified, her gaze unable to settle on anything)*

Thulatu: Well, I've had enough, enough, d'you hear? When I looked at Vusi, his ... twisted stillness in that box, all I felt was shame, the shame of silence worn like a hairshirt all these years. What kind of man have I been, timid as a sheep on the edge of your white world? Allowing myself to be shackled by my own tongue! A ... a servile mind, where's the ... grace in that? I might as well have been her mother's slave instead of her -.

Mia: What is he saying? What ... vile ... lie is he saying?

Thulatu: *(Leaning over couch from behind her, slowly, with great emphasis)* You know what I'm saying *(**Mia** stiffens. Pause)* You know who you are, whose ... flesh ... you ... are! *(**Mia** becomes rigid. Long pause)*

Mia: *(Jerkily fiddling with jewellery about her neck, holding it out to **Babo**)* Did I show you what Piet brought me for our anniversary? An exact replica of the seal of the British High Commissioner. Seventeenth century, I think he said. *(Pause)*

Spears and stones will crush ... my bones. See? See? *(Again holding out seal)* Twenty four carat ... the purest City Deep.

*Door opens, **Mia** leaps up. **Paul** enters hesitantly. **Mia** rushes to him, grips his arm*

Paul: My dear, I ... *(He pats her ineffectually without looking at her, extricates himself from her grasp. She sags. His gaze shifts continuously about the room. When he speaks, he addresses no one in particular)* I ... I'm afraid I was delayed ... an e-emergency case -. *(Pause)* You told her?

Thulatu: Not the details, no. I'll leave that to you. *(Pause. **Paul** goes to window, stares out)* You know, she could be your daughter after all, her head as deeply embedded in the sand as your own.

*Pause. **Babo** goes to **Mia**, embraces her. **Mia** does not respond. Her hands flutter continually as she smooths her dress, fiddles with her hair, jewellery. **Babo** leads her to sit.*

Babo: *(Staring at floor, to **Mia**)* Your mother ... Paul and Thulatu ... they knew each other when they were students in England.

*Before **Babo** has finished speaking, **Mia** rises, hands still fluttering. While **Paul** speaks, she moves about, blundering into furniture. She behaves as though she were blind and the room is totally alien to her. Equally, it appears she is searching out the familiar lines and angles of the room and its furnishings. She picks up the ornament she had so carefully placed on the table in scene one. Her hands flutter continuously as she feels it. She attempts to replace it dead centre on the table, but without the use of her eyes, she cannot succeed. She drops it on the table and moves on, her actions more jerky than before. She stops in front of glass bookcase, feels it, presses her palms flat against it and pushes again and again. She then drags her nails down the surface of the glass several times. The glass squeals as she does so.*

Paul: *(Without turning)* She ... your mother ... she d-didn't love me. It was *(His head jerks in **Thulatu**'s direction)* him she ... wanted. *(Pause)* When she discovered she w-was pregnant, we agreed it.

Thulatu: *You* agreed it.

Paul: *(Half turns but does not look at **Mia** as she moves about)* If y-you were ... if the baby were ... too dark to pass for a white, she'd remain in England. If not, she'd marry me ... return to South Africa. *(Pause)* I was w-willing to have her on any terms. *(Pause)* It was what she wanted for y-you.

*Pause. The glass squeals under Mia's nails. **Paul** turns at the sound, **Babo** rises. Goes to her.*

Babo: *(Places arm about her shoulders)* Oh Mia, I'm sorry.

***Mia** appears oblivious, continues dragging her nails down the surface of the glass. **Babo** pulls her gently away, leads her to sit as **Paul** goes for the brandy. **Mia** raises her legs, stares at her silk stockings. Swiftly she reaches to her ankles, dragging her nails along the silk towards her knees, tearing the stockings. **Babo** stops her as **Paul** is pouring the brandy. His hands are shaking. He spills a little, carries the glass to **Mia**, proffers it. **Mia** is staring blindly ahead, her eyes registering nothing. He holds the glass to her lips, the liquid spills down her chin. Her hand jerks upwards. knocking the glass and spilling the contents. It spills on her dress, the couch and carpet. She stares down, reaches suddenly for the lace antimacassar on the back of couch. Swabs furiously at the stains on couch and carpet, her breath coming in large gasps as though she were performing some strenuous physical feat. **Babo** tries to stop her.*

Babo: Mia, please don't. *(She pulls the lace from **Mia**, dropping it as she begins to stroke her. **Mia** becomes still, staring rigidly ahead)* Please, look at me. Please, look at me. God , I don't know what to say.

Paul: She's i-in shock. I ... I'll have to g-give her something.

Babo: *(Angrily)* Then what are you waiting for!

Paul: *(Looks about as though dazed)* M-my bag. *(To **Babo**)* She needs a ... a shot. I th-think I ... left it in the hall. She should be l-lying down. Will you help me?

*Together, he and **Babo** draw **Mia** from the couch, lead her from the room. **Thulatu** stands staring after them for several moments. Eventually he goes to sit, places his head in his hands. Long pause during which he raises his head several times as though listening. **Babo** re-enters alone, begins pacing.*

Babo: We shouldn't have. *(Pause)* It was wrong.

Thulatu: What is she? Sacred?

Babo: She wasn't able for it.

Thulatu: She had to be told. This palace. Why should she escape?

Babo: God's truth, if someone walked up to me in the street and said, 'Claus is not your father' I'd be thrilled.

Thulatu: Even if your real father turned out to be black?

Babo: You're not black.

Thulatu: Oh, and you think she noticed the difference. *(Pause)* You seriously think you'd sing for joy?

Babo: I'm not a racist.

Thulatu: I'm not sure what you are, Babo. *(Rises. Goes for drink. Pause)* The protest's fixed for next month. Perhaps then I'll finally get to see your ... colour.

Babo: What's keeping them?. The way she slobbered ... she's so ... tidy, normally! Her eyes ... *(shivers)* weird.

Thulatu: You'd better call them. I have to go soon.

Babo: Just go, then.

Thulatu: I've something else I want to say to her. *(Pause)* She has to tell them, she has to tell your family the truth!

Babo: No! D'you want to destroy her altogether?

Thulatu: You agreed to it.

Babo: Not all in one go.

Thulatu: I swore it over Vusi's body. You took my hand.

Babo: Thulatu, listen. I know her. I'm telling you, she won't be able to handle it. *(Pause)*

Thulatu: I should've taken her after her mother died. Her place was in the township, growing up with her brother, a spear in her hand.

Babo: Ending up dead like him too. *(Rises. Moves about. Bitter laugh)* You and Papa might be brothers! *(Sits)*

Thulatu: How is it you dare! *(Pause)* All those blank years ... I starved for news of her! *(Pause. Goes to her. Hunkers down. Takes her hands)* She'd a right to know! *(Bows head. Pause)* I need her, Babo. I can't go on if - *(Pause. Leaden, slightly drawn out)* Dead. *(Slight pause)* What a dull thud it wakes in the heart. *(Pause)* Don't fail me now.

Babo: They've been gone ages. An injection doesn't take that long. *(Pause. **Thulatu** makes as if to speak, hesitates, rises, moves across to bar)*

Babo: I can't face this dinner tonight if Mia isn't here, not with Papa -.

Thulatu: *(Intense, low, with rhythm of heartbeat)* De-dead *(Slight pause)* De-dead. *(Raises fists to slam on counter, but does not do so. Instead his arms jerk at each of following syllables)* De-de -. *(Pause. Sucks in air to regain control. Holds out his hand, palm upwards, stares at it, speaks while looking at his palm)* I held it against his chest. *(Slight pause)* When a heart ... stammers ... oh the silence is ... Well, I will not be silent! I have words enough to drown the world! *(Slight pause)* The protest's being held on open day. Lots of visiting government officials. We're taking over the campus. A twenty-four hour sit in. They'll be forced to listen, forced to hear the truth, God strike me if it doesn't have an impact! Well? You'll make the speech?

Babo: The speech?

Thulatu: Next month. The sit-in.

Babo: They'd kick me out of college, I, I don't know.

Thulatu: *(Bitter)* You don't know.

Babo: It's easy for you, you don't have as much to, to ... lose.

Thulatu: Oh yes? Apart from the skin off my back! But when has that ever counted for anything in this -.

Babo: Couldn't you get someone else? I'm lousy at making speeches.

Thulatu: It seems your conviction's only skin-deep.

Babo: It's not that! It's just ... I've never done anything so risky.

Thulatu: *(Indicates her)* One of the great white liberals, a, a breed of talkers! *(Pause)* A family with influence, power. What odds are you facing? May I ask? A few hours in a first-class cell until your Papa comes to bail you -.

Babo: I'd never ask for his help.

Thulatu: So they all say. Till they're detained.

Babo: You should know. You seem to ...*(Bitterly)* specialize in ... white women. *(Pause)*

Thulatu: Will you make the speech?

Babo: You're hard. Just like Papa. What, what is it with me? ... no matter which way I run I keep hitting into the same block of granite.

Thulatu: Well?

Babo: But even him. There's a way to get to him.

Thulatu: Will you?

Babo: I, I'll see. I'll think about it. But only if you promise you'll say nothing more to her today.

Thulatu: Agreed. But it won't end here.

Mia and Paul re-enter. Mia appears tense but controlled.

Babo: Oh, there you are! *(Pause)* Paul?

Paul: She's feeling b-better. I've given her a shot. *(Goes to stare out window)*

Babo: *(Goes to Mia)* Mia? You okay? *(Pause)*

Mia: *(Walks past Babo, picks up antimacassar from floor, sniffs)* Babo, how could you? The finest Irish lace. It cost a fortune. And the couch, the carpet!

Babo: But you ... *(Pause)* I'm sorry. *(Pause)*

Mia: *(To Paul)* How, how could you bring me up - ? *(Pause)* Why didn't you tell me before? *(Pause)* Look at me, I'm talking to you! See? See? My mouth is moving!

Paul: It was what she w-wanted for you. I only did as she asked. I ... th-thought the world of her.

Mia: What if I'd had a child?

Paul: I was s-sick when you married Piet. But you were so happy. How could I spoil it? You never had much of a life with ... me-me.

Mia: Sweet Jesus!

Babo: God, I'm sorry, Mia. It's such a mess.

Paul: The relief when you didn't get pregnant!

Thulatu: *(To Paul)* You reared her like an ostrich.

Mia: *(To Thulatu)* Get out!

Thulatu: You had to be told.

Mia: Get out!

Thulatu: Vusi! His name was Vusi! When I looked at his body ... a congested mass in the coffin -.

Mia: Stop it! *(Places hands over ears)*

Babo: *(To Thulatu)* You said -.

Thulatu: I said, 'Your sister will know of this.' I swore it!

Babo: *(To Thulatu)* D'you still want me to make that speech?

Mia: *(To Paul)* They'll be back from the farm soon. *(Moves about)* Take, take him away. *(Indicates Thulatu. Pause)* I have to talk to Elijah about dinner.

Thulatu: His name's Thembalethu. *(Pause)* Thembalethu, not Elijah.

Mia: *(To Thulatu)* What're you saying? What is he -

Thulatu: They've a right to their own names.

Mia: my uncle, or something? Maybe your whole tribe's waiting outside to be introduced? Well, bring them in, go on, all of them. What's a few more black faces between family?

Thulatu: It's all they own in this country.

Babo: Just go, will you?

Paul: I ... I'm afraid I'll have to go too. I'm on duty at four -.

*Mia goes to stare out window. **Paul** goes to her, hesitates, pats her shoulder. She is stiff, unresponsive. He presses a bottle of pills into her hand.*

Paul: M-my dear, I ... Take two of these when ... when you feel ... I'll see you in the morning. *(To **Babo**)* You'll s-stay?

***Thulatu** hesitates, watching **Mia**, then leaves with **Paul**. Pause. **Babo** goes to **Mia**, embraces her, leads her to couch.*

Babo: You poor thing.

Mia: When he said the words ... A mallet crashing in my chest.

Babo: It's been an awful shock.

Mia: Oh, if only it were a dream! Why me? Sweet Jesus, what'd I do to deserve this? Thank God you're here. This dinner. How'm I going to get through it? How? *(Pause)* You mustn't talk politics. Whatever happens, Babo. Promise me.

Babo: Y'might as well ask the grass to stop growing. Dammit, Papa and me in the same room?

Mia: You won't tell! Promise, swear to me!

Babo: I won't tell them.

Mia: How, how do I deal with this? No, no. I mustn't think of it now. After the dinner. Yes, yes. Then I'll. Yes, then. But you knew! Oh why didn't you tell me? How long've you known?

Babo: A while. He got Paul to ... introduce us. Thulatu's a lawyer -.

Mia: Don't mention his name! This dinner -. *(Slightly hysterical laugh)* Imagine! Piet was planning a nice reunion. The family together. Like old times.

Babo: Old times? Papa almost disowned Piet for marrying you so soon after Yolande's death.

Mia: Piet never loved that woman.

Babo: Papa thought the world of her. He'll never look on you as Jan's mother.

Mia: I love him. *(**Babo** places arm about Mia's shoulders)* Even Claus realizes that now. And now this!

Babo: Look, you don't know what Papa is. There are things I could tell you -. When I lived on the farm, when Mama was alive Papa ... Papa ... what he did ... the filth of it. *(Shakes head vehemently)* But what I'm saying is Yolande's dead. Mama's dead. I'm a lost cause. He's willing to include you because Piet and Jan are all he has left.

Mia: Oh, just when everything was going right -. When Papa finds out -.

Babo: It's a bit much calling him Papa. How come you've never called Paul 'Papa'?

Mia: That cold fish! He can't even bear me to touch him.

Babo: I can't bear to touch Claus.

Mia: What'll I do?

Babo: Let's just concentrate on getting through dinner. Look at me! I'm sweating already. Why was I invited? Why'm I staying? *(Harsh laugh)* Need I ask? A moth to a flame.

Mia: It's unreal. That's what it is.

Babo: Papa's up to something.

Mia: *(Rises)* Please, please! Don't make it any worse. Oh, give me yesterday!

Babo: *(Rises, hugs her)* Don't worry ... I haven't seen him in over a year. Things'll have cooled. Look can I take a quick shower? You should see the plumbing in my new flat! View's great though. *(Begins to move towards door)* We'll have a long talk later, sort it out.

Mia: This won't sort. It's worse than dirty linen. Oh, what'll happen? What'll I do? No, no. You go on. Have your shower. I've got to finish packing for Jan. His scouting trip -. They'll be back soon -.

Babo: Sure? *(Mia nods)* I won't be long.

Babo exits. Mia sits. Long pause.

Mia: I know what'll happen. I know. *(She jumps up. Begins pacing. Stops abruptly, stands rigidly. Begins pacing again, stops abruptly, stares about)* Such a mess. *(Begins tidying fastidiously)* A pigsty. A real pigsty. A sow would be cleaner, they'll say. No, no. Stop, stop it! Jan's packing. *(Grabs haversack and clothing, begins to move towards door)*. Finish Jan's packing. *(Exits)*

Scene Three

Drawing room

Piet and *Jan* *(wearing scout's uniform) are working on the battle display. Claus's voice carries through door from hall.*

Claus: Ja, I'm glad I made it. I promised Jan -.

Mia, *dressed differently, and* **Claus** *enter.*

Jan: *(To Claus)* Did you remember the knife?

Mia: *(Brittle tone)* Jan! Where're your manners.

Claus: *(Producing knife)* Anything for my favourite grandson.

Jan: Your only grandson.

Piet: *(To Claus)* Join me? *(Watches his father while he continues)* Sherry, Mia?

Mia: Brandy.

Piet: You never drink brandy.

Jan: *(To Claus, examining knife)* Deadly! It's much sharper than Papa's. The scouts'll be here any second. When we cross the Drakonsberg, we're camping out for two nights.

Claus: *(As they move to sit)* Ah, to be young enough to retrace the Great Trek! To pull ox and wagon over miles of bedrock. What an epic journey it was! *(Piet joins them with the drinks)*

Jan: *(Testing the knife)* Harder for us! We've no slaves now to push the wagons.

The men laugh as **Mia** *speaks.*

Mia: Jan! Don't talk like that!

Claus: More's the pity. Isn't Babo here?

Piet*: (To **Mia**)* You okay?

Mia: She's having a shower.

Piet: *(To **Claus**)* When they get to the camp site, they put on a play -.

Jan: We all put our names in a hat. I got stuck with playing a girl.

Claus: Which one?

Mia: Anna Steenkamp.

Claus: Ah zo, you have the most important lines.

Jan: Lucky for me she's only in it at the beginning. I'm playing one of the trekboers as well. Nobody wanted to be the slaves, so we decided to leave them out.

Claus: Hah! Sensible man. Ja, tell me what Anna has to say.

Mia: *(To **Jan** who is still fiddling with the knife)* Oh, he hasn't time. Go check you've everything packed, dear.

Jan: I have everything.

Piet: Come on, Jan. Let's hear you.

Mia: You might've forgotten something.

Piet: What's the matter with you? You spent hours helping him with his lines. I thought you'd jump at the chance -.

Claus: You wouldn't want to disappoint your old grandfather, would you?

Jan: Oh, all right. *(He rises, looking about for a place to stand. He pulls a lace antimacassar from the back of the sofa, placing it on his head, sniffs)* Yikes! It stinks!

Mia: Jan! Take it off! He really won't have time -.

Claus: Let him.

Jan: You're the British.

Piet: He's improvising.

Jan: *(He points at the three adults and begins in a solemn accusatory tone)*You ask us why we are willing to give up everything we know and love? Why we are prepared to endure much hardship and misery trekking across the impenetrable vastness of this land? We wish to go where we can be free to live by our own guiding principles, free to find a new home where we can preserve proper relations between master and servant. *(His voice takes on a sonorous note)* By emancipating our slaves you have placed them on an equal footing with Christians. This is contrary to the laws of God , the natural distinctions of race and religion. It is intolerable for any decent Christian to bow down beneath such a yoke. Wherefore we will withdraw in order to preserve our doctrines in purity. *(Jan mimes lifting a great weight on his back and begins a slow painful trudge across the room)*

Claus: *(As the men clap, murmur approvingly, **Mia** grabs the antimacassar from **Jan**'s head)* Uitstekend.

Piet: A chip off the old block, eh, Papa.

Claus: I just wish your mother had lived to ... *(He swallows. **Elijah** knocks, enters)*

Elijah: Excuse Madam. *(A horn sounds outside)*

Jan: Great! *(He pushes past **Elijah** as he rushes out)*

Mia: *(Hurrying after him)* Jan! You haven't said goodbye -.

Piet: Oh, leave him. *(To **Elijah**)* Help them load his gear. *(**Elijah** mumbles as he hurries out)*

Piet: What's that?

Elijah: *(Pauses, half-turns, eyes averted)* Said yes, Baas. *(Exits)*

Claus: He needs a tight rein, that kaffir. Your mother'd turn in her grave -.

Piet: Well, you've got news?

Claus: Ja-ja. Approved by all the branches. Had it straight from the horse's mouth.

Piet: Then I'm in?

Claus: Was there ever any doubt? A man with nothing to hide -.

Piet: Ah, it's splendid, Papa. *(Gulps drink, replenishes)*

Claus: You won't tell Mia. What your mother never knew -.

Piet: When - ?

Claus: You'll be sworn into the Westeinder cell at Friday's meeting. Replacing van der Meer.

Piet: Then he's out?

Claus: On his arse. The bastard.

Piet: We'd better be careful with Babo. If she ever suspected you'd used what she told me about him -.

Claus: The Broederbond's skilful at covering its tracks. But watch your tongue. She's a proper little ferret. And from what I hear, she's started to mix with some questionable types on the campus.

Piet: That won't go against me?

Claus: *(Shakes head)* We need all the information we can get.

Piet: But Babo'd never tell us anything.

Claus: When you wind her up, zo, amazing what she lets slip.

Piet: That's why you wanted us to invite her today.

Claus: Ja, worth a try. Now, tell me, what'd Jan say about the Windhoek woman?

Piet: It's true. She's been telling them the whites are treating the blacks unfairly.

Claus: Who the hell vetted her? Those teachers are handpicked.

Piet: Jan has a crush on her. I'd quite a job convincing him what she said was lies.

Claus: You see the damage a bloody Marxist can do? Undermining the whole educational structure.

Piet: It's only one teacher, Papa.

Claus: Use your head, man. Twenty, thirty boys, year in, year out. How many Afrikanerized children d'you think we'll have ten years from now? Verdomme, I'll wipe her name off the board -.

*Door opens and **Mia** enters, pauses reluctantly inside door.*

Mia: I hope he has enough sweaters. It's so cold in those mountains at night.

Piet: You're a worrier. *(**Babo** enters a little behind **Mia**. Tense silence. **Piet** rises, glances from **Babo** to his father and moves to drinks cabinet)*

Babo: Papa. *(Pause)*

Claus: You look well.

Babo: Never better. *(Sits with **Mia**. Pause)*

Claus: How ... is everything?

Babo: *(**Piet** hands her a drink and sits)* Such a vague word. What can you possibly mean? My love-life? My studies? Perhaps my new flat? Or the organization I've joined? Which 'everything' d'you wish to know about Papa?

Claus: Ah, zo, you thought to surprise me? I heard you'd joined the Black Sash.

Babo: I'd have thought one of your spies would've confirmed it by now.

Mia: *(Tensely)* Babo, please ... Piet?

***Piet** raises his hand to quieten her. **Mia** sits tensely. **Piet** watches **Claus** and **Babo**.*

Claus: If it's in the national interest -.

Babo: My foot. Everything you do is for the Volk, Papa, your precious nation of Afrikaners. And to hell with the blacks!

Mia: *(Slightly hysterical)* I should have given him more socks. If his feet get wet ... he could catch pneumonia. *(Pause. Everyone stares at her)*

Piet: *(Irritated)* Jan will be fine. What's the matter with you?

Babo: *(To Mia)* Did Paul ever tell you about Dr. Khumalo?

Claus: Paul? What would he know?

Babo: Miss Babo had a golly who was sick, sick, sick, 'n' she sent for the doctor to be quick, quick, quick -.

Claus: You've never left the nursery.

Babo: But the doctor never came -.

Claus: What would Paul know?

Babo: Khumalo. He used to run a clinic in Mamelodi. For blacks who'd been tortured in detention. *(Bitterly)* You know, the ones who officially slip on a bar of soap. Until he was detained himself. A week after they released him, four men shot Dr. Khumalo and his mother in their kitchen. The licence number of one of the cars spotted outside their house -

Claus: Zo, she's always had a wild imagination.

Babo: at the time of the murder was traced right to the commanding officer of the Pretoria Security Police.

Claus: Paranoid!

Babo: The government banned all news reports of the so-called investigation into -.

Claus: Ja-ja! Y'think the quack's scummy neighbours wouldn't lie through their teeth at the first chance of getting a policeman in trouble? We're not barbarians! We uphold the supreme principle of justice: innocent until -.

Babo: Killed in police custody.

Claus: Show me the policeman who was convicted of this crime. Where is he? Zo.

Babo: Out on the streets continuing his filthy work.

Claus: Is it my fault they're not long enough out of the trees? They have to be controlled -. *(**Mia** laughs harshly, begins grunting, scratching under her arms)*

Piet: Cut it out, will you? Have you been drinking? Babo, I try with them, believe me! After that rainstorm, I even gave them a full day to rebuild the huts in the kraal, for all the thanks I got. They're not like us. Look at the squalor they live in. They're like animals. *(**Mia** jumps up, moves about agitatedly)* I've nothing against them, but don't ask me to share our beaches. Surely it's better they've their own areas and we've ours?

Mia: *(To **Babo**)* Animals! I've used that word myself. See?

Babo: Oh, Piet. You sound just like Papa.

Claus: He's my son.

Babo: I mark it.

Claus: And you're my daughter.

Babo: No law says I have to like it. *(**Babo** rises, pours drink)* Still, I'm sure you can get your friends in the Justice Department to change that overnight.

Claus: Ja-ja. You should spend your mornings at your lectures instead of -. *(Pause)*

Babo: Of? *(Pause)* Hah! So, I'm being watched. Thanks. I'll be more careful in future.

Mia: *(High-pitched tone)* Jan has a cold. His sinuses. He always gets an attack in summertime. Hay fever, the doctor says. I hope he's -.

Piet: Christ , Mia! What the hell's the matter with you! *(Slight pause. To **Babo**)* You can't change things overnight. Unless you want a war on your hands.

Babo: Listen to Rip van Winkle!

Mia: *(To **Babo**)* You promised!

Claus: *(Drains his glass. To **Mia**)* Now my dear, any chance of us eating soon? Piet and I have some things to see to on the farm.

Babo: Getting a new batch of parolees, Papa?

Claus: *(Slams his glass)* You push me too far.

Babo: It was a simple question.

Claus: Don't smart-ass me.

Babo: You've just answered it. You wouldn't be so livid if you weren't still using slave labour to harvest your crops. God help them, they'd be better off in their overcrowded cells, being beaten by the police -.

Mia: I'll never forgive you for -.

Piet: Christ , Babo!

Claus: *(Leaps up)* Gott in Hemel! How dare you ... *(His hands curl into fists,* **Babo** *shrinks)* But for your mother I'd -.

Door leading to dining room opens. **Elijah** *enters*

Elijah: Excuse, Madam. Lunch is to serve.

They all turn towards him. **Elijah** *senses tension, backs out hurriedly.*

Mia: Yes, yes. *(She rises. Takes* **Claus**'s *arm, moves towards dining room)* Your favourite hors d'oevres, Papa. Fresh salmon with just a hint of lemon -.

They exit. **Piet** *rises. Glares at* **Babo**.

Babo: *(Pause)* When he's near me the world seems to ... tilt.

Piet exits. **Babo** *rises, breathing deeply, exits.*

Scene Four

Drawing room

Mia enters, wanders about.

Mia: *(Pours drink, gulps it, pours another. Wanders about)* Well, you're on your own, kid. No different to the way it's always been. *(Pause)* Except for Piet, oh Pietie, don't let me lose it now! Sweet Jesus, what'm I going to do? *(Stops abruptly, picks up antimacassar, places it on her head, points accusingly as Jan had done earlier)* By emancipating our slaves, you have placed them on an equal footing with Christians. This is contrary to the laws of God . The laws of God. *(Pause Swipes cloth from her head, sits, begins to rub jerkily at her face, arms, legs, with it. Pause. She sniffs the cloth, flings it from her, screams the following)* It stinks! Stinks! *(She curls into a ball on the couch, lights dim slowly to indicate passage of time. **Piet** enters the dusky room)*

Piet: Hey, beautiful lady! You asleep?

Mia: *(Starts)* What, it's not true! Who is it?

Piet: You okay? You look -.

Mia: Was it a dream, oh, was it?

Piet: Hey up! You're shivering. Feverish too.

Mia: Tell me I dreamed it.

Piet: Y'mean Babo? She's a bloody terror -.

Mia: I could've strangled her!

Piet: From the time she was knee-high, if Papa said yes, she'd scream no. It's worse since Mama died. She's had her knife in him -.

Mia: Oh, give me yesterday!

Piet: Listen! The Broederbond. I'm in. Can y'believe it? You could do with a brandy. What's got you drinking brandy? *(Pours drinks)* Only don't let on you know to Papa.

Mia: No, no, you mustn't tell Papa. You must keep it a secret. Is that possible?

Piet: Aren't you going to congratulate me? *(Raises his glass)* The Broederbond!

Mia: Babo says they're fanatics.

Piet: Babo doesn't know her ass!

Mia: She knows about politics.

Piet: Has she been getting at you? Is that, she'd do anything to get at Papa.

Mia: D'you have to join? You don't have to, do you? We're fine as we are.

Piet: You can't be serious! You know how much I've wanted -.

Mia: A bunch of fanatics!

Piet: The word according to Babo.

Mia: Babo didn't say it. I said it.

Piet: You just said -.

Mia: I said it!

Piet: What's the matter with you? It's the lifetime ambition of most Afrikaners.

Mia: Did they check you out? Did they? They didn't dig deep enough.

Piet: It's the best thing that could've happened. Think of Jan. His future's assured. I'm telling you, farming'll become just a sideline.

Mia: What's it all for? Answer me that! We've got enough, haven't we enough? Why d'you always have to reach for more? They're evil.

Piet: For Jan. This is for Jan.

Mia: For your father.

Piet: I want this, Mia. I want it. It can mean a career in banking, politics, industry, you name it.

Mia: You're a farmer.

Piet: Did I have a choice? You're always moaning at how tied to Papa I've been.

Mia: All I ever get from you is promises.

Piet: You're in a filthy mood.

Mia: Yes, filthy. I'm filthy. Sweet Jesus, how will I cope with it. Don't join, Piet.

Piet: Are you crazy? It's my one chance to be ... my own man. I'll have power, influence -.

Mia: How'll you use it? To keep the blacks down?

Piet: Listen, if anything's to be changed in this country, the Broederbond must have new blood, younger men like me, willing to adapt, move towards ... democracy.

Mia: Democracy? You mean one man, one vote?

Piet: Well ...

Mia: Will you do that? Will you, Piet? Then we'd all be equal.

Piet: Well -.

Mia: If you joined for that -. Y'think it'll come? Y'think it'll come? A big change like that? Then everything'd be all right! Oh when? How soon?

Piet: It's not that simple -.

Mia: I could help! I could do something! Join the Black Sash like Babo, chain myself to railings like those women -.

Piet: Hey up!

Mia: Yes, yes, you're right, you should join. Oh, I needn't've been afraid! *(Hugs him)* You're not Claus. It'll be okay. We were wrong to do nothing. We've been so lazy, but we'll change. We'll do it together, Piet. We'll make things happen -.

Piet: Wait a -.

Mia: I'll phone Babo in the morning. She'll know what I should do.

Piet: Christ! Will you -.

Mia: Oh, Pietie, how soon d'you join?

Piet: Hold on! Just hold on! It'll take a lifetime to bring about changes like that -..

Mia: A lifetime?

Piet: All we can try to do is -.

Mia: You said we'd have a democracy.

Piet: That's you all over, you twist things -.

Mia: My lifetime.

Piet: Papa was right. I should've kept my mouth shut. You say nothing to Babo, mind.

Mia: You mean not in my lifetime.

Piet: What's it matter to us? Where the hell are you getting this sudden interest in politics?

Mia: *(Sits, her body sagging)* A pipedream. To imagine it could happen. Stupid. But the other's a real ... nightmare.

Piet: You don't want to mind Babo, she makes it out to be worse than it is. Come on, you should be in bed. Any idea where my book is? *(Searches)* You know, the one on Antarctica? *(Pause)* What time did Babo leave? Christ, Papa was fuming all evening.

Mia: *(Low voice)* A family. Was it too much to ask? Like a fire on a winter evening. I fanned it so ... elegantly.

Piet: *(Searching)* Where the hell did I leave it?

Mia: Sweet Jesus, was it really too much to ask? *(Pause)* What chance've I got now? He won't let me hold on to Piet. I'm so cold.

Piet: A warm bed's what you need.

Mia: *(Pause)* No one. I've no one. Cold. Like a grave.

Piet: *(Goes to her)* You look as though you've seen a ghost.

Mia: *(Laughs hysterically)* You're close. Oh, you're close. Hold me, Piet!

Piet: Maybe I should call the doctor. You must've caught a bug. I've never seen you -.

Mia: Yes. I'm ... infected. It's been a terrible day, Piet, terrible. That black man! I've had the strangest feeling, it -.

Piet: Black man?

Mia: Won't go away.

Piet: What black man?

Mia: Eh?

Piet: You said 'black man'.

Mia: *(Frightened)* No. No. Did I? I didn't.

Piet: But you -.

Mia: Wait! Yes. In the shops today. He served me. So rude! Don't you find they can be rude?

Piet: The day of the Covenant? But the shops weren't -.

Mia: I'm cold.

Piet: Your hands are freezing.

Mia: On the inside. So cold -.

Piet: Come on. I'm putting you to bed.

Mia: The strangest feeling. I was looking through the wedding album. The negatives, in the pocket inside the cover? They fell out across the floor ... all those negatives. Piet, I could see through them, the tight weave of the carpet. They were so ... transparent. Like we weren't real, like I'd dreamed it all, the wedding, us. And when I picked one up, the only part of me that was white ... my hair. The rest was ... Since I looked at them, I, I can see through me. And Piet, there's nothing, there's nothing there!

Piet: *(His hand to her brow)* You're running a temperature, I'd swear. *(Draws her towards door)*

Mia: D'you hear ... me? Nothing! A cold, empty space.

Piet: You're ill. You're not yourself.

Mia: *(Laughs hysterically as they exit)* Then who am I? Who am I?

Scene Five

Drawing room

Enter **Mia**. **Thulatu** *is sitting. Jumps up.* **Mia** *begins pacing furiously.*

Mia: Why're you doing this? Why? Why've you come? You shouldn't be here. It's against the law. *(Pause)*

Thulatu: You're beautiful. Like your mother.

Mia: It's against the law.

Thulatu: *(Pause)* Looking at you, it's as though she never died.

Mia: Why are you doing this?

Thulatu: *(Reaching inside his jacket)* I've got an old photograph -.

Mia: I don't want to see it!

Thulatu: Your mother -.

Mia: She's dead. Dead! I don't want to know! Please go now.

Thulatu: We have to talk.

Mia: No! You've said all there was.

Thulatu: I'd like to ... to know you.

Mia: You're insane!

Thulatu: We're father and -.

Mia: *(Places hands over ears)* We're nothing! *(Pause)* An old photograph? What's this? Money! Is that what you're after?

Thulatu: You insult me.

Mia: You expect me to believe you have feelings?

Thulatu: I want to get to know you.

Mia: I want to forget you, don't you know that?

Thulatu: You've had time to ... adjust -.

Mia: Photograph. *(Harsh laugh)* And I'm the negative.

Thulatu: I've lost my son.

Mia: I'll lose mine!

Thulatu: You're all I have -.

Mia: How dare you! You've ignored me for thirty-six years. If your son hadn't died -. *(Pause)*

Thulatu: It was wrong, I know. But your mother married Paul. It ... You were swaddled in a white cradle ... behind my back, need I say it? *(Pause)* I loved her, despite what she did. I, I couldn't speak out, it would have destroyed her. *(Pause)* In the end, I agreed to the deception. Oh, she knew I would, knew me too well! *(Pause)* That's not the whole of it, I will be ... scrupulous. *(Faces her. Pause)* I was ... pulp! The thwarted bole of a baobab had more steel in its tender core! You know what makes us black. We're charred with servility. *(Pause)* I kept in touch, though. When I saw Paul at the clinic, I'd ask about you, I even tried to see you. He always fobbed me off. Eventually I gave up, it was too ... awkward between us. *(Pause)* I want you to tell them.

Mia: What clinic?

Thulatu: Hm?

Mia: You said, clinic.

Thulatu: For blacks.

Mia: Blacks?

Thulatu: Torture victims. When they're released from detention - *(With great intensity)* like Vusi. Your black brother.

Mia: Paul runs this clinic?

Thulatu: Funds it. Time and again I've wanted to publish the medical records. But he won't. He hasn't the guts -.

Mia: Sweet Jesus, have I ever been told the truth! He said he was helping poor whites.

Thulatu: That too.

Mia: What'd you mean, you want me to tell them?

Thulatu: Your family.

Mia: *(Frightened)* What? What? About Paul?

Thulatu: About you.

Mia: *(Sits abruptly)* I can't tell them about Paul. A clinic for blacks? Claus would -.

Thulatu: I want you to accept who you are.

Mia: I can't do it. Piet loves me, he loves me.

Thulatu: Then there's no problem.

Mia: But Claus -. Never! It's impossible!

Thulatu: I want to be able to come and see you -.

Mia: See me! You're never to set foot inside this house again, ever!

Thulatu: *(Rises)* If you don't tell them, I'll have no choice -.

Pause

Mia: So that's what it is. I knew. Really, deep down. These last weeks. I've had a ... dread. Chilling. I can't sleep for it.

Thulatu: I want to put things right -.

Mia: Your son is dead, you want to use me!

Thulatu: She was stubborn, so anxious to cover it up. The look on her face when she found out about you! Revulsion! Pure revulsion! Good enough to screw around with but not good enough to father -.

Mia: Stop it!

Thulatu: It's time I set things right.

Mia: You'll destroy me!

Thulatu: We'll take time, get to know each other.

Mia: Please, please, don't do this.

Thulatu: It's a god-send! I'm not saying it won't be hard. You'll have to face your feelings about me, deal with them, but think of what we can achieve together! In the end you'll be -.

Mia: Please! Leave me alone. You'll ruin everything I have. Everything I've built up -.

Thulatu: If they can't accept you as you are, then you're better off -.

Mia: You're doing this for spite.

Thulatu: Oh, is that it? It seems you haven't heard a word -.

Mia: It's cruel. Cruel.

Thulatu: Is it any more cruel than what happened to me? May I ask? I don't want to hurt you, but -.

Mia: You'll do more than that.

Thulatu: All your life you've been living a lie. So've I. So's Paul. It's time we stopped creeping around like guilty children. Otherwise, we have no future, this country has no future. What did Vusi die for? Fighting for the right to be human. He never denied who he was. He was never afraid to face it. You're an ... an ... imposter in this family. If you can't face who you are, tell them who you are, then what hope have we of ever wiping out racism?

Mia: You'll kill me.

Thulatu: Talk to Babo. You'll see I'm right.

Mia: Babo.

Thulatu: She's very fond of you.

Mia: Fond of you?

Thulatu: I must go. You'll tell them, then?

Mia: You're killing me.

Thulatu: I'm sorry you feel like that. I don't want to ... hurt you. But you'll thank me in the end.

Mia: In the end.

Thulatu: Good girl. Look, I'll be here, if you like. Babo, even.

Mia: *(Rises)* Stay away! You ... SCUM!

Thulatu: He died ten hours after the police slung him on the side of the road!

Mia: I won't listen!

Thulatu: Your black brother.

Mia: You're nothing to me, nothing! D'you hear?

Thulatu: Standing on a block of cement for six days, six nights.

Mia: *(Hands over ears)* Stop it!

Thulatu: *(While he speaks, **Mia** whimpers)*Whenever he fell, they whipped him. When his feet become too swollen, they tied him to the wall -.

Mia: Please, please -.

Thulatu: They worked in shifts. Seven, eight hours each. Round the clock. *(He makes circular gesture with his hand, continuing it through the following exchanges with **Mia**, until he's finished describing Vusi's torture)* Like this. Just like this.

Mia: Just like this.

Thulatu: Lashed with a sjambok till his skin opened.

Mia: ... till his skin -.

Thulatu: Wires attached to his fingertips, tongue, balls, toes -.

Mia: *(Moans)* No more -.

Thulatu: Sprayed in the face with teargas. His face a mass of open sores -.

Mia: No!

Thulatu: Thulatu's son. Born on a Monday, oppressed on a Tuesday, detained on a Wednesday, tortured on a Thursday, tortured on a Friday, tortured on a Saturday, died on a -.

Mia: *(Screams)* Stop it!

Long pause

Thulatu: I'll call next week.

Mia: You won't. I won't be here.

Thulatu: *(Moves towards her with outstretched hands)* Try to -.

Mia: Don't touch me! Just, go! Go!

Thulatu: *(Hesitates, moves towards door, stops, turns)* Until next week, then.

Mia: *(Moves to stare out window as **Thulatu** exits. She begins pacing as soon as she hears the front door slam. Stops. Stares about wildly. Begins to tidy fastidiously. Plumps cushions, stops abruptly, stares at seat of couch where Thulatu sat. Suddenly climbs onto couch. Speaking, she begins wiping her shoes as though she stood on a door mat)* The mark of his buttocks, his filthy buttocks! *(Jumps down, stares at couch. Hauls cushion, flings it across room, moves towards door, wiping her hands down her body as she speaks)* Wash, wash, scrub, scrub it off! *(Exits)*

Scene Six

Bedroom

*Double bed centre with bedside tables. Wardrobes stage left, with dressing table, mirror built in, two doors stage right, one leading to landing, the other to bathroom. At foot of bed, sarcophagus-like trunk stretching the width of the bed. The room is impeccably tidy. **Mia** in bed, propped against pillows, hands playing nervously with sheet. Enter* ***Babo***

Mia: *(Jerking upwards)* Well? What'd he say?

Babo: *(Sits on bed, takes Mia's hands)* I talked to him for hours. Hours! *(Pause)*

Mia: I'm finished.

Babo: He wouldn't budge. No matter what I said -.

Mia: Deep down, I knew.

Babo: I tried, I really tried.

Mia: He wants to destroy me for spite.

Babo: No Mia! Thulatu's not like that. If I thought that I'd -. No. Vusi's death has him knocked ... sideways. You don't know what Vusi meant to him.

Mia: Does he care what Piet means to me?

Babo: He loves you. He should stick by you.

Mia: What Piet should do, and what he's capable of doing are poles apart. You of all peole know him.

Babo: It might be the making of him.

Mia: It'll break me. *(Pause)* Oh, where will it end? *(Pause)* I know where. I can feel it coming -. *(Pause)* When is he going to - ?

Babo: I don't know. The protest's next Monday. Sometime after that, I suppose.

Mia: Couldn't we stop him?

Babo: How? All he's got to do is phone Piet. Or Claus.

Mia: Claus. I'm so afraid, Babo.

Babo: Look, I'll be here, I promise. I'll stay with you -.

Mia: Not knowing which day he might come. Waiting, waiting, oh, I'll go mad! I really thought there might be a chance. He said he was fond of you.

Enter **Paul**

Paul: W-what happened?

Babo: No dice.

Mia: You must talk to him. You know him a lot longer than Babo. A lot better. He'd listen to you, I know he would.

Paul: If he w-wouldn't do it for the woman he's -.

Babo *looks at him, shocked.*

Mia: Tell him it's really made me ill. Yes. That's it, just to give me breathing space. Then I can think what to do ... The woman he's -.

She stares at **Babo**. *Pause.*

Babo: Mia, no! *(To* **Paul***)* You malicious - !

Paul: *(To **Babo**)* You've never exactly tried to hide your taste in that ... kind of man.

Mia: You mean you ... and ... he?

Babo: Of course not! What do you think I am?

Mia: How could you! He's -.

Babo: *(Quietly)* Your father. *(Pause)* You really think I'm capable of - ?

Mia: It's disgusting! How can you, with someone like ... that?

Babo: *(To **Mia**)* I thought we were friends. *(To **Paul**)* What sort of fucking mind've you - ?

Paul: There's n-no need for that kind of -.

Babo: You bastard! This is your fault.

Mia: Go, go away, Babo.

Babo: Jesus, I don't believe this! So much for trust!

Mia: Just leave me alone. *(Pause)*

Babo: I'll call you later. We'll talk.

Mia: I'll be asleep.

Babo: In the morning, then. *(Pause)* I'll call in the morning.

Mia: I'd rather you didn't.

Babo: Look, I'm -.

Mia: Just leave it for a while, will you? I need to think.

Babo: I'll call anyway, to see how you are? You'll call me if you need to talk? *(Pause)* Promise me? *(**Mia** nods)* I'll come anytime you want. We'll sort things out, don't worry. *(Kisses **Mia**. **Mia** is unresponsive. Moves to door, stops)* Don't worry. *(Exits)*

Mia: Yes. I'll sort it out. My way. I should've seen that from the start. *(Pause)* At least I'll have control over how and when. That is something, isn't it?

Paul: I'll h-help you, I'll be here for you no matter what happens. God knows, I've done little enough -.

Mia: That's right. Both of you, patting me on the back, telling me not to worry. Avoiding the issue like the plague. Well, it is a plague, I'll grant you. Neither of you've faced what I'm staring at. What'll happen when I tell Piet! Answer me that! I'm telling you, I'll lose it all!

Paul: What can I say?

Mia: Nothing! It's what you've been saying all your life. Listen, it's a kind of relief knowing you're not my father. All those tepid years ... I used to think there was something wrong with me. Well, there was. I wasn't your child. Isn't that it?

Paul: I, I couldn't help the way I was with you. It wasn't deliberate, you m-musn't think that. *(Pause)* I grieved so much for her, I wanted to die. Only for the work, I'd've ... *(Pause)*. You were such a quiet little thing, I was blind to you. Always in the kitchen with Rachel. You seemed happy.

Mia: How would you know what I was? You were never there. How could you let him come like that, no warning, nothing *(Points at window)* You just stood there ... apart.

Paul: I couldn't stop him.

Mia: You never had a single photograph of her in the house.

Paul: I couldn't bear -.

Mia: You never mentioned her name.

Paul: It was difficult -.

Mia: For years you let me think she'd just gone off and left us. I was thirteen when you finally told me she was dead.

Paul: I loved her so -.

Mia: Did you really? Eh? Not even a twinge of resentment, of hatred, when she didn't choose you?

Paul: My God ! That's a cruel thing to say. But y-you're distraught -.

Mia: *(Pause. Harsh laugh)* Sweet lord, can y'believe it? Id've been better off growing up with ... with him!

Paul: You can't mean that! He's -.

Mia: Black!

Paul: An agitator. You'd've e-ended up like Vusi.

Mia: I may yet.

Paul: Babo too, if she doesn't watch out. Why she can't stick to her own kind -.

Mia: Why didn't you let him see me? He wanted to.

Paul: D-d'you think he'd have stopped at that? I promised your mother - *(Pause)*

Mia: Don't y'think it's cold? Is that window closed? Check it, will you?

Paul: My dear, it's sweltering. You're just feeling -.

Mia: How'd you know what I'm feeling! I'm losing myself. D'you hear? Where's this clinic for blacks? At least now I know the reason for your penny-pinching. That's something, I suppose. So where is it? I have to be treated. I'm suffering from ... from fugue.

Paul: Did you t- take those pills? Did you get any sleep?

Mia: When word gets out, I'll disappear! I won't exist. Already it's begun ... how d'you expect me to sleep? Isn't this nightmare enough? There's no safe place to sleep. Yes, yes, there is. One safe place. I'm saving it till last. *(Harsh laugh)* Like the best sweet.

Paul: What can I do? I can't reach you. My God, I've been so w-wrong. *(Pause)* If I'd told you when you were little, when colour meant nothing -

Mia: I need ... I'm fading.

Paul: You just get a ... g-grip on it. I'll fix it. He won't tell Piet or Claus, I swear to you. For all intents and purposes, you're white. No one need ever know -.

Mia: I, I know! You can't change that. My whole life's been a lie. A filthy, black lie. Y'want to go on with that? Haven't you had enough? Haven't I? Of course it'll come out. If not now, with him, then someday, sometime. Y'think I'd ever be able to relax spending my life looking over my shoulder?

Paul: I thought you -.

Mia: What if I ever had to have a skin test? All those allergies I get in the winter?

Paul: The likelihood of that -.

Mia: Look at this! *(Picks up newspaper, hands it to him)* Read it! *(**Paul** looks at paper)* Out loud.

Paul: There was widespread c-controversy over racial classification when a ten-day old baby was found abandoned near Port Elizabeth. *(Pause)* In order to classify the infant, named Victoria by the hospital staff caring for her, t-tests were carried out on her skin in a Port Elizabeth Police Laboratory. *(Pause)*

Mia: *(Grabs paper, reads)*As a result, the infant was classified coloured.

Paul: I know h-how you must feel, but -.

Mia: That's nothing. That's all nothing. That's a load of ... of crud! D'you know what it is? *(Pause)* I have to face it. *(Pause)* That's it. I can't deal with any of it till I do. *(Pause)* D'you know the awful thing? *(Pause)* Finding out they're not animals. That's the worst lie I've been living. That's ... indefensible! *(Pause. Laughs)* Shall I tell you a dirty secret? I've always been black. *(Laughs)* Oh, it's true. That's true. *(Pause)* You're only black if you have nothing. Starvation, that's the stipulation. Oh, I've ... hungered! Who should know that better than you! A medusoid man o' war, all sting and no blood. What is it that spills in your veins, what kind of arctic sludge? *(Pause)* Why d'you think I jumped at the first man who - ? Marriage delivered me to a warm bed, a candle-!it table, my very own dumb waiter. *(Pause)* Except the lobster bisque was always bitter - too well seasoned by the cook. The cook, y'see, is the waiter's *(Slight pause. Intense, fearful)* Papa. *(Pause)* D'you suppose they feel it when they're boiled alive? D'you suppose the blacks feel it when they're shot alive? Why d'you suppose the cook hates them so much? The dread of too many mouths, less broth? I've been on a low moral diet for too long. I'm overweight. Look at me!

Paul: My dear, I -.

Mia: D'you suppose I can shed it? *(Pause)* As sure as there's a hell for blacks, the cook will sniff it out. *(Sniffs)* It's not an appetizing smell.

Piet enters.

Piet: How's the patient today?

Paul: Oh, eh, fine, fine. She'll s-soon be on her feet again. I must be on my way. *(He kisses **Mia** swiftly)* See you tomorrow, my dear. Piet. *(He exits)*

Piet: What's his hurry? *(Pause)* How d'you feel? *(He leans to kiss her. She turns sharply away)* Am I so distasteful?

Mia: I am.

Piet: What is it with you lately?

Mia: I thought you were at the farm.

Piet: I came home to have lunch with you. I thought you'd like -.

Mia: I'm trying to diet. I'm not hungry.

Piet: Good. Neither am I. *(He tries to caress her)* It's been ages ...

She stiffens. Pushes him away.

Piet: What the hell's -. If you'd agree to see a doctor -.

Mia: Paul's a doctor.

Piet: I didn't mean him. He's your father.

Mia: My ... father's a lawyer.

Piet: *(Takes her hand)* Mia, you need help. Please. I can't bear to see you -. *(She pulls her hands away from him)* Christ! *(Pause)* You look at me. There's hatred in your eyes. What've I done?

Mia: Not hatred. Not for you.

Piet: Tell me, what'm I supposed to have done? I'm in the dark.

Mia laughs harshly.

Piet: It can't go on.

Mia: I'm in the dark.

Piet: You heard me. Either you get up out of that bed, behave like a normal wife or ... you see a doctor. Talk to somebody. I can't take much more -. Whatever it is you're blaming me for, I'm sick of it.

Mia: Please let Jan come to see me. I need -.

Piet: Are you crazy? These last few days, you wouldn't even look at him.

Mia: I, I wasn't myself. *(Laughs)* I'm still not.

Piet: He'd be better off on the farm with Papa at the moment.

Mia: Don't give him to Claus! Please! He's too fond of his cooking already.

Piet: You're paranoid.

Mia: I'm afraid of him.

Piet: Papa?

Mia: A man who always knows what he wants.

Piet: It's what I admire most about him.

Mia: He'll destroy me.

Piet: You're living on another planet.

Mia: Yes. No. A black hole.

He exits.

Mia: *(Screams)* Piet!

He returns. Stands silent.

Mia: Please. Stay with me.

Piet: So y'can hurl more insults at my father.

Mia: I, I need you to stay.

Piet: I've a meeting at two in the city. Papa's picking me up.

Mia: Don't go. Please. Just this once, stay. Talk to me.

Piet: You've built a wall between us. You're going to have to knock it down yourself.

Mia: The wall is in me.

Piet: More riddles? What d'you take me for? A bloody fool? *(Car horn sounds)* For Christ's sake, pull yourself together!

He exits. **Mia** *leaves bed. Pulls a heavy book from underneath it. Returns to bed, opens it, searches the table of contents.*

Mia: Definitions of Race, 240 *(Turns pages, searching, reads aloud)* 'A white person is defined as any person who in appearance obviously is, or who generally is accepted as a white person, but does not include any person who, although in appearance obviously a white person, is generally accepted as a coloured person.'

She stares at the page, slams the book closed, flings it across the room. She gets out of bed, rummages in a drawer, takes a pair of sunglasses, puts them on, returns to bed, stares about the room, stares at the skin on her arms, shoulders, pushes the bedclothes away, stares at her legs, jumps from bed. Rubs white cold cream on the lens of her glasses, returns to bed, puts the glasses on, re-examines her skin, lies back, pulling the covers over her head.

Scene Seven

Patio of farm outside Pretoria

Table with sun canopy, chairs. Chess set. Drinks on table. French windows leading off at back of stage. **James** *and* **Sipho** *kneeling, dressed in green sacks, with string tied around middle of Sipho's, each with bucket and rag placed before them. Sound of crickets.* **Sipho** *has cuts on his arms, face.*

James: Keeping us waiting is all part of it. Patience!

Sipho: I thought 'Scutta' was only played in the cells.

James: The manager here was once a policeman. He's still fond of the game. But! He'll only beat us if we lose.

Sipho: I'll never get it done in time. *(Places hands over ears)* Those fucking crickets!

James: The thought of that sjambok lashing your back is enough to move mountains. The secret is to push the rag back to the bucket, damming the water. I've seen men squeezing it out of sheer nerves before it's halfway back.

Sipho: I'm still sore from that donkie piel.

James: The newcomer's welcome. So now you know who'sbaas, eh?

Sipho: Those fucking crickets!

James: Switch them off.

Sipho: Ha. Ha.

James closes his eyes in concentration. Places his hands over his ears, slowly removes his hands, opens his eyes.

James: There, you see? What'd I tell you? *(The crickets are still chirping. Sipho stares at him)*

Sipho: Yeah.

James: Aw, you didn't try hard enough, brother.

Sipho: Yeah and you tried too hard.

James: You got to believe in the power.

Sipho: There's only one power I believe in right now. *(His actions indicate the beating he's had)*

James: The power of the mind. Mind over matter. That's what it is.

Sipho: Is that what it is?

James: You switch them off same way you shut the Boers out. That's what it is. How you live through it. Come on, come on, try it. Concentrate. *(Places Sipho's hands over his ears)*

Sipho: You been here how long?

James: Long enough to switch those fucking crickets off! You interested?

Sipho: Okay, okay.

James: Close your eyes. Concentrate. Squeeze those bastards out of your ears. That's it. That's it. *(As he removes Sipho's hands, the chirping ceases.* **Sipho** *stares about in amazement)*

Sipho: Hey, brother! *(Slaps* **James** *on back, almost knocks him over)* I'll get some sleep tonight.

James: Easy, easy. The bones are brittle.

Sipho: I'll never get it done in three minutes.

James: That's what the last man said. He was nearly shitting himself.

Sipho: What happened?

James: He shit himself. *(Laughs. Pause)*

Sipho: What did they get you for?

James: Out without my Pass book.

Sipho: But the Pass Laws've been abolished, don't you know that?

James: Then why'm I here? Where'd you hear that?

Sipho: In all the newspapers.

James: Ah, you don't want to believe everything you read in the papers. *(They laugh)*

Sipho: Yeah, now blacks can eat in five-star restaurants.

James: Shit, just when I lost my credit cards. Aw, I'll eat in the cheaper places.

Sipho: And end up back in jail? The cheaper places are still out of bounds. Only the best for us, the very best. You need the works for those places ... black tuxedo, bow tie.

James: That all? *(He pulls at string around Sipho's waist, hauls off his own sackcloth. He's wearing black shorts)*

Sipho: Stop, stop it! If he comes -.

James: *(Ties string in bow about his neck, stands, struts about)* Y'see? *(Indicates himself)*

Sipho: Cut it out!

James: Y'like my black tuxedo? *(Poses)* Hand sewn in heaven by the great tailor himself. *(Turns his buttocks to **Sipho**)* Seat's a little shiny but shit, I've been wearing it since I first looked a wholesome piece of thigh in the eye.

Sipho: He's coming!

*James hurriedly dons sack, kneels, returns string to **Sipho**. Pause. James cranes to see.*

James: My heart! He's not.

Sipho: I thought he was. *(Pause)*

James: What about you?

Sipho: My wife works for a Madam in Pretoria. Sometimes I sneak in to see her. The bastards caught me without a 'midnight special'.

James: Before, or after?

Sipho: After. *(They laugh)*

James: Jesus, brother, some expensive screw. How long've you got?

Sipho: They selected me for parole yesterday. Eight months to do.

James: *(Nods)* Harvest time. Be glad it's wheat. I once got paroled to a wine farm outside Cape Town. They operated the 'tot'. Cheap wine twice a day instead of a fair share of food.

Sipho: You took it?

James: It got me through the days, the smell of the compound, the sour mealie. We were locked in at night, same as here ... forty men and a bucket. This isn't so bad. There's room to lie without touching off the next man.

Sipho: Unless you stretch. *(Loudly)* It stinks.

*Samuel enters, wearing white jacket and shirt, necktie, black trousers. Goes to chess set in play on table, makes move, walks in front of two parolees, surreptitiously slips **James** a gun before returning indoors. **James** tucks gun into his underpants.*

Sipho: What the - ?

James: *(Quietly)* Now you know why I'm not complaining.

Sipho: If you're caught -.

James: I'm dead. Won't be missing much, right?

Sipho: It's a life.

James: Yeah, but what kind? I've had all I can take, brother. What are we? Blacks? Animals? Insects? Filth? What?

Sipho: If you had a life you wouldn't know what to do with it.

James: Give me a life, then I'll worry about what I'm living for. That's luxury, hey?

Sipho: I have a wife. Kids.

James: That's your excuse.

Sipho: You calling me a coward?

James: I'm saying I've had enough.

Sipho: You married?

James: I have a woman.

Sipho: She wouldn't want you to get yourself killed.

James: For all I know, she could be dead. I was working in the mines at Kimberley. When I came home for Christmas, the township was flattened. 'This area has been re-zoned for whites only'. Took me weeks to find out she'd been sent to the Transkei. Then they caught me without my pass. Seven months in jail before they took me to court! If you're black and you don't fight, you'll rot.

Sipho: You'll rot if you do.

James: At least the smell of myself'll be more pleasant.

Sipho: I wish you luck, brother, but I don't want any trouble.

James: If you're breathing, you're in trouble.

Sipho: I'm afraid of the police. I'm afraid of the army. I'm afraid of whites.

James: Blacks are afraid to piss in this country.

Sipho: All I want is peace, time to watch my children grow up.

James: To this?

Sipho: I don't want to die.

James: We all have the skin disease. You either lie down and you die -.

Sipho: You believe in God ?

James: Or you fight and you die -.

Sipho: Do you?

James: Believe? I've seen Him, brother! - a big black man, his fist raised, a spear in his hand, his eyes burning with the fire of the townships -.

Sipho: Aw, you won't be serious.

James: You hear Him? Listen! *(He raises one hand in a clenched fist over his head, lays other hand across his heart)*
God our father, I kneel to say,
Thank you for this gun today,
Thank you for the bullets too,
I'll use it wisely, promise you.

Sipho: Stop it!

James: *(Intensely)* God our Father, which art in South Africa, justice be thy name, thy liberation come, thy salvation be done not as it is in Namibia, but as it is in Lusaka, give us this day our daily weapons, our military training and forgive us our past timidity as we strive against our white oppressors and lead us not to Apartheid but deliver us from its evil, for thine is the non-racial kingdom, the power and the victory forever and -.

Sipho: Those fucking crickets are back!

James: Head down! Deep breaths, deep.

Sipho: You're not going to -.

James: Not now.

Enter ***Vos****, carrying a quirt. He whips it through the air, the plaited braid making a whirring sound.*

Vos: You stinking munts had a good rest? Well, you got two minutes. *(He cracks quirt.* ***Sipho*** *and* ***James*** *immediately spill water over tiles, begin a frantic race to mop up.* ***Vos*** *looks at his watch while cracking the quirt continuously)* Who's baas, eh? Swartgatte!

Enter ***Piet***

Piet: *(To* ***Vos****)* Enough! I've told you before I want none of that here.

Vos: I take orders from your father.

Piet: My father isn't on this patio.

Vos: He leaves the men in my hands.

Piet: Does he know you beat them up?

Vos: He's never had any complaints about my efficiency.

Piet: Look at this man! *(Goes to* ***Sipho****, tears the back of his sackcloth, winces)* You're an animal! Take him to the kitchen. Those cuts need -.

Enter ***Claus*** *carrying file of papers.*

Claus: Get these kaffirs out of my sight! I've told you, Vos, early morning when I'm not using it.

Vos: Sorry, sir. *(Kicks at* ***James*** *and* ***Sipho****)* Get a move on, you bloody commies. *(The men jump up, move off in the direction of the farm)*

Piet: Wait. *(To* ***Claus****)* Those cuts need attention.

Claus: Are you mad, maan? Next thing they'll be looking for hot dinners. *(To* ***Vos****)* Get them out of here!

Vos: Sir. *(He exits, ushering the men before him.)*

Piet: Why d'you let him?

Claus *moves to table, stares at chess game as he speaks.*

Claus: Hah! That Samuel's a clever get. Thinks he's foxed me. He'll have a hairy wait.

Piet: It's not the first time, Papa.

Claus: Right, you smart little kaffir! *(He makes a move)* Let's see you squirm -.

Piet: It's happened too often since you hired that brute. Unproductive, even. How can they be expected to work after that?

Claus: You know, I could almost admire how he plays. Best thing I ever did was teach him after your mother died. *(Pause)* How many times've I told you? Forget them. They've skins thick as rhinoceros hide. They're so used to it, they've become immune.

Piet: Or we have?

Claus: What?

Piet: Nothing, nothing, Papa.

Claus: Get your priorities right, man. Those are animals out there, lazy good-for-nothing criminals who'd stab you in the back soon as look at you. The only law they understand is the whip. The day you stop sniffing their fear, is the day we're finished. What's the matter with you anyway? You're like a man's got a bee buzzing in his pants.

Piet: It's Mia.

Claus: *(Pours drinks. They sit)* She's still the same?

Piet: I found her wandering in the garden last night. Naked. Washing herself in the dew. Good for the skin, she said. It was freezing, Papa.

Claus: You've got to deal with it before it gets any worse.

Piet: When she finally began getting up again, I thought she was better. Then, when I found her giving all the silver to Elijah -. What the hell'm I going to do?

Claus: I told you, that new sanitorium out near Garsfontein is like a first-class hotel.

Piet: ... She'll never forgive me.

Claus: Ja, I'll never forgive you if you don't. Even if you can cope, what about Jan? Y'think I want the only grandson I've got exposed to that kind of thing? Why not let him come here until you decide what to do?

Piet: I sent him to the Vorster's yesterday. He'll stay till -.

Claus: I see far too little of him. This house should be full of grandchildren. If Yolande had lived -.

Piet: Helmut is his best friend. You know what boys are like.

Claus: You mean Mia wanted him to go there. That woman's always twisted you round her -. What in hell's wrong with her? How long's it been? Something must've brought it on.

Piet: Three, four, weeks. Maybe more.

Claus: Anything unusual happen at the time?

Piet: I'm sick thinking back.

Claus: Something sparked it off. Think, man. Did you quarrel?

Piet: She was like that. I came home one day. She was different.

Claus: When?

Piet: Feverish. That's it! The day we were last together for dinner!

Claus: Babo?

Piet: The row. You think - ?

Claus: I think nothing. Yet.

Piet: We went to the farm.

Claus: She was with Babo when you returned?

Piet: *(Shakes head)* On her own. Talking gibberish.

Claus: They used to be thick as thieves before Babo started her politicking. Could be she's been getting at Mia.

Piet: I don't know what she thinks I'm made of. The place is falling apart. Elijah keeps pestering me. He doesn't seem to have a clue. She won't even bother to get dressed most days now. Can you imagine! Mia, of all people, she was always so capable! I never thought -.

Claus: She needs psychiatric help. Zo. Having your wife in a sanitorium, it's no dishonour on a white family. The Americans have made it fashionable, acceptable, ja?

Piet: I'll be lost without her. I hate the house when it's empty.

Claus: Zo. You and Jan can come here.

Piet: I always leave the radio on. It kills the silence.

Claus: Has Babo been since?

Piet: No, Mia won't talk to her.

Claus: Come. *(Picks up file)* Time to meet the broeders. *(They rise)* Why not invite Babo over? Tell her you're worried. Get the two of them in the same room. See what happens.

Piet: If there's a ... scene I don't think I could face it on my own. Would you - ?

Claus: *(As they move to exit)* Thursday night?

Piet: Thanks, Papa. Maybe it'll sort itself out.

Claus: Don't bet on it. Say nothing to Babo about my coming. Otherwise, she won't show. Ja, she's had a hand in this, I can smell it.

They exit.

Scene Eight

Bedroom

Room in total disarray: Bed unmade, clothing, books heaped about, etc. **Piet** *is pacing,* **Mia** *on the bed, head in hands. He stops, turns, looks at her.*

Piet: Say something. *(Pause)* Will you say something?

Mia: Claus.

Piet: I don't need Papa to tell me what to do.

Mia: Claus.

Piet: You're crazy. He was right.

Mia: You've always needed him.

Piet: Look at this place -.

Mia: Look at me!

Piet: I can't stand it. *(Goes to tidy up)* I've never lived in such a -.

Mia: Look at me.

Piet: You won't even let Elijah in to clean -.

Mia: Look at me!

Piet: I'm sick looking at you!

Mia: So you're going to have me locked away. Disposed of. Like I was -.

Piet: Stop saying that.

Mia: A black.

Piet: For the last time - you need help.

Mia: Picked up off the street. 'Idle and undesirable'. What section is that? 50, 50A, 30?

Piet: I want you to get better. I want everything to be like it was. We were happy, weren't we?

Mia: *(Picks up newspaper, searches)* Undesirable? That's easy, every black, every coloured, every Indian. Idle? Unemployed

... most of them are that. A decorative domestic engineer might escape it. *(Pause)* Here. 29. But which act? Internal Security? Blacks Act? I'm so confused. Oh, what does it matter? They've got him anyway, on one pretext or another. Fined 500 Rand, or 190 days in jail. Of course, he couldn't afford to pay. Which of us can?

Piet: Has Babo been getting at you?

Mia: Him? Or me? *(Laughs)*

Piet: While I'm out? Has she been here?

Mia: Of course, I could afford to pay it. If it were me. But then, I'm accepted.

Piet: I'll ask Elijah.

Mia: It won't last, though. Nothing ever does. *(Pause)* I'm not mad.

Piet: I'm not saying you're -. Look, it's no big deal. It's even considered fashionable nowadays to be seeing a psychiatrist. What about Heidi Moulin, she's been going to one for years.

Mia: *(Strangled laugh. Pause. Sings in delicate, wistful tone)* Poor Heidi Moulin , wipe your mouth it's a-droolin', 'n we know which blood is rulin' but it's too late ... to tell your mother ... to stop foolin' around. *(Pause. To **Piet**)* Not yet. *(Pause)* You can't lock me away.

Piet: Christ, this is a vicious circle.

Mia: *(Laughs)* They'll be angry.

Piet: Who?

Mia: She is incurable, they'll say. Take your wife away from here, Meneer Schuurman, or we'll remove her by force. She is here illegally. Take her back to her homeland.

Piet: Of course they can cure you. Lots of people have breakdowns.

Mia: This is a breakapart. Apartheid. There is no cure.

Piet: Nothing's that black and white.

Mia laughs hysterically. **Piet** *goes to her, raises his hand, then drops it. He shakes her.* **Mia** *sobers.*

Mia: Clever boy.

Piet: Don't talk down to me! *(Pause)* I'm my own man.

Mia: You don't fart without his permission! *(Pause)* Oh, has my vulgarity shocked you? Forgive me!

Piet: What's got into you? I married you.

Mia: When he was in Lesotho.

Piet: For years afterwards - working with him on the farm nothing but days of silence, yes, he made me pay! I never complained to you. Never regretted it.

Mia: You never let me forget the sacrifice you made. I've never stopped paying for it.

Piet: What the hell's that supposed to mean?

Mia: Every time he came here, I could have been part of the furniture. And you, falling over backwards, grovelling. 'Goodbye, Papa, thanks for coming, Papa'. We've always stood in his shadow. *(Pause)* Darkening.

Piet: It was never like that.

Mia: I've never been separate, ever. You've been my sustenance. Filtered through your father. Sometimes I've had a chilling dread that if Claus weren't around to look at you with respect in his eyes, you wouldn't exist. You feed on him. Then I wouldn't exist either. I'd fade away, blend into the wallpaper like your mother, smiling apologetically, too timid to open her mouth.

Piet: Mama was quiet. That was her nature.

Mia: I even dressed to please him. 'It's lovely on you, you know I like it. But you know how Papa is, he's so conservative. Perhaps something a little less revealing?' And like a fool, I'd change. Well, I can't change my skin. I can't!

Piet: That's all in the past. You're being neurotic. He accepts you now.

Mia: He won't accept me.

Piet: I have to be with him, work with him.

Mia: Not when he knows.

Piet: The farm is my life. One day it will be Jan's. *(Pause)* Is it a crime to be fond of your father?

Mia: I was afraid he would win. That he'd take you away from me. Now he'll take me away from you.

Piet: No, he won't. I promise. *(Kneels before her, takes her hands in his)* It's all in your mind.

Mia: Is it? Is it? Show me, then. *(Kisses him)* Make love to me. Make love to me now.

Piet: *(Pushes her away)* I can't. I can't just switch on like that. *(Pause. He moves away)*

Mia: Has your Papa been telling you sex with me is a fruitless activity, since I can't supply him with a grandson?

Piet: You bitch!

Mia: You can't switch on? You've never yet managed to switch yourself off.

Piet: Shut up!

Mia: You know, when I think of it, it's been the only ... constant. An electric current, you might say. But does it count as ... warmth? Every night for ten years, not including lunchtimes? Oh wait, apart from these last weeks and those shopping trips to Jo'burg with Babo. But that was years ago, and even then you made up for it when I came back. Did I ever tell you I had a headache? I was too tired?

Piet: You wanted it as much as I.

Mia: I didn't want it half as much as you.

Piet: You're lying.

Mia: I accepted it because I was afraid not to. I thought at least if I kept you satisfied in bed, Claus couldn't get to you, I'd be able to hold you. Even when I didn't want it, I accepted it gratefully, a sign that you loved me.

Piet: *(Throttles her)* You bloody hypocrite! The whole thing was a lie, a fucking lie.

Mia: He was there, even in the bed between us. I might as well have slept with your father. It would have been a more honest prostitution.

Piet: Tart! *(Pause)* Why, why didn't you tell me this before?

Mia: There's more. Oh, there's more.

Piet: I bought you clothes, jewels, this house -. I thought you were happy. You were happy. You wanted those things.

Mia: I'd never had them before. I thought they'd - warm me.

Piet: Did I ever complain when you ran up bills? You never stopped spending money.

Mia: My compensation. I became a well-dressed mannequin, a ventriloquist's dummy, to tempt you, to woo your father. *(Leaves bed, begins changing into black slip)* I lost my substance. *(Pause)* It disappeared into my string of pearls, my mink stole, my shimmering gowns -.

Piet: The way you've been dressing lately, I'd say you've lost your self-respect.

Mia: Wait till you see my new image! It goes with my new substance. The real me! *(She rubs black eye shadow on her cheeks, turns to him)* Well, d'you still find me attractive without the clothes, the jewels?

Piet: You're pathetic.

Mia: You can always sell them when I'm gone. Or better still, use them for the next wife. But make sure it's another Yolande you marry, from a nice Afrikaner family. Otherwise your Papa won't approve.

Piet: *(Reaches out, grabs her, begins to shake her)* That's enough, enough. D'you hear?

Mia: *(Begins to hit him, using both fists)* Yes, Papa, no, Papa, three bags full, Papa. *(**Piet** pushes her onto bed, falling with her)* Notice it's Baa Baa Black Sheep.

He kisses her

Mia: You want me?

Piet: Yes.

Mia: Like this? I smell. I'm ... *(Laughs)* ... undesirable.

Piet: I like the smell of you.

Mia: There's a dark side to my nature ... I'm tainted.

Piet: Don't talk.

Mia: Tell me! Have you ever had a black woman?

Piet *stops. Sits up. Head in hands. Pause.*

Mia: Have you ever had a black woman?

Piet: No.

Mia: You're lying.

Piet: All right, I'm lying. Are you satisfied?

Mia: I hear if you close your eyes, it doesn't feel any different. You, you always make love with your eyes open. Do you think you can close them from now on? *(Pause. Takes his hand, puts it to her cheek)* This is my new substance. *(Slides his hand down over the black slip along her body)* And this.

Piet: *(Jumps up, moves away, turns)* What're you saying? *(Pause).* Spit it out, for Christ sake! *(Pause)*

Mia: *(Kneels on bed)* Paul is not my father. *(Pause)* Paul is not my father. *(Pause)* Paul is not my - father. The nail is home.

Piet: Mia, for Christ sake ... you need help. Of course he's -.

Mia: Phone him. He'll tell you. *(Pause)* Go on. *(Pause)*

Piet: What're you saying? Just what the hell are you saying?

Mia: I'm saying there's an accidental black spot in my lineage, a dark birthmark on my nether horizon. I'm saying my father is a Capey. Cape coloured. His skin's the colour of peanut-butter. I'm saying my grandfather was black. Black as the ace of spades. *(Laughs)* Just think, I had my very own life-sized gollywog and never knew it. Imagine what a difference that could have made to my ... wonderful childhood! I always loved music. D'you think I could have been a black and white minstrel in my youth? *(Pause)* That's what I'm saying. Don't you hear what I'm saying? I hear the words. They're outside my head, clear as a bell, skewering the sky on a quiet morning. Oh, isn't innocence bliss! When I look back now I can see that compared to this, I was positively rapturous! *(Long pause)* I have black blood in me. Black as coal. Black as pitch. Black as hell. **(Piet** *sits diminished, in a chair.* **Mia** *picks up hand-mirror)* Hard to believe ... apart from the eyes and the hair. *(Turns to* **Piet)** That woolly hair! D'you suppose they're related to sheep? *(Turns back to mirror)* Though she does tan easily - the merest whisper of the sun, you know? You've always said how lucky I am, in this climate! *(She laughs. Pause)* That is the secret of my forked tongue, the hiss and scrape of his sickle writhing in the jungle of my mother's pouch. *(Pause)* I had no words, either. I have no pity for you. This should have been no tragedy. A mere hiccup. Take a deep breath and count -. Except I haven't learned to breathe deeply. I'll hiccup to death. What? So quiet? No questions? You've been fucking a black bitch for ten years and you've nothing to say? *(Pause)* All that fucking, was it worth the price?

Piet: Stop it.

Mia: This is my new language: it goes with my new substance.

Piet: When - ?

Mia: You know when. Paul brought him that day. And Babo.

Piet: Who is he?

Mia: One of twenty-eight million ... Blacks, Indians, Coloureds ... they all look alike, don't you know that?

Piet: Who is he?

Mia: Who am I?

Piet: My God , I can't believe it!

Mia: I can't not believe!

Piet: Who knows?

Mia: I do.

Piet: Who knows?

Mia: You do.

Piet: Nobody else?

Mia: Not yet.

Piet: I don't know what to say, what to do. *(Pause)* I can't tell Papa.

Mia: You will.

Piet: I can't. He'd -.

Mia: You'll tell him. You won't be able to stop yourself.

Piet: No, no. I have to think. *(Gets up, paces)* I can't -.

Mia: You'll tell him because you tell him everything. Because you're afraid.

Piet: Hoe jou bej!

Mia: Afraid he'll find out one day. Know you've lied to him, cheated -.

Piet: I can't take any more. *(Moves towards door)*

Mia: Where're you going?

Piet: Out! Anywhere! Away from you. You're driving me crazy. *(Slams door)*

Mia: *(Screams)* Back to Papa! Go! Go on! *(Pause)* It's done. *(She drags coverlet about her shoulders. Pause)* Go quickly, Piet. And tell him. Quickly! I'm tired. So tired. *(Pause)* The nail is home.

ACT TWO

Scene One

Drawing room

Piet and Claus are present. Piet pours drinks.

Claus: What time'll Babo be here?

Piet: Papa, I've got to talk to you.

Claus: You should get her down here now.

Piet: Who? I don't think she'll come down.

Claus: Then what the hell am I doing here?

Piet: Those early days - we were so happy. Were we happy?

Claus: You're beginning to sound as woolly as your wife.

Piet: I could never wait to get home to her.

Claus: Did you tell her I was coming?

Piet: I didn't get much sleep last night. Papa -.

Claus: I might as well be hitting my arse off the sky. Why isn't she here?

Piet: She's - not the same.

Claus: You mean she's worse? Did you phone the sanitorium?

Piet: Worse? *(Nods)* It's worse. But she's more *(Pause)* lucid.

Claus: Go and get her.

Piet: She's -. You'd think it was my fault. Is it my fault? *(Slight pause)* She won't come down. She's been there all day.

Claus: You should never've waited till it got to this.

Piet: She's locked the door. Won't answer me.

Claus: We may have to break it down. Babo! I'll get answers if I have to -.

Piet: I have the answers.

Claus: Was ist los? Was? *(Pause)* Out with it, man.

Piet: *(Begins pacing)* You won't find this pleasant, Papa. *(He pours drinks, gulps his own)*

Claus: Don't use those words. The last time you said them your mother died.

Piet: Sorry. *(Pause)*

Claus: Go on. *(Pause)*

Piet: Mia ... *(Pause)* Mia has mixed blood. *(He laughs nervously)* Flowing in her veins. *(Pause)*

Claus: Impossible! I had her checked myself. Her mother's blood is English to the last drop. *(Pause)* There's no black blood -.

Piet: Not her mother.

Claus: She has to be pretty sick to talk like that. Sooner she's in hospital -. We don't want rumours. *(Pause)* Not her mother.

Piet: Her father.

Claus: There's no -.

Piet: Paul is not her father. *(Pause)*

Claus: He's on the birth certificate.

Piet: He's not her father! *(Pause)*

Claus: Gott in Hemel! *(Pause)* Who?

Piet: I don't know.

Claus: Who?

Piet: She wouldn't tell me. Only that he's coloured. *(Pause)*

Claus: A hotnot! You work, sweat all your life, for ... to see your son marry a -.

Piet: She said some hard things. I've never seen her like that -.

Claus: Thank God your mother's dead.

Piet: Mama wasn't a ... *(Pause)* She wasn't.

Claus: Go on. Say it. If you have the guts. *(Pause)* Tell me what I am. *(Pause)* Tell me what you are. What that ... woman of yours is. How long has she known?

Piet: That day. Before dinner.

Claus: Gott in Hemel, how stupid we've been. The little slut tricked us. No wonder she got you to marry her the minute my back was turned.

Piet: No. No. She didn't know until -.

Claus: You believe that? She's tricked you.

Piet: That day. That's why she's behaving -.

Claus: You know why you married her.

Piet: Ask Babo. She was here.

Claus: You know.

Piet: *(Rises, paces)* It's hot in here. That blasted air-conditioning -.*(Sits slumped. Pause)*

Claus: You know.

Piet: I don't know what to do.

Claus: God verdomme, did you have to marry her?

Piet: I fell in love.

Claus: Schutt! You married her because you wanted to get her in bed. You couldn't wait. What was it? The smell of the munt?

Piet: *(Rises, pours himself another drink)* You shouldn't talk to me like that, Papa. *(Pause. He laughs)* Maybe she smelled the racist in me. *(He laughs again)* She smelled the beast.

Claus: Zo. She can't stay here.

Piet: That's how she sees me.

Claus: You can't send her to the sanitorium.

Piet: She doesn't want to go.

Claus: It's out of the question now.

Piet: I can't manage her on my own.

Claus: Use your head, man. If she sees anyone here she'll spill it. It'll be all over the city in no time. Can you see the Vorsters inviting your coloured wife to dinner?

Piet: Every inch. Every inch of her is white.

Claus: It'd be better if she went away. *(Pause)* For a time. *(Pause)* The U.K. She still has relatives there.

Piet: I can't do that to her Papa.

Claus: I'll have no trouble getting her a visa. *(Pause)*

Piet:: I couldn't.

Claus: Ja, face it, man. If she stays, she'll ruin your life. Jan's. Why d'you think she's been told now? Either Paul is up to something, or the bastard who fathered her. Babo ... you think she'll keep her mouth shut, hah? There's nothing Babo'd enjoy better than watching me squirm. As for her! *(Jerks his thumb towards ceiling)* Y'think the state she's in, she'll sing dumb?

Piet: I don't know anything anymore.

Claus: Her birth certificate's falsified. Right now she's up in that bedroom illegally. In this neighbourhood illegally. She can't breathe without obtaining the right documents.

Piet: The Mixed Marriages Act was repealed -.

Claus: I'm talking about the Population Registration Act, the Group Areas Act.

Piet: Married to me, her mother being white -. She might get away with being classified white.

Claus: Until the authorities take into consideration the lies on her papers. Our only hope is that you're not legally married to her, otherwise -. If you refuse to split from her, you could end up being reclassified into her population group. Jan would have to leave that school. Go to one for coloureds. And you know what they're like. You'd be forced to live in a coloured area, you'd lose your vote, you'd be a nothing.

Piet: You could try -.

Claus: Ja, I know all the right people. But the price? Y'think anyone'll want to know us after this? The Broederbond? We'll be out on our ear as soon as they get a sniff of it. Left to blunder in the wilderness. It'd cost me everything I've built up for you, for Jan. If you can't think of yourself, think of Jan. It'd cost him his future. Educationally, socially, politically, culturally! Can you really be selfish enough -? He's the innocent in all this, the one with most to lose. His blood is pure, he's every right to his heritage. *(Pause)*

Piet: Just for a while. A few months, I'll say.

Claus: Prima. You'd better get her down here. The father must be silenced.

Piet: Give you time to get over the shock.

Claus: As for Paul, there are ways of dealing with him. Babo is another matter.

While these last words are spoken, **Mia** *enters dressed in a black slip. Her cheeks are stained black.*

Mia: And what are the ways of dealing with me?

Piet *rises.* **Claus** *does not look up.*

Piet: You're ... *(Indicates her attire)*

Mia: My shadow. The emperor's new clothes. The-what-you-can't-see-you-believe-is-me. Good evening Mia. Good evening ... Papa! You're looking well, Mia. That black is most ... becoming. Why, thank you ... Papa! Black's always been one of my favourite colours. Didn't you know that? Not yours, is it ... Papa? Still, from what I hear ... *(Pause. She looks at* **Piet***)* it's most men's -. Of course I've had too few men on which to base such a definitive statement, but drawing from the wealth of my own private experience, when it comes right down to it, silky French knickers wouldn't be quite au fait in bed, if they weren't black.

Piet: Mia, please -.

Mia: Mia, please, go crawl under a stone and don't come out. Stay there, Mia, stay there till you're -.

Piet: It's not like that -.

Mia: Tell me what!

Piet: *(Goes to her, tries to lead her to sit. She shakes him off, but does sit, opposite **Claus**)* We need to talk.

Mia: Tell me!

Piet: *(Sits)* Look, it's not a pleasant situation for any -.

Mia: *(Laughs)* Oh but it will be, won't it ... Papa?

Claus: *(Looks at her, indicates her attire)*. You've no shame.

Mia: *(Laughs)* But I thought you'd appreciate my honesty, my willingness to show my true colours. To be what I am.

Claus: Who is he? His name?

Mia: Oh, what is it? *(Picks up small, unfinished wood carving from table, tugs scouting knife from it, drops it on the table)*

Piet: It was to be a surprise. He forgot to take it to the Vorsters'.

Mia: Jan, Jan. *(Caresses the carving, lifts it to her face, slowly moves it over her cheeks)*

Claus: What's his name?

Mia: There's love in it. A child's love. Don't do it, Piet!

Claus: I'll find out.

Piet: Just for a little while. A little while. I promise. Not the sanitorium. *(Pause)* You've always said you'd like to visit those cousins -. This'd be a good time -. *(Pause)* Just for a while. Until we, until you ... get over it. The shock. Then, when ... you come -. *(Pause)* No one need ever know.

Mia: *(Bitterly)* You kept your word. After all these years. *(Pause)* I'm to go, finally. *(Laughs)* With one slight omission. My husband. *(Pause)* For good.

Piet: Just until -.

Mia: For good.

Piet: Mia. Please. Try to understand -.

Mia: For good.

Piet: No, I swear it -.

Mia: I'm afraid for Jan. You and - *(Indicates **Claus**)* What will you tell him? *(Pause)*

Piet: You're not well -.

Mia: What will you tell him?

Piet: I don't know.

Mia: Let me -.

Claus: Nein! You'll upset him.

Mia: Piet? I've washed him, fed him, read him stories. He's my son.

Claus: You have no son. *(Pause)*

Mia: I have nothing. *(Laughs)* One of the lost tribe. *(Rises, pours herself a drink .**Babo** enters, stops, stares at **Mia**)*

Babo: My God ! *(Pause. Looks at men, then back to **Mia**)*

Mia: I have no God, either, come to think of it.

Babo: Jesus! What've they done to you! *(Moves to embrace **Mia**)*

Mia: It is what they will do. *(Returns embrace)* Dear Babo. It might be infectious.

Babo: Oh, why wouldn't you see me? I've been worried sick. Paul told me a little. But not this. *(To **Piet**)* Damnit, why didn't you tell me? You just kept saying she wasn't well.

Piet: These last days ... it just spiralled suddenly. She's been locking herself in, refusing to see anybody. I don't know what I'm doing anymore.

Mia: Mia is here. She is not a non-citizen. She has not been vetoed. Yet. *(Pause)*

Babo: *(To **Piet**)* What's going on?

Mia: Reforms. *(Laughs)*

Claus: Stay out of it, Babo.

Babo: When you do!

Claus: Piet's made up his own mind.

Babo: And South Africa is a non-racial, multi-party state. Mark it.

Claus: Ja-ja!

Babo: *(To **Piet**)* What? *(Pause)*

Claus: She's going to England.

Piet: Just until Papa ... we ... sort things out.

Babo: You bastard!

Claus: *(To **Babo**)* I need his name.

Mia: I need a priest. I could call him Father, he could call me child. *(To **Babo**)* D'you think he would, a white one? *(Goes for drinks)* There's a bad taste in my mouth.

Babo: *(To **Mia**)* For God 's sake, fight them!

Mia: With what!

Babo: Tell them to go to hell. *(Points to **Claus**)* You think he'll ever let you set foot in this country again?

Piet: That's not true -.

Claus: A thorn in my flesh.

Mia: I'm gone already. I can't come back.

Babo: You'll never see Jan again.

Mia: HE can't see ME. I'm a negative. *(She laughs)*

Babo: Don't give in! Come and stay with me.

Claus: Over my body.

Mia: Not 'in', I'm giving 'up', I'm no longer acceptable -.

Babo: None of my friends are racists.

Mia: To myself.

Babo: They'll all accept you.

Mia: EXCEPT ME! *(Harsh laugh)* You can't convert a racist, don't you know that? A question of acceptability? Yes. But whose? *(Points to **Piet** and **Claus**)* Y'think I care about their attitude? Look at me! The stink in my eyes! I've been taught it ... to hate, to fear, to despise. Now it's rebounded, caught me by the throat. I've no courage to fight what's inside. The white part of me is filled with a revulsion, a loathing that's been learned ... with the alphabet!

Babo: You can unlearn.

Mia: All my life I've been flushing shit down the toilet. Do you think I can eat it now?

Babo: What you feel, it's based on a - a myth - an immoral ideology -.

Mia: A,B, C, D the blacks are not as good as we. W, X, Y, and Z we're so clever, they're thick in the head, let's shoot all the bastards dead. Don't you know? We've twisted it into a scientific fact! Do you know the truth about truth? It's man-handled! *(Pause)* All I've come to face is a sense of what they suffer -.

Claus: Spare me the martyrdom.

Babo: That's a start -.

Mia: It's counterfeit! *(Pause)* You think I would've realized it if I didn't know I had mixed blood? *(Bitter laugh)*

Babo: Jesus, how did I escape? *(She embraces **Mia**)*

Mia: It's the children you must start with.

Claus: No way're you going to get your hooks into my grandson.

Babo: What'll you do?

Mia: I'm happy to go.

Babo: Piet - ?

Claus: Leave him alone.

Babo: And to hell with Mia!

Claus: Yes, to hell with her.

Piet: Don't say that, Papa.

Babo: The worm has spoken.

Piet: You shut up!

Mia: Farther than countries. Farther than fathers. *(Laughs)*

Claus: More bloody trouble than she's worth.

Piet: Don't, don't talk that way!

Babo: She's your daughter-in-law. Part of your family.

Claus: Never! She's a hybrid. A sin committed by black and white. Look at her! A slut! A mutation. She belongs to a bastard race -.

Piet: STOP IT! *(While he speaks, **Babo** grabs scouting knife from table, stabs it into wooden surface)*

Babo: You animal! You filthy animal! How dare you! You of all people. I know what you are, I've seen it, out there on the farm! Well, it's time Piet was told -.

Claus: Shut up!

Mia: In the beginning was the thought and the thought was with white and the thought was godwhite.

Claus: *(To **Piet**)* Y'hear her! She's witless!

Mia: A sin *(Nods)* The elders preach it from the pulpits: God has proclaimed it, white is the mastery of race.

Babo: You can't still believe that bullshit. Even the churches are finally admitting Apartheid's a heresy.

Mia: But not a sin. They won't say it's a sin.

Piet: For God's -.

Babo: God's a defrocked bone-man in every white cupboard!

Mia: I'm in a prison, Babo. There's a wall in my cell. There's no light there, no light. *(Moves towards **Babo**. Stops and strokes Jan's carving, picks up the knife)*

Piet: We could all use a drink. *(As he prepares drinks, **Mia** moves past him towards the door, carrying the knife)*

Piet: Mia! Wait. *(He reaches out to her)*

Mia: Don't touch me! *(She recoils, her hand reaching to rest on the back of couch as she steadies herself)*

Piet: Where are you going?

Mia: *(As she speaks, her hand clenches to a fist. Drawing the antimacassar on the back of couch into her grasp)* To break it down. My hands are bleeding from ... trying to climb it.

Piet: I'll get you a brandy. We've got to -.

Mia: One night in a dream, I straddled it, looked down into the humming silence, the talking dark. *(She exits with the knife, antimaccasaar trailing from her other hand)*

Piet: Mia, wait. *(He moves to follow her)*

Claus: Leave her.

Piet: You stay out of this, Papa!

Babo: Pigs've learned to fly!

Piet: Shut your mouth! I won't send her away, Papa. I won't.

Claus: You'll lose everything.

Babo: Go, go.

Piet: We'll manage. *(He exits. Pause)*

Babo: Dear Piet ... it was a long time coming.

Claus: It's not over yet.

Babo: Don't try to persuade him!

Claus: She can come back. When she's better. By then, there'll be ... improvements, attitudes are changing -.

Babo: After an election rigged to create more panic among the whites so the Nationalists can rein in even tighter?

Claus: You're as corrupt as the rest of us ... playing your little paper games. Easy, isn't it, when you have a strong safety valve?

Babo: If I'm ever detained, you'd be the last person -.

Claus: I'll know about you before the kwela-kwela reaches the station. *(Pause)* You ever asked yourself why you're doing this? Ever analysed those high-minded motives of yours?

Babo: I don't know what you're talking about.

Claus: Ja? You're not fighting for black liberation. You're fighting me.

Babo: It won't work, Papa.

Claus: You don't give a curse about the blacks.

Babo: That's not true.

Claus: You sell yourself to them - anything to escape it. You've become a tart, a black man's whore because you can't face yourself. You don't care if they live or die. All you're interested in's provoking me.

Babo: God, you're sick. If I were a man I'd -.

Claus: You might as well be! You don't know how to be a woman!

Babo: You bastard! You stinking, rotten bastard! How dare you talk to me like that! You think you know what I am? You know nothing. I know what you are. I saw you! That day in the kitchen. With Ruth.

Claus: Shut up!

Babo: You're lily-white paws all over her. Ramming your filth into her. Mama on the verandah drinking herself into a stupour.

Claus: *(Rises)* I'm warning you, shut up!

Babo: You forced her! Even then, a child, I could see it. Too clearly.

Claus: That's a lie. She was willing. She wanted it, strutting about, twitching her fat hips!

Babo: She was your servant. Would you've kept her on if she'd refused? Every black in this country is prostituted.

Claus: Ja-ja. It fits. A string of black men sneaking in and out of your flat. What were you doing? Evening the score?

Babo: My God! -. *(Pause. Sits, slumped. Pause)* No matter which way I turn. *(Pause)* What, what are we? *(Pause)* Goddam you! Afrikaners? A Christian minority? *(Harsh laugh)* Dutch ingenuity, German efficiency, French civility? A race of mongrels, pimps, rapists. *(Pause)* I saw her eyes. When I opened the door. Staring ... wounded ... she didn't even see me.

Claus: Enough!

Babo: The pain. The sickening disgust ... *(**Claus** slaps her face. She falls onto couch, covers her face. He turns his back. Pause)*

Babo: *(Stands)* You're wrong about me. But it doesn't matter. You know why, Papa? Because you are the system incarnate. The whole oppressive, evil regime. Fighting you, fighting it, there's no difference. But you're right about one thing. *(Pause)* Playing paper games, isn't enough. When it comes to a war between good and evil, human and animal, there's only one choice, one dignity. Remember that, Papa. *(Pause)*

Claus: *(Without turning)* You've joined.

Babo: You're way behind. I left the Volk long ago.

Claus: Then you'll perish.

Babo: Preferable to rotting from your plague of Afrikanerdom. *(She moves towards the door. Stops)* If Mia doesn't stay here I'm telling Piet about Ruth. Mark it. *(Pause)* You can try convincing him of how much she wanted it. *(She exits)*

Claus moves slowly across to drinks, pours himself one, gulps it, returns to couch, sits, head in hands.

Claus: She was willing. Willing.

*Pause. **Piet** enters.*

Piet: She won't open the door. *(Pause)* I told her. Again and again. You're staying here. We'll sort it out. I promise. You're not going anywhere. I'll take care of you. She wouldn't answer. *(Pause)* Not even when I promised to bring Jan home. *(Pause)* Babo gone? *(Pause)* Papa?

Claus: That her mother drank -. Because of that? Nein, nein. She won't land that at my door.

Piet: What I said *(Pause)*, is that I won't send her away -.

Claus: Mijn Gott! She would've made a brave man!

Piet: I won't send her away.

Claus: It's late. Let's talk about it tomorrow.

Piet: I won't, Papa.

Claus: We have a regional meeting at ten. You haven't forgotten?

Piet: What's the point? When they find out about Mia -.

Claus: Zo. We might find a way of keeping it hidden. Let's sleep on it.

Piet: If she comes out in the morning, I'm not going. I have to talk to her, make her understand -.

Claus: This meeting's important.

Piet: So is Mia! I want some time off, Papa.

Claus: If she doesn't come out, come with me. We can talk then. Decide what to do. When the meeting's over, you can come straight back, ja? (*Claus* moves towards door, *Piet* follows)

Scene Two

Bedroom

*The room is tidy but the bed unmade. It is clear that only **Mia** has slept there. She pulls the covers straight, the sheet turned down just below the pillow. Pillow still carries indentation from where her head has rested. The antimacassar is on the floor. She takes suitcase from wardrobe, begins to pack. She is wearing dressing-gown over black slip. Her cheeks are stained black. A thesaurus lies open on bed beside suitcase. As she packs while speaking the following, she glances a couple of times at the book, her gaze skimming the words.*

Mia: Amalgam, alloy, admixture, blend, compound, combination, composite, conglomeration, fusion, skip 'h', no wait, heterograft, that's good ... infusion? Go on, medley, miscellany, mixture, mishmash, melange, merger? Mongrel? Save that. Patchwork, pastiche, potpourri, tangle. Transfusion? (*Pause*) No. No. No. Not even mongrel. Hybrid. Offspring of a tame sow and a wild boar, child of a free man and a slave, wait, free woman and a slave. Offspring of a tame boar and a wild sow, no, you just can't beat that. Hybrid. I'll never be able to look at another cross-bred plant. *(Laughs)* I'll never have to. *(Raises hand, as though pointing at someone)* Take a memo: Dear Piet, please, no plants, no flowers. Or I'll turn in my grave. And most definitely, no white Italian marble, nor black South African granite. Perhaps that stomach-churning sea-green Connemara stone would be more appropriate? Shaped like an x to mark the spot, the ... final signature? She was sick of it, you can say. *(Looks around room)* Neat, neat. Yes. *(Goes to dressing-table, gathers jewellry boxes, goes to door, opens it, sticks her head out. Whispers)* Thembalethu! *(Louder)* Thembalethu! *(Roars)* Thembalethu! *(Walks back in, spots knife on bedside table, places it in drawer, begins to pack jewellery in case.* **Elijah** *knocks, sticks his head in)*

Elijah: *(Softly)* Madam? *(Pause. Louder)* Madam?

Mia: It's you, is it? Yes. There you are. Come in. Come on.

Elijah: I phone Baas now, Madam?

Mia: I'm feeling very happy today. I'm going away, Thembalethu. A long way. Isn't it a nice morning? Don't you think?

Elijah: I phone.

Mia: Did I say it right? *(Pause)* No, I don't need a taxi. *(Laughs)* I'm under my own steam.

Elijah: Steam? You catching train? First you talk to Baas.

Mia: Why?

Elijah: Baas, he said to phone him. He said if Madam she unlocks door, Elijah must phone. He come home then. He left you note. *(Holds out note)* Home soon.

Mia: *(Takes note, places it on bed without reading)* Then I don't have much time. No, forget about that.

Elijah: He get angry if -.

Mia: It's okay. I'll phone him in a minute. First I want you to take this. Everything. *(She indicates the case)*

Elijah: Where you want I should put it?

Mia: Your wife. What size is she?

Elijah: Size?

Elijah: Maybe these things will fit her.

Elijah: No, no, Madam. She will not fit.

Mia: The jewellery too. Maybe you could sell it. Buy some things for your family.

Elijah: No, Madam, I cannot. Baas, still he is angry over the forks. He explain you not ... I know this thing. Before I work, my wife in Soweto? When the small one died, she was strange for a long time. I know. But she better now. I have work. I send money every month.

Mia: I've no use for them.

Elijah: You wear them. They for you. For here.

Mia: Wouldn't they fit your wife?

Elijah: If she wear them she in trouble. They not for the township, they for here. For you.

Mia: I'll tell Piet, you needn't worry -.

Elijah: Baas, yes, but worse our neighbours.

Mia: Neighbours?

Elijah: They see my wife in these, they smell white, they ask questions.

Mia: You can tell them -.

Elijah: They find own answers. They make big trouble for us. We can die. If you black and you well off then you a sell-out. You doing something you shouldn't. Maybe informer.

Mia: Informer?

Elijah: The police, the soldiers, they pay big money for names of people who protest, students who organize the boycotts, the committees for the evicted, you know? If you see a black with the money then you ask ... Where he find money to pay high rents? To buy meat? To wear new clothes, drink in the shebeens? And you know. Only blacks you can trust is they stay poor. I stay poor. *(Pause)*

Mia: What have I been? *(Pause)*

Elijah: You phone Baas now?

Mia: Did I get it right? Did I?

Elijah: Yes, Madam. *(Pause)*

Mia: Do you know what I'm talking about, Thembalethu?

Elijah: I know you not well -.

Mia: Do you?

Elijah: No, Madam.

Mia: Your name.

Elijah: Elijah: name is Elijah.

Mia: Babo said -.

Elijah: The police, they put it on my papers. I cannot change. I am registrated. Registered. Thembalethu cannot work. Elijah can work. That is the way -.

Mia: You have a right to be called by your name.

Elijah: Madam. This good job. I happy with Elijah. Money is good. I need to work.

Mia: How can you say the money is good?

Elijah: Money is good. Baas is good. Very fair. He pay more than most whites pay.

Mia: A lot less than any white would get. How can you be thankful for that?

Elijah: I want no trouble.

Mia: I don't understand.

Elijah: It is difference. For you. For me. I phone Baas now?

Mia: At least let me give you some money. *(Goes towards bag on dressing-table)*

Elijah: No, Madam. I cannot have it. This make trouble. I go.

Mia: I can't connect. Anywhere. I'm ... homeless. *(Pause)* Please, let me do something? I, I won't see you again.

Elijah: *(Hesitates at door)* The books, Madam. If you don't need.

Mia: Books. Yes, books. Books?

Elijah: Of Master Jan's. Old ones. The box on the attic. School books you keep there.

Mia: You want those?

Elijah: For the children.

Mia: Don't they have books?

Elijah: Is not cheap, the books.

Mia: At school?

Elijah: Is not free the school, is not free the books.

Mia: *(Sits, head in hands)* It wasn't that I couldn't. I wouldn't. I wouldn't look.

Elijah: Is okay, Madam?

Mia: Take them. Take them all.

Elijah: Thank you, Madam. First I call Baas.

Mia: First take them. Bring them to your shed at the bottom of the garden. Then you can call him. *(Pause)* Yes, go. *(Pause)* What is it?

Elijah: Is a good thing. *(He exits. Pause)*

Mia: *(Laughs)* It's a good thing. *(Pause).* For me, what is it? A blind stab? *(She dumps thesaurus into suitcase, drags suitcase down, shoves it under bed)* The nail ... almost ... almost. *(Pause. Looks around room)* Yes. Yes. Yes. *(Takes off gown. Hangs it in wardrobe, goes to the mirror)* A little loose on the chin, a little flabby at the midriff. But otherwise ... not bad for a thirty-six-year-old hybrid. *(Peers at her face)* Losing my colour? *(Opens make-up box, stains her cheeks darker)* Can't have you going off looking pale and wan and miserable. *(Goes to drawer, removes knife, bottle of pills, takes black eyebrow pencil from dressing table, carries everything to bed, sits, rises. Goes to bathroom. Returns with glass of water. Halfway to the bed, she stops abruptly)* My blue dress! My lovely blue creation! It's been there weeks. That fat black cow! *(Goes to her handbag, roots in it, pulls out a ticket)* Elijah. He can collect it. Her fat black fingers drooling all over it. 'Dry clean, Madam. Certainly, Madam.' Well she can't have it. She can't! Keep your paws off it, you filthy munt! *(She stiffens rigidly. Pause Throws herself on bed, heaving. Pause. Sits up slowly, opens the pills, begins to take them one by one with water as she speaks. All her movements are leaden)* Y'see. Babo? Y'see Babo? I can't unlearn. To know it is not what I should be, that's the killing thing. *(Pause)* To be what you should and not to know why, is also a crime. Be careful, Babo. *(Pause)* But the terrible, the terrible, is coming to know it only by default. How can I live with that? *(Pause. Puts a handful of pills in her mouth, swallows with water. Checks bottle is empty)* Perhaps mongrel is a better word after all since some hybrids prove superior in nature to what went before. *(Pause. Screams, pointing accusingly)* Let the verdict be given, the sentence be passed! Mia Schuurman, you have been found guilty! To have no conscience is to be sub-human: to come to know it by counterfeit is despair: to try to live with it is suicidal: to die with it is the solution. *(Pause. She begins to slow down in speech and gesture)* I desire to be that which I've never been in this house. Separate. To break out, break away, break apart. Apartheid ist der Zeitgeist. *(Pause)* The wherewithal to take my life has been supplied courtesy of my ex-fathers, for which I humbly thank them ... a divine Trinity united in my godhead. Blessed be their union! *(Laughs)* The doctor's pills and the butcher's knife. The one to anaesthetize, the other to operate. Something must be said of a third party, a black spirit who's been shadowing me. It was he who diagnosed me the carrier of an immoral disease fatal to humanity. Please note all three should be given an honourable mention in the credits. *(Pause)* There will be no post-operative phase. No jaded re-runs. *(She marks a ring around each wrist with the eyebrow pencil. Examines each wrist)*

A bracelet of black

Blood about the bone.

The nail is home.

The pickaxe poised

To ring the stone.

(The following words are uttered in jerking gasps as she cuts her wrists)
Now, Mia! Now, Mia! Run! Run! Run! Run from the wall, the song in the stone. *(She doubles over on the bed)*

Scene Three

Bedroom

Piet , Thulatu, Paul and Babo. Piet sitting on trunk seat at foot of bed, head in hands. The undersheet is still covering mattress. But the top sheet has been drawn with the quilt into a pile near the bottom of the bed where Mia fell forward. A tiny trickle of blood is startling bright against the whiteness of the sheet. Mia's pillow still carries the indentation of her head. Throughout the scene, characters look at, or go to the bed as various emotions fuel them. Long pause during which Babo notices antimacassar on floor, picks it up. She fiddles with it, bunching it up, twisting it etc, as she moves about. She goes to bed, tries to touch it, but can't. Moves away.

Babo: She was always so ... delicate. *(Stares at antimaccasar as she speaks)*

Paul: *(To Thulatu)* This is your doing! You b-bastard!

Thulatu: Yes, that's it, isn't it? I'm the black bastard!

Paul: Any w-white man her mother would've slept with ... I'd've felt the s-same.

Thulatu: Y'think by now I haven't learned to smell it!

Paul: She should've s-stuck to her own kind! *(To Babo)* You're no b-better than she was! You and -. *(Indicates Thulatu)* Two years ago he'd've been thrown in jail. There was a law against -.

Babo: Black-fuckie-white?

Paul: My God , you've no s-sense of -.

Babo: *(To Paul)* Jesus. You're a -.

Thulatu: Racist.

Paul: If we're not on your s-side, we have to be against you!

Babo: *(To **Paul**)* Did Mia know how you felt?

Thulatu: She had a nose.

Paul: *(To **Thulatu** and **Babo**)* Y'want to come out s-smelling of roses at my expense. W-we're all to blame. All of us.

Thulatu: Some more than others.

Paul: That's right. *(Indicates himself)* T-try to pin it -.

Thulatu: I was talking about me. Me!

Paul: Oh, I thought -. *(Pause)*

Thulatu: *(To **Paul**)* Did her mother want her to know?

Babo: *(To **Thulatu**)* You and your anger! Goddamn you! You destroyed her!

*Claus enters on Babo's last words, goes directly to **Piet**, grips his shoulders. **Babo** moves away. **Piet** doesn't look up.*

Claus: There'll be no publicity. *(Looks at the group, examining **Thulatu**)*

Claus: *(To **Paul**, indicating **Thulatu**)* The father, I presume?

Babo: What's this? An unwanted pregnancy?

Claus: *(To **Thulatu**)* We've no need of you here. The funeral will be private. Family only.

Babo: New-found loyalty eh, mijn Führer?

Claus: *(To **Thulatu**)* Your name, kaffir?

Babo: Don't! *(To **Thulatu**)* He's liable to have you assassinated by the security police once your back is turned. Mark it: once your back is turned. Remember Khumalo -.

*During the following exchanges of dialogue, **Piet** rises, goes to stand by bedside. He stares along its line, his gaze suddenly arrested by the pillow. He winces, reaching out, his hand several inches above the indentation as he strokes the air gently. Stops, drops to his knees, takes the edges of the pillow in both hands and buries his head in the indented part, bringing the edges up around the side of his head. He rolls his head a little to and*

*fro in the pillow, then still. Pause. Lifts his head slowly, staring at the
pillow, smoothes the edges of it.*

Babo: ... murdered one month after my father made casual
inquiries -.

Claus: Shut your bloody mouth!

Paul: *(To **Thulatu**)* Tell me what to do. The m-medical
records I'll publish them. T-torn and gutted like r-rag dolls.

Claus: A nest of vipers. Ja I might've known. *(To **Paul**)* You
won't get away with this. *(To **Thulatu**)* None of you.

Babo: Mark what he says. My father is clairvoyant. He can
predict, with great accuracy, the dates of people's deaths.

Claus: *(Moves towards **Babo** with raised arm)* You bitch!

Thulatu: *(Moves in front of **Babo**)* At your peril ... Baas. *(Pause)*

Claus: I never forget a face.

Thulatu: There's no file on me.

Claus: Yet.

Piet: *(Roars)* Jan! *(Stands, looks about in confusion)*

Babo: *(Goes to him, leads him to sit)* Piet. Oh, Piet.

Piet: How? How can I tell him? What do I say? Where is he?
(Stands) The Vorsters. Yes. Bring him home. *(Pause. Sits, howls)*
HOME! *(Pause)* Four hours ago she was breathing. Talking to
Elijah. The seconds ticking, bringing her closer. Closer. Then,
it's done -. The spilling between the seconds. *(Pause)*

Paul: *(Voice breaking. Beside bed)* For G-god's sake!

Babo: Don't -.

Piet: *(Pause)* How will I tell him? How?

Babo: You don't have to yet. I'll be here. I'll help you,

Piet: How did it get to this? He'll ask me. How did my
mother get to this? Did she see my wood carving, Papa?
What'd she say? *(Pause)* Is that exactly what she said? Why
wouldn't you let me see her? Why, Papa? Why? Why'd she do
it?

Claus: *(Sits other side of **Piet**)* Ja. It's difficult, I know. *(Pause)* He was ... fond of her. But he's young, resilient. He'll get over it. *(Pause)* You too, given time. I know you don't think it now, but look at me. When your mother went ... But it passes. You pick up the pieces. You learn to live with it. You must, for Jan's sake. He needs his father. Even, one day ... you might find ... when you're over it ... you change ... you can't see that now ... but it's true you change ... you might even ... find someone else ... have children, who can tell?

Piet: *(Rises)* What is this - ? I killed my wife to please my father. It's not enough, d'you hear! He wants more. More grandchildren. Two wives dead. And he's looking to the next. *(Pause. To **Claus**)* I've tried, tried. All my small, narrow life. None of it's enough for you.

Babo: *(Looking at **Piet** . Quietly, intensely)* Look, Mama! A man!

Piet: What do you want on the death certificate? 'Natural causes?' *(Pause)* We each took her wrist and slit it for her.

Claus: Ja, now, you'll drive yourself insane thinking – *(Points to **Paul** and **Thulatu**)* That pair! I've no doubt they've been in cahoots for years -.

Paul: *(Broken)* I should have t-told her long ago. It was the shock that -. *(He moves towards door)*

Claus: *(Pointing to **Paul** as he exits)* Y'hear that? **(Paul** exits)

Piet: You and I Papa. She was close to the edge, yes, so help me, I couldn't see it. But we ... shoved, you and I. I've let you do it. What'll you say to Jan? What? How'll you tell him we killed his mother?

Claus: She wasn't his -.

Piet: She was more a mother than you've ever been a father!

Claus: Listen -.

Piet: No! You listen! I worshipped you! Strong, brave, the kind of man I wanted to be. You knew that! I wanted nothing more than to please you, win your respect. I even married Yolande! The only good thing that came out of it was Jan. The rest was hell!

Claus: You were always weak. Even Babo had more -.

Piet: Your scouting knife! Your knife! It's you! *(Pause)* Old Mothodi – he must've been seventy. You and those others, forcing him to sit in a slimy puddle, shaving his head - because he dared to have white hair! You took it then - after I spewed my guts up – 'You won't have this knife till you're man enough'. *(Pause)* I'm not much, Papa. Mia was right. All my life I've been trying to hide it. I've been living a bigger lie than hers. I'm a sham, a weak, frightened sham! What is her lie in comparison to that! Nothing, it's nothing. There was no deceit ... she wasn't even guilty of that! I'm the deceit! Don't you understand what I'm looking at? She died because I have no balls!

Babo: Pietie, listen -.

Claus: *(To **Piet**)* Don't put yourself through this. *(Points to **Babo**)* Y'think she couldn't've stopped it? All she had to do was come to me.

Babo: *(To **Claus**)* Never!

Thulatu: *(To **Babo**, indicating **Claus**, with disgust)* God's my witness, I'd no idea!

Piet: A queen has died.

Claus: She was -. Don't exaggerate, man!

Piet: Get out, Papa!

*During following exchange of dialogue between **Piet** and **Claus**, **Babo** moves to bed, stands staring at it, trembles. She reaches out towards the bunched sheet, tries to touch it, hesitates, arm in mid air. **Thulatu** goes to her, puts his arm about her shoulders, withdraws her arm. They stand close together.*

Claus: *(Rises)* You dare to speak to me, your own father ... !

Piet: I have no father. *(Pointing to **Thulatu**)* I had as lief he were my father.

Claus: I don't know you!

Piet: You never wanted to. Something happened when you were here last night. Something you'd never understand. I

wanted to accept Mia exactly as she was. D'you hear me? I
didn't care about her blood. When I found her there on the
bed, the revulsion, the shame I felt was for the colour of my
own skin. *(Pause)* Her death - just the tip of the iceberg, the tip
of it. That's what's most cruel. That is what I can't live with. I
never want to see you again!

Claus: *(Moves towards door)* Y'think you can manage on your
own. Zo. Try it! See where it gets you. You can't breathe
without me! You can't piss without me to hold your hand!

Piet: The death announcements will state who Mia really is.

Claus: Ja? No newspaper will touch you after I make a few
calls.

Piet: Word will still get round! I'm going to take a pickaxe to
the ice. I'm going to hack and burrow and bore until chunks
of it drift into every sea, become beached on every shore.

Claus: Zo, talk! You'll do nothing in the end. *(Pause)* After all
I've done for you -.

Piet: Because of what you've done TO me! TO Mia! *(Pause)*
Go. Go. Go on. *(They look at each other. **Piet** sits, withdraws into
himself. Long pause. **Claus** turns to **Babo**)*

Claus: *(Hand reaching out)* Babo?

Babo: *(**Thulatu** comforts her)* Put a spear in my hand! Put a
spear in it! Oh, yes, I'll make the speech, the words will ... rip
the air! *(Her voice breaks)* D'you know who he made the casual
inquiries from? Do you? *(Pause)* He had no respect. Not for
any of us. People need respect. If they don't get it, it drives
them to do ... the things he does ... somehow we're right there
with him at the very core. All ... stained! *(Pause. Crying)* It
wasn't just hating him. It wasn't just that ... was it? Oh, I want
to tear my heart out! *(Crying broken)* I do care. I do, don't I? I
know what's right. Surely that counts? *(Long pause)* We've got
each other. We'll manage. *(Pause)* Won't we, Pietie? *(Pause)*
You're strong. You can see your way clearly now you've faced
what you are. *(Pause)* I'm lost, blinded in a maze. I'll arrive,
but I won't know why I travelled.

Piet: *(Roars)* Mia!

Scene Four

Patio

*Claus and **Reunert** standing, facing one another. **Reunert** is hugging a file. **Claus** is disturbed. Both men are tense. A folded wheelchair is pushed almost out of sight behind a chair or plant in a corner.*

Claus: *(Holding out hand)* The report, man!

Reunert: Look, I'm sorry, Sir, deeply -.

Claus: *(Goes to French window, voice raised)* Samuel? See if she needs ... anything ... a drink ... zo? *(Listens ... hesitates, turns to **Reunert**, hand again outstretched)* Stomme, give it!

Reunert: *(Reluctantly handing it over)* Look, I realize you're upset. I mean, if she were my daughter -.

Claus: *(Carrying report to table)* Ja-ja, remarkable powers of observation. *(Opening it)* Is that why we gave you the job of police commissioner? *(Pause. **Reunert** speaks while **Claus** leans on table, reading)*

Reunert: Unfortunately, she was taken to one of the smaller stations across town. *(Pause)* We were swamped. Literally swamped. We annexed the sports complex at the university. A lot of them were held there, initially. If she'd been taken there, I could have -. It was mayhem, mayhem, Sir, believe me. It took us days to find out who we'd detained, who'd slipped through. *(Pause)* Of course, the smaller stations don't have photographs. Lists of names, certainly, but *(Pause)* a question of the administrative costs, you understand? *(Pause. **Claus** sits slowly. **Reunert** speaks with emphasis)* If she'd given her name, it wouldn't have happened. *(Pause)* It was unfortunate ... in the general melée ... if she'd been taken to me ... *(Pause)* It was an unfortunate oversight.

Claus: Oversight! You dare to call this *(Slams file on table, stands)* an oversight!

Reunert: I mean, you, we didn't foresee her being taken out of my jurisdiction -.

Claus: Animals! *(Pause)* She doesn't smoke! *(Pause)* I want that bastard's hide! *(Suddenly stiffens).* A tetanus shot? *(Peers at file, searching till he finds the words again. Turns on **Reunert**)* Und why was she given such a -.

Reunert: A, a mere precaution, Sir, at the hospital -.

Claus: Zo?

Reunert: I told them to give her one.

Claus: Verdomme! Tetanus?

Reunert: The dogs were let loose on them in the courtyard.

Claus: Gott in Hemel!

Reunert: That servant of yours seems a capable sort of ... of ... He seems able to ... manage her ... though perhaps you might like to consider some private nursing ... I can give you some names -.

Claus: His hide, d'you hear?

Reunert: Actually, she was quite ... fortunate. If it hadn't been for your son and his enquiries, she might still be -.

Claus: My son?

Reunert: He became quite a nuisance, I gather. Just as well, for her sake. When his name was brought to my attention that's when I put two and two -.

*Enter **Samuel**, goes to wheel chair, opening it as **James** enters behind him, carrying **Babo**. He places her in it, stands watching as **Samuel** hunkers down, gently moving her slumped shoulders to centre her. **James** glances across at **Claus** and **Reunert**, then back at **Samuel**. As he looks down, he wriggles, shifts slightly, passing his hand fleetingly over the area of his genitals. The entire action gives no more than the merest suggestion of the discomfort of the gun in his underpants. When he has completed the action, **Samuel** looks up at him. Slightest pause. **Samuel** nods. **James** leaves, heading towards farm. **Samuel** positions **Babo** at one end of patio and leaves, heading indoors. As he does so, **Babo** slumps a fraction sideways. Long pause before **Claus** can bring himself to turn and look at her. **Reunert** moves about, ill at ease, speaking as he does so.*

Reunert: A few weeks rest – all this will be just a, a memory. *(Pause)* You think they won't recover, but I've seen it, yes, Sir. *(Pause)* I mean, some of them, no matter how many times they're detained, and you think, that's the end of them, they're broken, once and for all, a couple of months later, there they are, large as life, boycotting shops, spouting about freedom.

*(Enter **Piet**)*

Piet: Where is sh- ?

*Sees **Babo**. Pause as he stands transfixed. His mouth works, but he cannot speak. He moves slowly across patio, stands before **Babo**, his shoulders like lopped branches. Babo's hand flaps ineffectually and she mumbles, her tongue lolling in her mouth. His legs buckle. He drops to his knees. Raises his hands to touch her, but cannot. His head bows slowly. Pause.*

Claus: *(To **Reunert**)* I want his hide!

Reunert: You're upset.

Claus: You bastard, I'll nail you for this!

Reunert: I make allowances. A man has a right to -.

Claus: Where is he?

Reunert: Be angry.

Claus: You owe me.

Reunert: He's being transferred.

Claus: I want him out.

Reunert: It's the best I can do in the -.

Claus: *(Slams fist on table as he speaks)* Out! D'you hear, man?

Reunert: I suggest you ... control yourself, Sir.

Claus: That bastard's walking around scot-free -.

Reunert: He wasn't to know she was your daughter.

Claus: Is that any reason to treat a woman -.

Reunert: He was doing his duty, like any other policeman. He had his orders.

Claus: Ja, you think I'll leave it at that? Zo, watch. I'll make waves big enough to drown both of you.

Reunert: Who will you complain to? Yourself? Sir?

Pause. **Claus** *sits. Pause.* **Piet** *howls, a protracted sound that is at first low, rising in pitch and density till it fills the air. It is an agonized, pain-filled howl that echoes the vowel sound of 'home' which he uttered in the previous scene after Mia's death. Pause. He begins to weep silently, his body shuddering.* **Reunert** *collects his file and withdraws quietly.* **Claus** *rises, goes to stare out across the farm, his profile to* **Piet***.*

Piet: *(Regaining control, lays his head in Babo's lap. Babo's hand flaps on arm of wheelchair)* Mia was right. There are no words. *(Pause)* Babo, oh, Babo. *(Pause. Lifts head, turns to address* **Claus***)* Do you know what she was saying when she slit her wrists? Do you? *(Pause.* **Claus** *does not turn)* These things are beyond words. *(Pause)* D'you know what that makes us? Do you? *(Pause. Strikes his chest)* Well, Mia's here now ... Here! Every time you look me in the face, she'll be staring at you! *(**Babo** mumbles.* **Piet** *turns to her, strokes her hair, face, shoulders, arms, rubs her hands as he speaks)* Oh, what is it? What is it? Babo? Babo? Are you in pain? Is that it? You should be lying down. *(Rises. To* **Claus***)* Has Samuel made up her bed yet? *(Claus's shoulders jerk. Pause)* I'm staying. *(Pause)* I'll put the camp bed up in her room. *(Pause)*

Claus: Where is Jan? *(**Piet** exits through French windows. Pause.* **Claus** *glances swiftly at* **Babo***, sits, drinks, pours another.* **Babo** *stiffens suddenly, her face contorts as though she is screaming, but no sound is emitted.* **Claus** *observes this, calls for* **Piet** *before* **Babo** *has completed the action)* Piet! *(Pause).* Piet! *(Pause).* Samuel! Schnell! *(Pause)* Schnell! *(**Babo** slumps again. Pause.* **Samuel** *enters wearing sloppy old T-shirt, old slacks.* **Claus** *stares at him)*

Samuel: Wanted something, Baas? *(Pause)* Something, Baas?

Claus: She's saying something again. *(They look at* **Babo***)*

Samuel: Not now. Only silence

Claus: She was.

Samuel: She needs help.

Claus: The doctor said -.

Samuel: Not his. Proper kind.

Claus: Zo?

Samuel: You know.

Claus: He's the best there is.

Samuel: No.

Claus: What d'you want? A bloody medicine man?

Samuel: Miss Babo needs proper kind.

Babo mumbles unintelligibly. They both look at her.

Claus: *(Looks at Samuel)* What? What is she saying?

Samuel: Not sure. *(Moves to Babo, bends over her)* Miss Babo?

Babo mumbles again.

Claus: Ja? What is it?

Samuel: Think she's cold. *(Goes towards French windows)*

Claus: Where're you going?

Samuel: Get rug. *(Exits. Pause. Returns, wraps rug about Babo's knees)* There, warm. *(To Claus)* Proper kind.

Claus: He's the best there is.

Samuel: Can't help. Doesn't know this sickness. *(Pause)* Doesn't know torture.

Claus: She wasn't ... wasn't -.

Samuel: I know. Samuel knows. Seen many. Only one man -.

Claus: Who?

Samuel: Can help. Takes time. Works.

Claus: Who?

Samuel: Black man.

Pause Babo's arm slips off the arm of the wheel chair. Her body tilts a little to one side. Samuel goes, props her upright.

Claus: Black. *(Pause)* Black.

Samuel: Takes time. Long time. But works.

Claus: Get him.

Samuel: Can't. Too busy to come. I take Miss Babo. Go there.

Claus: He can come here.

Samuel: Won't come. Too busy. Clinic. Treats many. There.

Claus: Get him.

Samuel: Can't. *(They look at each other. Pause)*

Claus: When?

Samuel: Tomorrow. Morning. Early. *(Pause)*

Claus: He'll make her better? *(Pause)* Won't he? *(**Samuel** moves towards French doors)* Wait! Your move. *(Indicates chess set on table)* You haven't taken it.

Samuel: No

Claus: Make it now.

Samuel: Have work.

Babo *mumbles again, her tongue lolling in her mouth.* ***Samuel*** *goes to her, bends, listens while* ***Claus*** *watches.*

Claus: What is it?

Samuel: Wants water.

Goes to table, ***Claus*** *pours water, hands him the glass.* ***Samuel*** *takes it to* ***Babo***. *She slobbers it.* ***Samuel*** *returns glass to table, heads again towards French doors.*

Claus: Wait! *(**Samuel** stops)* I need you here ... If she talks ... I can't understand. *(Pause)* We might as well play the whole game. *(Pause)* Pass the time.

Pause. ***Samuel*** *turns, moves to table, makes his move.* ***Claus*** *stares at board, then at* ***Samuel****.* ***Claus*** *makes move.* ***Samuel*** *makes another move, speaking as he does so.*

Samuel: Check.

Claus: What? *(Pause. He stares at board)* I taught you everything you know. Everything! Y'must be mad if you think you can beat -.

Samuel: *(Sits. Pause as* **Claus** *stares at him)* We see. No more. The old way. *(They continue playing. Every few moments* **Claus** *glances at* **Babo**, *pours himself another drink)*

Claus: You think she's okay, ja?

Samuel: *(Glances at* **Babo***)* For moment. *(Pours himself a drink. Pause as the two men stare at each other.* **Claus** *looks down at chessboard, makes a move as* **Samuel** *drinks)*

Claus: I'll come with you. Where is this clinic?

Samuel: You stay here. *(A loud shot rings out.* **Claus** *starts, half rises,* **Samuel** *calmly continues to play as though he heard nothing)*

Claus: What's that?

Samuel: *(Lifts his head, listens)* Probably wild animal. *(Pause)* Not good on farm. *(Pause)* They shoot to kill. *(He stares intently at* **Babo** *as if he were listening, though* **Babo** *does not say anything.* **Claus** *notices him)*

Claus: What? *(Looks at* **Babo**, *then* **Samuel**.*)* What?

Samuel: Ssshh ... *(Pause. Goes to her, bends, listens)* Tired she says, very tired. *(Looks at* **Claus***)* She wants to lie down. *(Pause)*

Claus: I didn't hear her.

Samuel: I did.

Claus *moves reluctantly towards* **Babo**, *attempts to lift her.* **Babo** *flails her arms at him. He stops. Pause.*

Claus: *(To* **Samuel***)* Will you - ?

Samuel *lifts her, carries her indoors.* **Claus** *sits, head in hands. Pause. Looks at wheelchair while he speaks the following:*

Claus: Your mother never knew. That's not why she drank. *(Pause)* She was willing. *(Pause)* Willing! *(Pause)* D'you hear me? *(Pause. Next two words imitate police commissioner's voice)* Yourself? Sir? *(Pause)* Damn your courage! *(Pause)* Damn your eyes! *(Pause. He swipes his arm across table, knocking everything to floor)*

Afterword

In the Talking Dark was the first play I wrote. In part it was inspired by Hilda Bernstein's novel *Death Is Part of the Process*, which had impressed me very much, not least because of the politics, the meticulous and moving way she had exposed the rotten core of Apartheid.

Someone once told me I was black, and maybe I am, under this pink Irish skin; at least, maybe that's one dimension of me. My heroic people when I was a teenager were my mother, Jesus, Muhammad Ali, and Martin Luther King: my mother and Jesus for loving me unconditionally no matter what shenanigans I got up to, Muhammad Ali for being passionate and angry about how badly blacks were treated, and Martin Luther King for his 'I have a dream' speech about justice and equality and peace. I had a lot of other heroines too, only I didn't know them till later, women who braved ridicule and marched for my right to have my Child Allowance Book assigned to me.

When I write fiction, I'm unable to divorce the politics from it. I believe the forced migrations of poor and hungry and disenfranchised people in a highly politicized world makes of every birth, every baby's first intake of breath, a political act in the eyes of our power-structured planet, instead of what it should be, a loving, wondrous act of creation in fruition.

I don't know if this illumines the play in any great way, but somehow it's all in there, bits of me that seethe at our capacity for injustice and cruelty, bits that long for love to be unconditional, bits that cry to and at and with humanity at the core of this great big expanding silent humming divine universe which I'm both at one and at odds with.

Dolores Walshe
Dublin
2001

Biographies

Mary Elizabeth Burke-Kennedy is Artistic Director of Storytellers Theatre Company. She was a founder member and resident director of Focus Theatre, Dublin from 1975 to 1983. During that time she wrote and directed for the company *Daughters* (Dublin Theatre Festival 1975), *Alice in Wonderland*, *The Golden Goose*, *Enter the Photographer*, and *Curigh the Shapeshifter* (Dublin Theatre Festival 1980). In 1981 she wrote *The Wind of the Word* for Team Theatre Company and wrote and directed *The Parrot* for the Dublin Theatre Festival in 1983. She was commissioned by Cork Theatre Company in 1984 to write *Women in Arms*, for which she was nominated for the Susan Smith Blackburn Award. This was followed by *Uncle Silas* (adapted from the novel by Sheridan Le Fanu). For Storytellers Theatre Company she has adapted *Esther Waters* (George Moore), *Emma* (Jane Austen), *Hard Times* (Charles Dickens), *Wuthering Heights* (Emily Brontë), *Silas Marner* (George Eliot), *The Mayor of Casterbridge* (Thomas Hardy), *Oedipus Rex* (Sophocles), and *The Star Child & Other Stories* (based on three of Oscar Wilde's fairytales). Other adaptations include *The Nose* (Gogol), and *Albert Nobbs* (George Moore). She has written extensively for children's television, *The Rimini Riddle* (R.T.E.), and *Beachcomber Bay* (Channel 5).

Síofra Campbell lives and works in New York City.

Emma Donoghue was born in Dublin in 1969. She is a playwright, novelist and historian who now lives in Canada. She followed up her first play, *I Know My Own Heart* (1993) with another Glasshouse production at the Project Arts Centre, *Ladies and Gentlemen* (1996), a play about vaudeville stars of the 1880s, which was published by New Island Press. *Kissing the Witch* (adapted by Donoghue from her 1997 book of fairytales), was commissioned by the Magic Theatre in San Francisco. Donoghue is also known for her radio plays on RTE and BBC Radio 4. Her novels include *Stirfry* (1994), *Hood* (1995), and *Slammerkin* (2000).

Anne Le Marquand Hartigan lives in Dublin and works as a poet, painter, playwright, and prose writer. Three of her plays have been produced in Dublin: *Beds* (1982), *La Corbière* (1989), both part of the Dublin Theatre Festival, and *Jersey Lilies* (1996), a trilogy, in which Hartigan both directed and acted. She has published four collections of poetry: *Long Tongue* (1982), and *Return Single* (1986), were published by Beaver Row Press; the award winning *Now Is a Moveable Feast* (1991), *Immortal Sins* (1993), and prose, *Clearing the Space* (1996), were published by Salmon. Her play *The Secret Game* won the Mobil Playwriting Competition in 1995. She has won many other awards for her poetry and visual art.

Michelle Read began her career as a writer/performer working as a stand-up comic on the London comedy circuit. Since moving to Ireland in 1991 she has continued to act and has written four new stage plays. Her second play *Romantic Friction* won a Fringe First for new writing at the 1998 Edinburgh Festival and is being adapted for BBC Radio 4. Michelle is co-artistic director of the theatre company ReadCo and she is also a founder member of the Dublin Comedy Improv.

Dolores Walshe began writing in earnest in the second half of the eighties, and got a lot of encouragement from winning a number of things, including the O.Z. Whitehead/SIP/PEN Playwriting Award, Listowel Writers' Week Playwriting Award, the staging prize in the Mobil International/Royal Exchange Theatre Playwriting Award which produced *In the Talking Dark*, the Irish Stage and Screen/Andrew's Lane Theatre Playwriting Award which produced *A Country in Our Heads*, and the James Joyce Cultural Centre's Jerusalem Bloomsday Award for Short Story. A novel, *Where the Trees Weep*, and a short story collection *Moonmad*, have been published by Wolfhound Press. Walshe has received a bursary in literature from the Arts Council of Ireland, and a development grant from the Irish Film Board.